REGULATING PATIEN

CW01095380

Systematically improving patient safety is of the utmost importance, but it is also an extremely complex and challenging task. This illuminating study evaluates the role of professionalism, regulation and law in seeking to improve safety, arguing that the 'medical dominance' model is ill-suited to this aim, which instead requires a patient-centred vision of professionalism. It brings together literature on professions, regulation and trust, while examining the different legal mechanisms for responding to patient safety events. Quick includes an examination of areas of law that have received little attention in this context, such as health and safety law and coronial law, and contends in particular that the active involvement of patients in their own treatment is fundamental to ensuring their safety.

OLIVER QUICK is Senior Lecturer in Law at the University of Bristol. He teaches undergraduate and postgraduate courses in Criminal Law, Medical Law and Public Health Law. He has published widely in these areas, and is co-author (with Nicola Lacey and Celia Wells) of *Reconstructing Criminal Law* (Cambridge University Press, 2010). He has carried out original empirical research into how UK prosecutors and experts interpret the controversial crime of 'medical manslaughter'. He obtained his PhD thesis from the University of Wales, Cardiff, and has been a visiting scholar at the University of Western Australia, Boston University and the National University of Singapore.

This series of books was founded by Cambridge University Press with Alexander McCall Smith as its first editor in 2003. It focuses on the law's complex and troubled relationship with medicine across both the developed and the developing world. Since the early 1990s, we have seen in many countries increasing resort to the courts by dissatisfied patients and a growing use of the courts to attempt to resolve intractable ethical dilemmas. At the same time, legislatures across the world have struggled to address the questions posed by both the successes and the failures of modern medicine, while international organisations such as the WHO and UNESCO now regularly address issues of medical law.

It follows that we would expect ethical and policy questions to be integral to the analysis of the legal issues discussed in this series. The series responds to the high profile of medical law in universities, in legal and medical practice, as well as in public and political affairs. We seek to reflect the evidence that many major health-related policy debates in the UK, Europe and the international community involve a strong medical law dimension. With that in mind, we seek to address how legal analysis might have a trans-jurisdictional and international relevance. Organ retention, embryonic stem cell research, physician assisted suicide and the allocation of resources to fund healthcare are but a few examples among many. The emphasis of this series is thus on matters of public concern and/or practical significance. We look for books that could make a difference to the development of medical law and enhance the role of medico-legal debate in policy circles. That is not to say that we lack interest in the important theoretical dimensions of the subject, but we aim to ensure that theoretical debate is grounded in the realities of how the law does and should interact with medicine and healthcare.

Series Editors

Professor Graeme Laurie, *University of Edinburgh*

Professor Richard Ashcroft, *Queen Mary, University of London*

REGULATING PATIENT SAFETY

The End of Professional Dominance?

OLIVER QUICK

University of Bristol

CAMBRIDGE
UNIVERSITY PRESS

University Printing House, Cambridge CB2 8BS, United Kingdom

One Liberty Plaza, 20th Floor, New York, NY 10006, USA

477 Williamstown Road, Port Melbourne, VIC 3207, Australia

314-321, 3rd Floor, Plot 3, Splendor Forum, Jasola District Centre, New Delhi - 110025, India

79 Anson Road, #06-04/06, Singapore 079906

Cambridge University Press is part of the University of Cambridge.

It furthers the University's mission by disseminating knowledge in the pursuit of education, learning and research at the highest international levels of excellence.

www.cambridge.org
Information on this title: www.cambridge.org/9781108464888
DOI: 10.1017/9780511844386

First published 2017
First paperback edition 2018

A catalogue record for this publication is available from the British Library

Library of Congress Cataloging in Publication data
Names: Quick, Oliver, author.
Title: Regulating patient safety : the end of professional dominance? / Oliver Quick.
Description: Cambridge [UK] ; New York : Cambridge University Press, 2017. |
Series: Cambridge bioethics and law ; 35
Identifiers: LCCN 2017000015 | ISBN 9780521190992 (hardback)
Subjects: LCSH: Medical errors – Prevention – Law and legislation. | Patients – Legal status, laws, etc. | Patients – Safety measures. | Medical care – Law and legislation. | Medical law and legislation.
Classification: LCC K3601 .Q85 2017 | DDC 344.04/1–dc23
LC record available at https://lccn.loc.gov/2017000015

ISBN 978-0-521-19099-2 Hardback
ISBN 978-1-108-46488-8 Paperback

CONTENTS

ACKNOWLEDGEMENTS

I would like to thank the University of Bristol Law School for giving me the time and support to write this book. Periods of study leave have allowed me to develop my thinking and engage with key figures from the world of patient safety research. In particular, a three-month stay at the Law Faculty of Boston University was invaluable for broadening my horizons. Thanks to Fran Miller and Stephen Marks for their warm hospitality and friendship during that stay, and to the following for sharing their wisdom with me: David Bates, James Conway, Robert Hanscom, Linda Kenney, Lucian Leape, Michelle Mello and Diane Pinakiewicz. I am grateful to the Society of Legal Scholars for helping to fund this visit through its Research Purposes Fund.

Draft chapters were greatly improved by the comments of Lois Bibbings, Judy Laing, John McWilliams, Michael Naughton, Ken Oliphant, Tony Prosser, Celia Wells and Richard Young. The discussion about coroners and patient-centred care benefitted enormously from the input of Nicholas Rheinberg and Vikki Entwistle. At Cambridge University Press I am indebted to Finola O'Sullivan for being a constant source of encouragement, and to Julie Hrischeva for steering the book through the production process. Allan Alphonse and Sathish Kumar, from Integra Software Services, managed the copy editing and proof stages with care and efficiency.

Most of all, thanks to my wonderful family – my mother, Susan and late father, Peter, for their endless love and support, and to Maria del Mar, Carmen and Roseanna for making me a proud husband and father, and reminding me that there is much more to life than writing a book!

Introduction

There is nothing new about efforts to ensure the safety of patients. After all, the most famous principle of medicine is the Hippocratic instruction to 'first, do no harm'. Yet, whilst healthcare aims to heal patients it also causes harm. Although this should be no surprise given the many risks associated with providing healthcare, the problem of medical harm has not been well described. The history of medicine has tended to focus on success stories rather than failures (Wootton 2006). It is only during the last half century that serious attention has been devoted to identifying and understanding medical harm. The headline figure from various studies across the globe is that around 8–12 per cent of hospitalised patients will experience an adverse event in relation to their treatment in advanced healthcare systems (Vincent 2010: 54). This translates into a high number of preventable deaths, estimated at 180,000 each year in the United States, and the striking claim that this would equate to three jumbo jet crashes every two days (Leape 1994). There is now sufficient data to suggest that such claims, far from exaggerating the scale of the problem, are likely to underestimate it. Recent analysis suggests that medical error is the third leading cause of death in the United States (Makary and Daniel 2016). This clearly represents a major public health problem, but one which has been slow to capture the attention of the public, medical professionals and policy makers.

However, the problem of medical harm is no longer a professional secret. Two landmark reports published at the turn of the twentieth century marked its arrival as a major public issue. In the United States, the Institute of Medicine report 'To Err is Human' (1999) noted that deaths caused by medication and surgical errors were the tip of the iceberg. The report famously claimed that medical errors accounted for more deaths than road traffic incidents, workplace injuries and breast cancer. Beyond the human cost of lives lost or damaged, there are also financial costs and the potential for damaging trust, so important in the therapeutic context. In the United Kingdom, a Department of Health publication called 'An Organisation with a Memory' (2000) had the same effect of putting medical error on the political agenda. This has been accelerated somewhat by the revelation of a number of episodes of poor care leading to preventable deaths and injuries. Amongst the many examples that attracted significant media attention were those involving paediatric heart surgery at the Bristol Royal Infirmary and the large scale neglect of patients at the Mid Staffordshire NHS (National Health Service) Foundation Trust, both of which are described in Chapter 1.

The study of error and harm has evolved into the more ambitious task of improving the safety of patient care. Whereas the study of error tended to look back and measure harmful events, concern with safety looks forward and attempts to avoid and ameliorate such events (Vincent 2010: 31). The scope of patient safety is potentially vast; most of the decisions, policies, treatments and communications that take place within healthcare have implications for the safety of patients. It thus extends beyond drugs, devices and doctors, to include issues of a multi-disciplinary workplace culture, the relationship between patients and professionals, the design and funding of health systems, cleaning and portering services within hospitals, the effectiveness of healthcare administrative staff and the infrastructure within which care takes place. I experienced an example of the latter shortly before the writing of this introduction; it also illustrates the difference between focusing on patient safety rather than medical error. On the 25th March 2016, my wife was in labour for the birth of Roseanna, our second daughter. She requested an epidural for pain relief, and as the anaesthetist prepared to insert the needle into the 'epidural space' of my wife's spinal cord, the hospital power supply failed, as did the backup generator. This left us in complete darkness without the reassuring sight and sound of the foetal heart rate monitor, causing panic for all in the room. Thankfully, no harm was done as a result of this failure in the power supply. Despite the apology from the blameless anaesthetist, there was no medical error to speak of or any real harm. But the safety of care was compromised during those long five minutes in the dark. We certainly didn't *feel* safe during this short time.

This increased tendency to frame a range of issues, from infection control, the language competency of staff, to the use of telemedicine services such as NHS 111 as issues of patient safety is a positive development. However, such is the obvious attraction of the 'patient safety argument' that it can also be used to mask ulterior motives. In April 2016, the dispute over a new employment contract for junior doctors in the English National Health Service was a prime example.

The Secretary of State for Health, Jeremy Hunt, sought to negotiate new terms which no longer regarded working on Saturdays as justifying 'out of hours' pay. According to the Government, this was part of its aim of creating a seven-day NHS and was justified by concerns about the safety of care in hospitals over the weekend. This was vigorously contested by the British Medical Association, who also cited safety concerns about doctors working longer rotas as part of its position in rejecting the contract. Numerous studies were cited on both sides of the debate, although none were able to arrive at clear explanations for the so-called 'weekend effect' whereby more patients die in hospitals over the weekend (Wise 2016). However, there was little doubt about the potency of framing the debate as one about patient safety, even though this conflict raised important issues about the funding of medical services, including the remuneration of medical staff, and the quality of evidence relied on to support health service reforms. This dispute also raised doubts about the dominance of the medical profession, something which this book is centrally concerned with.

Objectives, Structure and Scope of this Book

The theoretical context for this book stems from the sociology of the medical profession. In particular, it takes as its starting point the main theoretical contribution about the status of the medical profession during the last 50 years – the professional dominance thesis associated with the work of Eliot Freidson. This regarded professionalism as the preferred model of managing medical work, as opposed to market and bureaucratic alternatives, and celebrated a high degree of medical autonomy and trust. It defended professional dominance of the clinical, economic and political aspects of medical work, and left little space for external evaluation or lay scrutiny. The sensitive issue of medical harm was kept in house so that there was limited public knowledge about the many costs of medical error. As discussed in the opening chapter of the book, whilst the idea of dominance has long been challenged, and alternative models of the relationship between the profession and the state posited, Freidson's model has remained an accurate conceptualisation. However, this book will argue that professional dominance is ill-suited to the challenging task of improving the safety of care. This task requires a different form of professionalism that embraces patient safety as its priority. This is a significant challenge involving issues of education, training and culture.

It also requires an evaluation of the role of regulation and law, and in particular a consideration of which regulatory approaches and legal duties are best suited to improving patient safety. This book will also argue that patients (and their carers) should play a more prominent role in securing their own safety. Patient safety is an issue of public health, and it is legitimate and necessary to fully involve patients in the pursuit of safer care.

Chapter 2 begins by tracing the history of attempts to measure and understand medical errors and the more recent shift towards understanding risk and safety. Despite the work of some early patient safety pioneers such as Ernest Codman, the systematic study of errors and safety in medicine has been slow to emerge. Indeed, one leading commentator was moved to describe the lack of serious interest in the safety of care as negligent (Vincent 1989). Happily, the problem of medical harm has now attracted interest from a number of different disciplines, including medical sociology, health services research, psychology, policy and medico-legal studies. Greater interest in patient safety is highly significant from a professional dominance perspective. The shift from medical error being a private professional problem to an issue of public health challenges traditional notions of professional autonomy and responsibility. However, despite this interest and the emergence of what has been called the science of improvement and implementation (Marshall et al. 2013), there remains a dearth of data on whether or not care is safer, and if it is, a lack of understanding about the possible reasons for this.

The concepts of regulation and trust, and the relationship between them, are examined in Chapter 3. Regulation is an important concept within the social sciences and has given rise to a vast literature. In terms of healthcare, interest has tended to focus on the regulation of the medical profession, mainly through institutional self-regulation, and more recently of healthcare systems. There has been much less attention given to regulating the *safety* of care. However, this is now a busy area with the creation and constant reinvention of regulatory agencies that monitor the quality and safety of care. This chapter adopts a positive view of regulation as a collaborative enterprise between the state, the profession and the public to prioritise the safety of patients. However, this positive view of regulation is not shared by professionals who have tended to associate it with discipline and sanction. Professional regulation thus faces a challenge in terms of its legitimacy and relevance for practitioners.

The concept of trust has long been central to caring relationships and to the privileged position of professional dominance reflected in self-regulation. However, discussions about trust have tended to be simplistic and one dimensional – for example, exploring whether or not patients trust or distrust their doctors, or whether trust has increased or decreased. Chapter 3 presents a more detailed understanding of trust and considers its different dimensions within the healthcare setting. It might be thought that greater public knowledge about safety failings might lead to decreased trust in medics and medicine. However, there have been few investigations into the relationship between trust and patient safety. A nuanced and positive conception of trust is proposed which is better able to protect patients and enable more productive patient–professional relationships to evolve. In particular, it is argued that trusting patients may nevertheless be vigilant about the safety of the care they receive.

Chapter 4 examines the increasingly complex relationship between regulation and patient safety. Until relatively recently, this was confined to the work of individual regulators such as the General Medical Council, which was established in 1858. For the bulk of its existence, the GMC has focused on dealing with cases of professional misconduct involving alcohol addiction or inappropriate sexual relations with patients (Smith 1994). Whilst such cases are clearly significant in terms of protecting patients, the Council has historically avoided investigating the errors or poor performance of practitioners. However, a crisis of trust, partly connected to the high profile regulatory failures exposed by the events at Bristol and Mid Staffordshire discussed in Chapter 1, has led to significant changes to the structure, remit and ethos of professional regulators, introduced following damning public inquiry reports (Kennedy 2001, Smith 2004). Changes to the landscape of professional regulation have extended beyond the GMC. Reflecting a loss of trust in the ability of self-regulation, new regulators in the form of the Professional Standards Authority for Health and Social Care and the Care Quality Commission have been created to oversee the work of individual regulators and to monitor the quality and safety of healthcare organisations. The crucial questions of how regulation might impact the behaviour of healthcare professionals and which approaches appear best suited to improving safety are also explored in this Chapter.

Chapters 5–7 consider the role of law in seeking to protect patient safety. The meaning of law is potentially very broad here given that most laws about the design and delivery of medical care will have implications for the safety of patients. However, these chapters examine established mechanisms within civil and criminal law for responding to medical harm. In terms of civil law, this largely means clinical negligence litigation and examining whether tort law and the civil justice system helps or hinders patient safety. Literature reviews and studies from both the United Kingdom and the United States have been unable to conclude that the tort system helps produce safer care. However, this has not prevented commentators strongly defending the so-called deterrent effect of tort law and others being equally forceful in condemning it as counterproductive. Chapter 5 considers the evidence about the relationship between different liability systems and the safety of patients. It considers the experience of systems in New Zealand and Scandinavia (which have abandoned fault liability) as well as initiatives within the tort system that appear better aligned to the pursuit of safer care.

Criminal law has generally been regarded as something of a last resort for dealing with grossly negligent medical care. Historically, this has involved occasional manslaughter prosecutions following fatal medical errors, although there has been concern about a possible increased propensity to prosecute cases over the past twenty years (McDowell and Ferner 2013). Chapter 6 explains that the prosecution of a small number of individual practitioners is driven by notions of blame and justice rather than concern about improving safety. However, the expansion of criminal law during the past decade has created other mechanisms that are more consistent with attempts to regulate patient safety. Prosecutions of healthcare organisations for corporate manslaughter or for regulatory offences enforced by the Health and Safety Executive and the Care Quality Commission are not only more appropriate, given that medical harm is more often caused by organisational rather than individual failings, but are also more likely to encourage policies, protocols and practices for safer care.

Relatively few deaths associated with medical error end up as criminal cases. Far more result in investigation by coroners. Chapter 7 argues that coroners have an important public health role in trying to ensure that lessons are learned from tragedies and that safety is improved for the future. This includes commenting not only on failures at local level, for example at a particular hospital, but also on failures of regulation and of delivering safe care within the NHS. The work of coroners in this context can also be understood as part of the challenge to professional dominance as it represents a further opportunity for external, and often adverse comment on the quality of medical care. Whilst coroners are primarily interested in pursuing facts rather than fault, those called to give evidence at inquests experience similar cross examination, scrutiny and the possibility for public shame which is central to criminal trials; they are essentially accounting for their conduct and are aware that coroners may refer cases to regulators or prosecutors.

Whilst law and formal regulation are important, they are somewhat distant from the daily business of doing medical work. Chapter 8 therefore considers the more relevant role that professionals can play in terms of raising concerns about patient safety and apologising when things go wrong. This chapter will consider the important day-to-day role of professionals in monitoring safety, whether through raising concerns about clinical competence, or unsafe working environments caused by staff shortages or inadequate equipment. It describes the negative experiences of several well-known healthcare whistle-blowers who have raised safety concerns. The culture of the medical profession, and indeed the health service, is central to this, particularly as it applies to the sensitive subject of safety. Creating a culture of safety is complex but openness and honesty are critical to it. This chapter focuses on two aspects of openness most significant for this book. First is the need for professionals to raise safety concerns, whether about individual incompetence or organisational failings that cause or risk avoidable harm to patients. This has traditionally been labelled as whistle-blowing, but has also been described in more neutral terms as the freedom to 'speak up' about safety. Secondly, and closely connected to this, is the need for professionals openly to disclose harmful adverse events to their patients through a legal duty of candour.

Finally, Chapter 9 considers the role which patients and their carers can play in terms of helping secure the safety of care. Efforts to improve safety have tended to focus exclusively on the education, training and regulation of professionals, and more recently on the regulation of healthcare organisations. However, this chapter will argue that it is legitimate and necessary to involve patients and their carers in this task. Patients are uniquely placed to comment about and question safety, given their involvement in all aspects of care, unlike the wide range and number of healthcare professionals treating them at different times. Successfully engaging patients with the safety of their care challenges the prevailing culture of medicine where doctors have traditionally dominated and left insufficient space for the input of patients and their carers. This chapter will examine how patients and carers can make valuable contributions to the study and delivery of safer healthcare, with reference to some powerful examples of failures to involve them sufficiently.

Patient safety is an issue of global public health and the same issues are relevant to different types of health systems. However, countries take different approaches to the design and funding of health systems, and have different regulatory and legal environments in relation to patient safety. This book focuses on developments in the United Kingdom, and in particular in England. Since the devolution of powers in 1998, the United Kingdom has had four different health systems, with Northern Ireland, Scotland and Wales making their own health policies with the UK government responsible for the National Health Service in England. Whilst these systems still share much in common, the powers and approaches of national sector regulators such as England's Care Quality Commission, the Regulation and Quality Improvement Authority in Northern Ireland, Healthcare Improvement Scotland and the Healthcare Inspectorate Wales are different. Professional regulatory bodies, such as the General Medical Council, have a UK-wide jurisdiction. Whilst this book predominantly focuses on the position of the United Kingdom, and within this on England, reference is made to material and initiatives from Australia, New Zealand and the United States. Despite the focus on developments within the United Kingdom, the arguments made and conclusions drawn in this book are also likely to be relevant to the provision of safer care in other jurisdictions. The pursuit of patient safety requires a multi-disciplinary approach, and this book brings together material from various disciplines including medicine, law, sociology, psychology and health services research. In line with Charles Vincent's plea to social scientists (2009), it aims to make a positive contribution towards understanding and improving patient safety rather than being unduly critical.

1

The Rise and Fall of Professional Dominance

This chapter provides some context to the discussion that follows by offering a brief history of the modern medical profession and its regulation. It engages with the literature on the sociology of the professions in order to understand how they have been theorised. The notion of professional dominance, which originated during the so-called golden age for the professions in the 1960s, is examined. This theory, advanced by Eliot Freidson, observed how the medical profession controlled the clinical aspects of medical work, including the exclusive right to evaluate the quality of such work. Whilst alternative theories have been advanced to describe the relationship between the profession, the state and society, the dominance thesis has been dominant. However, several societal shifts, in particular the rise of consumerism and managerialism, make it timely to question whether the idea of dominance remains apposite, or indeed appropriate. The merits of professional dominance have been further doubted following evidence about the scale of safety problems within healthcare, and especially after the fallout from high profile medical disasters. This chapter will argue that a new style of professionalism is required that prioritises safety and allows space for patients to make a contribution to ensuring their own safety.

Theorising Professions

The growth of professions has been described as a 'defining characteristic' of industrial societies (Johnson 1972: 9) and has inspired a vast literature exploring the process of professionalisation and the idea of professionalism. The term profession is widely used and its meaning assumed, but considerable academic debate has surrounded its definition. Eliot Freidson, perhaps the foremost sociologist in this area, stressed the difference between two usages: a 'broad stratum' of occupations linked by some form of higher education, and a limited number of occupations that generally share 'particular institutional and ideological traits' (1994: 16). Universal consensus over defining professional traits has proved a difficult task, not least because, as Wilensky explains: 'Many occupations engage in heroic struggles for professional identification; few make the grade' (1964: 137). The most commonly cited traits include specialised education and training, knowledge monopoly, service-orientation, work autonomy, self-regulation, and a high degree of trust between the professional and client. According to Wilensky:

> Any occupation wishing to exercise professional authority must find a technical basis for it, assert an exclusive jurisdiction, link both skill and jurisdiction to standards of training, and convince the public that its services are uniquely trustworthy (1964: 138).

Despite disagreement surrounding the definition of professions, there is no doubt that medicine is a profession; as Freidson explains, 'if anything "is" a profession, it is contemporary medicine' (1970a): 4). It has always been, and continues to be the model for other health care professions. Yet just as there is no one definition of 'profession', it would be misleading to characterise the medical profession as a single unified entity. Historically, physicians, surgeons and apothecaries were legally distinct groups under the authority of three different bodies: the Royal College of Physicians, the Company of Surgeons (the Royal College of Surgeons from 1800), and the Worshipful Society of Apothecaries (Waddington 1984: 1). Relations between elite institutions such as the General Medical Council, British Medical Association and the Royal Colleges have been marked by tension and rivalry, and such historic divisions have not made for an 'effective fighting force' when the profession is on the offensive (Salter 1998: 101). This lack of unity and overall leadership also characterises the modern medical profession (RCP 2005: 25). Within the profession there is the obvious distinction between those working in primary and secondary healthcare settings, with the latter split into several specialities, each with a different sub-culture. Whilst this book draws on material and discusses issues of relevance to all health professions, it focuses on the medical profession as the dominant force within healthcare, setting the tone for the organisation and regulation of other health professions.

Most theorising about professions has focused on two central aspects: the moral value of professions and a sceptical monopolisation critique. The moral dimension stems from the structural functionalist approach of Emile Durkheim (1964), which values professions as providing a means of ensuring social order. This normative view was developed by Talcott

Parsons (1947) who saw professions as acting in the public interest and providing a stabilising effect to counterbalance the crude excesses of the capitalist state. An alternative theory, rooted in the Chicago school of sociology of Everett C. Hughes and Howard S. Becker, focused on professional monopoly and social closure. For Hughes (1958: 78)

> An occupation consists, in part, of a successful claim of some people to licence to carry out certain activities which others may not, and to do so in exchange for money, goods or services. Those who have such licence will, if they have any sense of self-consciousness and solidarity, also claim a mandate to define what is proper conduct of others toward the matters concerned with their work.

This 'power' approach can be traced to the work of Max Weber. According to Weber (1968: Chapter 11), society is made up of self-interested individuals who, in order to gain monopolies and privileges, seek to exclude others from their group. This approach is primarily concerned with the question of *how* occupations become professions. Occupations first need to construct a marketable commodity, for example expert medical or legal services. However, becoming a profession demands social and market closure. A number of scholars have focused on this aspect of professionalisation (Berlant 1975; Larson 1977; Abbott 1988). Eliot Freidson blends these theoretical backgrounds in making the most significant contribution to our understanding of professions and professionalism. In his last major work, Freidson defends professions as the best form of occupational control and as legitimate monopolisation. For Freidson, professionalism exists 'when an organized occupation gains the power to determine who is qualified to perform a defined set of tasks, to prevent all others from performing that work, and to *control the criteria by which to evaluate performance*' (2001: 12, my emphasis), where neither consumers or managers can control what professionals do. It is superior to market or bureaucratic control in having a 'logic and integrity of its own' (2001: 11) and allowing for judgment and discretion. Crucially, it depends on a high level of public trust in order to flourish. Before discussing the contemporary challenges to this ideal type of professionalism, and preparing the ground for an alternative vision, the key concept of autonomy will be unpacked.

Medical Professional Autonomy

The trait theory for distinguishing professions from occupations is inevitably limited, prompting theorists such as Everett Hughes (1958) and

Eliot Freidson (2001: 13) to focus on wider questions about the sociology of work. But amongst the traits traditionally associated with professions, trust and autonomy are arguably the most important and are also inter-related. High autonomy is generally only conferred on groups who are trusted. The concept of trust, and in particular, the significance of chan-ging trust relationships between patients and doctors, is fully explored in Chapter 3. Autonomy is generally understood to mean control over one's own actions, but in this context has two distinct meanings. First is the autonomy of individual practitioners at the micro level to decide how they conduct themselves and practise medicine. Second is the autonomy of the profession as a whole at the macro level, reflected in the control exercised by the institutions of self-regulation. Individual professional autonomy may be further distinguished into three distinct yet interre-lated areas: economic, political, and clinical or technical autonomy. For Freidson, technical autonomy, that is, control over diagnosis, treatment, education, training, evaluation and discipline is at the very core of professional dominance. Unsurprisingly, the profession has been protec-tive of its autonomy, particularly in relation to clinical work and the *evaluation* of this work. The exclusivity of professional judgment in terms of defining and dealing with error is the most jealously guarded aspect of autonomy. As the Merrison inquiry into the regulation of the profession noted (1975: 3), it is the 'essence of professional skill that it deals with matters unfamiliar to the layman, and it follows that only those in the profession are in a position to judge many of the matters of standards of professional conduct'. This aspect of technical autonomy, which incorporates defining and dealing with medical errors, and more broadly the management of the safety of patients, is the main focus of this book.

Whilst the modern medical profession is characterised by a high degree of autonomy and trust, this has not always been true. In the latter part of the seventeenth century, the family and community, rather than medical practitioners were responsible for taking care of the sick. As Freidson explained 'Official medicine, however, had only a loose, variable connection with the general cultural beliefs of the population and was more a learned than a practicing profession' (1970a: 12). Poor economic status, preference for alternative methods, and the use of unqualified practitioners meant that demand for official conventional medicine was small (Waddington 1984: 182). Indeed, much medical work was part time and supplemented by other incomes. This low demand for a national market in healthcare was reflected in the reliance on local guild-like corporations rather than national institutions. Given that demand for official medicine was condensed amongst those of higher income and status, the doctor-patient relationship became a system of client control (1984: 191). Under this patronage system, as Jewson explained, it 'was the patient who judged the competence of the physician and the suitability of the therapy. The wealthy and influential threw their support behind whatever practitioner pleased them, and withdrew it from those in whom they were disappointed; thus it was the client who held ultimate power in the consultative relationship' (1974: 375). In short, medical autonomy was constrained under this patronage system where patients were not the 'passive creatures of mythology' (Corfield 1995: 141).

However, with increased demand for medical care in the nineteenth century, particularly from the lower socio-economic sector, the patronage system diminished in importance to doctors. No longer reliant on a few for their work, the balance of power shifted within the doctor-patient relationship. The rise of the urban middle class in the second half of the nineteenth century created an expanding market for services and provided the conditions for professionalism. As Johnson neatly observes, 'the Industrial Revolution opened the floodgates of professionalisation' (1972: 52). Changes in the structure of medical education were particularly significant to the development of medical autonomy. The localised apprenticeship system was gradually replaced by the teachings of university medical schools and centralised hospitals which became the 'secular cathedrals' of medical science (Corfield 1995: 161). Importantly, this formal institutional setting 'encouraged shared experiences with other students and, by so doing, facilitated the development of a common professional identity and sense of professional community' (Waddington 1984: 202). Medical practitioners were beginning to gain control through the dominance of professional rather than lay values.

This period witnessed the growth of specialist medical journals, most notably *The Lancet* in 1823 and the *British Medical Journal* in 1840. A further 148 were in circulation by 1850 (Corfield 1995: 141). The foundation of medical associations, notably the Provincial Medical and Surgical Association in 1832, which became the British Medical Association in 1852, hinted at a spirit of increasing professional unity (Loudon 1992). More generally, Perkin noted the 'enormous expansion' of professional associations from the end of the nineteenth century (140 between 1880 and 1990) as reflecting the rise of professional society (1990: 20). The 1858 Medical Act placed professional control on a statutory footing; in addition to seeking public protection against bogus doctors or 'quacks', the Act established the institutional structure of the modern medical profession. In particular, the legislation enabled a degree of social closure through effectively creating a monopoly for medical services. Although unqualified practice was not illegal, there were advantages attached to registration, for example a monopoly of practice in all public institutions. This took on considerable significance with the growth of the public sector from the late nineteenth century onwards (Waddington 1984: 147).

In the second half of the nineteenth century medicine began to resemble a homogeneous occupational group. In short, regulation was delegated to doctors. A professionally dominated Council permitted professional control of medical practice. This freedom from external supervision reflected increased public trust and marked the beginnings of medicine as a modern profession. The 1858 Medical Act represented the formal manifestation of the profession-state bargain where the profession committed to long training, hard work, expertise, and competence, in exchange for trust, autonomy, high pay and status. Professional regulation is thus based on a contract with the state, with the General Medical Council representing the institutional product of this arrangement. Despite doctors jealously protecting their autonomy, the relationship between medicine and the state became one of mutual necessity. Institutions were reliant on the state for their authority and funding, while the state depended on the institutions to care for the sick, to maintain a productive population and for educative and research purposes (Fox 1994: 1219). Professions straddled the boundary between the private and public, and the secret and open. Although independent, they were also dependent on the state to provide statutory protection (Vincent 1998: 23). Perhaps this is best conceptualised as a triangular relationship between the profession, civil society and the state. Public trust in the medical profession is central to this social contract. Undoubtedly, tensions have increased within this triangular relationship and led to a re-evaluation of the basis for trust, which is examined in Chapter 3, and a redesign of self-regulation, explored in Chapter 4.

The Dominance of Professional Dominance?

Professionalism crystallised during the twentieth century. In the United Kingdom the creation of the National Health Service in 1948 represented a significant concordat between the profession and the state. As Salter remarked (1999: 98), the 'medical profession gained money, status and the power to protect and regulate its privileges; the state gained a healthcare system to protect and regulate its populace'. This led to what many regarded as a golden age of the professions in the 1960s, and this is when the professional dominance theory emerged. Rooted in the Chicago school of sociology of Everett C. Hughes and Howard S. Becker, it is most closely associated with the work of Eliot Freidson (1970a and 1970b). Although writing in an American context, the main thrust of Freidson's argument was nevertheless applicable to the UK profession. This position held that medicine, relative to other healthcare professions, had achieved true organised autonomy and immunity from external review. It legitimately controlled the content of work and dominated other health professions and patients. In short, for Freidson paternalistic professional control was preferable to the alternatives of market or managerial control.

In one of the classic works on the sociology of the medical profession, Freidson argued that the defining features of professions, compared with occupations, were autonomy and self-regulation. Medicine had, according to this thesis, ensured control over all aspects of work; moreover this was 'legitimate, organized autonomy' (1970a: 71). As noted above, autonomy has many manifestations, relating to economic, political and clinical aspects of work. Even if the profession did not dominate the social and economic organisation of work, it controlled the most important aspect of professional autonomy, the technological part of work. For Freidson, autonomy of technical evaluation, in other words the 'recognized right to declare such "outside" evaluation illegitimate and intolerable', is at the core of professional autonomy (1970a: 72). Reflecting his overriding interest in the broader institutional environment, Freidson's professional dominance thesis referred to the collective (rather than individual) notion of autonomy. Thus whilst conceding that aspects of individual doctors' autonomy may be eroding, Freidson claimed that at the macro level, institutionalised professional autonomy survived through medical control of the supervision and management of medical care, including dealing with medical failure. Essentially, this involved the profession enjoying exclusive control over evaluating the quality of medical work, including defining and dealing with error. There was little room for external regulation or patient involvement within this model of professionalism. As Dingwall neatly summarised, 'the dominant profession judges others without itself being judged' (2006: 85).

Freidson's theory was soon challenged by other sociologists of the medical profession. In particular, two theories predicted the decline of the professional dominance model: the deprofessionalisation thesis (Haug 1973) and a Marxist theory of proletarianisation (McKinlay and Stoeckle 1988). The deprofessionalisation thesis was defined as 'a loss to professional occupations of their unique qualities, particularly their monopoly over knowledge, public belief in their service ethos, and expectations of work autonomy and authority over the client' (Haug 1973: 197). For Haug, this was a developing process signalling diminishing prestige, status and trust in the profession. Five main reasons are cited for this. First, concerns the erosion of professional monopoly over access to knowledge, mainly through the technological assault on knowledge and professional performance by computers. As Haug explains, scientific professional knowledge can be 'codified', broken into bits stored in a computer memory, and recalled as needed. No longer need it be preserved in the professional's head or in books alone (1973: 201). Professional dominance is thus challenged by technology: '[t]he accessibility of this intellectual warehouse has already taken away some of the professional's knowledge monopoly, and will undoubtedly continue to do so' (1973: 202). The use of the internet and smart technology and the effect of this re-balancing of knowledge between professionals and patients has made this prediction particularly prescient (Jutel and Lupton 2015). In addition, the increase of general education has contributed to the de-mystification of medicine, with declining deference leading to increased willingness to challenge doctors. Furthermore, increased specialisation means that the profession is increasingly reliant on other professionals and non-professionals, thus further dispersing power. The emergence of professions allied to medicine also challenges its dominance of the work domain.

In terms of the division of labour, the medical profession is now surrounded by a number of professions, some of which are in competition with each other for work. For example, the Health and Care Professions Council regulates 16 different professions (HCPC 2016). The role of nurses has also changed, notably with the rise of the nurse practitioner, undertaking some of the work previously performed by junior medics (Royal College of Nursing 2010). Unsurprisingly, the growth of professions allied to medicine has led to a more multi-disciplinary approach to healthcare. Whilst doctors remain powerful figures in such teams, their dominance has diminished somewhat. At the same time, medicine has become increasingly specialised and reliant on expensive drugs and technology.

One of the consequences of scientific advances is that medicine has become less personalised and tends to treat diseases rather than people with diseases (Leape 2010), echoing what Ivan Illich termed the depersonalisation of diagnosis and therapy (1977a: 30). Advances in medical technology and increased specialisation of medical work make it less meaningful to refer to a single homogenous entity. The proliferation of consumer self-help groups has been a further thorn in the side of dominance. However, revisiting her thesis fifteen years later, Haug (1988) accepted that history had not by that point fully borne out her claims. It arguably makes much more sense when we think about the modern day medical profession.

The proletarianisation thesis is based on the Marxist theory that workers in capitalism lose control of their work. For example, changes in work conditions, such as deskilling from increased specilisation, the hierarchy and bureaucratisation of workplace regulation through rules and managerial control, and the increase of lay influence leads to alienation and decreased professional autonomy (McKinlay and Stoeckle 1988). The burgeoning evidence-based medicine movement, the proliferation of guidelines and the role of institutions such as the National Institute for Health and Care Excellence (NICE), are consistent with this de-skilling argument. Freidson's work also set the scene for broader attacks on the dominance of medicine, as opposed to the medical profession. Most notable amongst these was Ivan Illich's fierce and farsighted attack on the counterproductive ills of medicalisation (1977a) and what he saw as the disabling effect doctors have on patients (1977b). Illich savagely criticised various forms of iatrogenesis – clinical, social and cultural – which he claimed rendered individuals overly reliant on medicine and medics, and ultimately made for an unhealthy society. The ills of medicalisation have continued to attract criticism (Skrabanek 1994; Fitzpatrick 2000; Light 2011) and been applied in relation to a number of medico-legal settings such as abortion (Sheldon 1997) complaint handling (Mulcahy 2003) and electronic-pharmacies (Glover-Thomas and Fanning 2010).

Initially, Freidson remained unimpressed and unmoved by these challenges to the professional dominance thesis. In response to the deprofessionalisation thesis, whilst accepting the growing influence of computers, Freidson noted that storing and interpreting such knowledge remained a professional domain. Although constrained by clinical guidelines and protocols, given the profession's role in developing these, it remained dominant. In response to the proletarianisation thesis, although accepting that aspects of individual autonomy may have diminished, Freidson maintained that the autonomy of the profession at the macro level was intact. Crucially, physicians retain control over evaluating *each other's work*. Although external pressures altered the environment, 'members of the profession administer and perform the new functions of control pushed onto it by external forces' (1986: 71). For Freidson then, rather than *losing* control, the profession merely *adjusts* to manage the new situation created by the pressure of external forces. Writing in 1991, Elston echoed Freidson's conclusions in a British context, for example, playing down the significance of changes at the General Medical Council, notably procedures for dealing with professional performance and increased lay membership. According to Elston, such changes look more like 'uncomfortable adjustments than a major waning of either the medical profession's institutionalised technical autonomy or of their social and cultural authority' (1991: 84). However, Elston also acknowledged that this conclusion might be premature, which has proved to be accurate given her subsequent claim that medical sociologists would no longer deny a reduction in medical autonomy and status over the past 20 years (2009: 19).

Some have questioned the merits of advancing theories such as 'professional dominance', 'de-professionalisation' and 'proletarianisation' on the basis that they only characterise one trend in the profession – society relationship. For example, Light is critical of the UK sociological literature for the assumption that the 'Anglo-American ideal of the autonomous independent professional is the theoretical centre for analysis, rather than as a cultural ideal by certain professions at certain times in history' (1995: 31). He proposes a model of 'countervailing powers' as a better way of understanding profession-state relations. According to this view, the State is able to dilute professional autonomy and authority and instead focus on scrutinising performance and increasing accountability (1995: 31). This involves analysing interactions between the main actors, and an appreciation that dominance by one party encourages counter-moves by other main actors to redress power imbalance. The main limitation of this approach is that by focusing on the profession-state relationship it overlooks the role of patients as meaningful actors in the process. This book will argue that modern professionalism, and its theorisation, has to be more patient centred. This means recognising patients as true partners in their healthcare and involves encouraging patients and their carers to play a more active role in ensuring the safety of care. The context for this rethinking of professionalism has been marked by the rise of consumerism and managerialism, which will be briefly discussed here. It has also been influenced by a series of high-profile cases of medical failure that have caught public and political attention. Before outlining the key characteristics of this reformed professionalism, some understanding of this context is necessary.

Consumerism and Managerialism

Modern society is undoubtedly consumerist. In healthcare, this has manifested itself in terms of increasingly well-informed and engaged patients and their willingness to comment, complain and seek compensation about substandard medical treatment. Many (including patients themselves) may resist the label 'consumer' on the basis that public goods such as health and education should be based around caring rather than consumerist relationships (Mold 2010). Nevertheless, a consumerist mentality has influenced the delivery of key public services such as education and health (Simmons, Powell and Greener 2009). Viewing patients as consumers is a central feature of the increasing marketisation of public services, as is the emphasis on competition and choice in the delivery of modern healthcare services (DOH 2015a), which has been subject to fierce criticism (Pollock 2005; Tallis and Davis 2013). The increased reliance on private medical insurance and areas where patients commonly pay for treatment – such as fertility services and cosmetic surgery – also normalises a consumerist approach to healthcare. The possibility of patients paying top up fees to help fund expensive treatments (Jackson 2010), and the increase of health tourism (Reisman 2010) further illustrate the rise of health consumerism. And whereas once health services were perhaps resistant to criticism and complaints, healthcare organisations now actively encourage patients to provide public feedback on their experiences via websites such as NHS Choices or I want Great Care.

Consumerism has coincided with the rise of managerialism. The role of managers in healthcare has undoubtedly increased over the past 30 years. This can be traced to the NHS Management Inquiry of 1983, led by Roy Griffiths, which expressed surprise that the NHS lacked meaningful evaluation of its performance against set criteria. In a short report, it noted that 'Businessmen have a keen sense of how well they are looking after their customers. Whether the NHS is meeting the needs of the patient, and the community, and can prove that it is doing so, is open to question' (Griffiths 1983: 10). Unfortunately, this is still open to question. The report stressed the need to recognise patients as consumers and marked the introduction of general management and economics into healthcare. Significantly, by seeking to change the balance of power between doctors and managers, it challenged the assumptions of the NHS. As Klein explains (1995: 151), to 'ask whether the right goods were being produced and to question the adequacy of standards was ... to threaten the secret garden of professional autonomy'. Increased managerial monitoring of the quality of medical work has occurred within the general context of greater scrutiny of other public services such as education, social services, and local government. This changing ethos for regulating the public sector has been referred to as New Public Management (Hood 1991) or new governance. In terms of medicine, this has meant an increased emphasis on clinical governance, standards, performance measurement and increased competition.

The status of managers increased with the enactment of the National Health Service and Community Care Act 1990, which by introducing markets and contracts into the NHS encouraged greater managerialism. The context for this shift was the Thatcherite ideology of a free market economy for services, including health, but also a strong state (Farnham and Horton 1993). This was part of a wider attack on professional groups, especially public-sector professionals, as profligate and inefficient (Perkin 1990). The influence of managers increased with the introduction of Clinical Governance in 1998. Section 18(1) of the Health Act 1999 placed a legal duty on healthcare providers to have 'arrangements for the purpose of monitoring, and improving the quality of healthcare which it provides for individuals', which has been amended by subsequent Health and Social Care Acts. This established a statutory duty of quality on NHS organisations and thus created an increased need for management. Many of the changes to healthcare regulatory landscape discussed in Chapter 4, particularly the rise of the Care Quality Commission as a system regulator, has placed an onus on healthcare managers to ensure compliance with fundamental standards of care. Whilst the empirical evidence about the role of managers in contributing to safety is somewhat thin (Parand 2013), obvious ways in which they can make a contribution include efforts to encourage a safety culture, the implementation of evidenced based best practice, and compliance with open disclosure policies. For example, Feng et al. (2011) have empirically demonstrated a statistically significant association between management safety commitment and the culture of patient safety, additionally finding that management commitment was a predictor of patient safety culture.

However, the extent to which increased managerialism has decreased medical power or dominance is less clear. The increase of managerialism, alongside the demise of traditional self-regulation (discussed in Chapter 4) clearly has implications for the profession's dominant position in the social contract with the state. However, the empirical base for the claim that managers dominate professionals is somewhat thin. For example, clinical governance activities have tended to be led by medical professionals (Dopson 2009: 46). Indeed, some have suggested that rather than weakening medical power, increased managerial regulation strengthens the position of the medical profession, given the reliance on expertise which continues to be valued and trusted (Kuhlmann 2006a: 192). However, it is undoubtedly the case that medical work is now subject to managerial concepts and constraints, and that this has had some effect on medical dominance.

Scandal and Scrutiny

In this consumerist and managerialist era, the work and regulation of the medical profession has been subject to an unprecedented degree of scrutiny. Robert Dingwall's observation in 1999 that these were not propitious times for the profession has transpired to be quite an understatement (1999: 131). As will be explored in subsequent chapters, the number of complaints and negligence claims about healthcare have increased markedly, as have criminal and coronial investigations into deaths associated with medical error. The media has been active in reporting on medical failure (Davies and Shields 1999), and the government has (somewhat belatedly) given sustained attention to the problem of patient safety and begun to tackle the shortcomings of self-regulation (see Chapter 4). There have also been numerous high profile public inquiries, mainly into failings around safety and consent, that have amply illustrated the many problems with ensuring patient safety (Kennedy 2001; Smith 2004; Francis 2013). Whilst there is no space to examine all of these, it would be remiss not to remember the most important episodes which have had significant implications for the regulation of the profession and the degree of public trust vested in it (which are discussed, respectively, in Chapters 3 and 4). They provide an important context that has shaped debate both about regulation, professionalism and the problem of how to improve patient safety.

The first of these involved the inquiry into paediatric heart surgery at the Bristol Royal Infirmary. Reflecting its profound effect, and akin to other infamous disasters such as Lockerbie, Chernobyl and Zeebrugge, the events and aftermath have been commonly referred to by the single word 'Bristol'. It involved paediatric cardiac surgery performed by two surgeons, James Wisheart and Janardan Dhasmana, at Bristol's Royal Infirmary, between 1990 and 1995. This involved two surgical procedures – arterial switch operations for the transposition of the great arteries and surgery to correct atrioventricular septal defects, also known as 'hole in the heart' operations. Concerns were voiced by Stephen Bolsin, then a consultant anaesthetist at the hospital, who began recording operative results to test his unease over the length and outcomes of operations at Bristol, which he believed compared unfavourably with those at other centres. Dr Bolsin expressed his concerns to the hospital chief executive, Dr John Roylance, and then the Department of Health. The surgeons were stopped from performing operations in 1995.

In June 1996, parents of deceased and brain damaged children made a complaint to the General Medical Council in what became the longest and most expensive case in its history. Aggrieved parents claimed that 55 children died and 13 were left brain damaged after undergoing surgery at the hospital. The two consultant surgeons, James Wisheart and Janardan Dhasmana, were charged with serious professional misconduct for continuing to perform cardiac operations despite a high rate of mortality and morbidity; Wisheart also stood accused of misleading parents by underestimating the risks that their children would be exposed to. The then chief executive of United Bristol Healthcare Trust, Dr John Roylance, was similarly charged with serious professional misconduct for allowing the operations to proceed. Counsel for the GMC presented evidence that Dr Wisheart's mortality rate for correcting the hole in the heart operations was 54 per cent, which compared unfavourably with the national average of 13.9 per cent. One in two of his patients undergoing this procedure were dying as opposed to the one in seven across the country. Of the 13 arterial switch operations performed by Dr Dhasmana, nine resulted in death which compared badly with the 90 per cent national survival rate (Dyer 1997: 967). This evidence was subject to a debate between another consultant at the hospital – who claimed that the surgeons were only judged on 4 per cent of their paediatric surgical caseload in these proceedings (Dunn 1998), and Dr Bolsin – who maintained that the mortality figures were excessive (Bolsin 1998a).

After a 65-day hearing, in which 67 witnesses responded to more than 2,500 questions from counsel and the Professional Conduct Committee, the allegations were found to have been proved against the doctors. James Wisheart and John Roylance received the ultimate penalty of being erased from the medical register, whilst Janardan Dhasmana was banned from operating on children for three years (Horton 1998). It was not only the three doctors who were being judged; the Bristol Royal Infirmary, the General Medical Council and medical profession as a whole were effectively on trial. The Bristol heart surgery affair represents a watershed in the history of the medical profession. The emotive nature of multiple death and injury of young babies following allegedly incompetent heart surgery, ensured that it captured the attention of the profession, the public and politicians. It led to a high profile public inquiry chaired by Professor Ian Kennedy (2001), which made a number of recommendations, many of which have been implemented and are examined later in this book. It has transformed the context of medical regulation; as the editor of the BMJ explained, echoing W. B. Yeats, after Bristol it is a case of 'all changed, changed utterly' (Smith 1998).

Bristol was widely regarded as a disaster for the medical profession. It was soon followed by another, more disturbing one. In January 2000, Dr Harold Shipman, a General Practitioner, was convicted of killing 15 of his patients after prescribing and administering lethal doses of morphine. The true toll of his killing is believed to have far exceeded this. A public inquiry, led by Dame Janet Smith, was established to investigate the surrounding systems that failed to prevent such mass murder (Smith 2005). Unlike Bristol, which revolved around the technical deficiencies of otherwise well-intentioned heart surgeons, Shipman was an evil killer. However, despite this important difference, both raised issues about the regulation of the medical profession and the safety of patients. The vast six-volume inquiry report contained stinging criticisms of the GMC and numerous recommendations for reforming it, as well as suggesting changes to the coronial system and to the monitoring of General Practitioners. A number of these reforms have been enacted and will be discussed in Chapter 4.

The final noteworthy episode in this period of scrutiny of medical work occurred at Mid Staffordshire NHS Foundation Trust. Between January 2005 and March 2009, hundreds of patients suffered harm and in some cases died due to shortcomings in the standards of care at the hospital. These failures included medication mistakes and neglecting to ensure patients received basic hydration and nutrition. It was reported that the poor standards of care contributed to an estimated 1,200 unnecessary deaths (Smith 2009), although this figure has been the subject of considerable debate. However, it is clear that many patients suffered harm due to unacceptably poor standards of care, and also that some members of staff had raised concerns about the safety of care to the hospital management. These events were investigated by a high-profile public inquiry chaired by Robert Francis QC, and the final report contained no less than 290 recommendations (Francis 2013). The Government was quick to respond by accepting that further reforms to strengthen the regulatory and legal frameworks for ensuring safe care were necessary (Department of Health 2014).

A proper understanding of the recent history of the medical profession and its regulation cannot ignore the impact that 'Bristol', 'Shipman' and 'Mid-Staffs' have had. There have been other so-called medical scandals during this period, but none which have captured public and political attention as much as these. Their combined effect has been to create a sense of crisis around the regulation of professionals, patient safety and the healthcare system generally. They have undoubtedly acted as catalysts for significant reform of the regulatory and legal environment that will be explored in this book. They have also encouraged reflection on the concept of professionalism, and what this should mean given the increasing emphasis on patient safety.

Re-thinking Professionalism: Protecting Patients and Professions?

In the final section of this chapter, a sketch is provided of the main positions taken within this book. It will be argued that the professional dominance era is coming to an end, if somewhat belatedly, and that this offers a welcome opportunity to radically reconsider the nature of medical professionalism. Increased knowledge about the problem of patient safety provides an important context for designing a more appropriate notion of professionalism, which is protective of both patients and professions. The idea of protecting patients is perhaps self-evident: improving the quality and safety of healthcare is clearly protective of patients. But embattled professions, stung by what some regard as an unwarranted assault on their integrity (Tallis 2004), might wonder how this can also be protective of professions. After all, the rise of consumerism and a greater emphasis on patient empowerment has coincided with the most turbulent time in the history of the medical profession. But this book will argue that a new patient-centred form of professionalism can also be protective of the profession, and is preferable to alternative models that allow markets or managerial led bureaucracy to dominate. Such models increase the risk that professionals may act in ways which put the interests of organisations before those of their patients (Mechanic and McAlpine 2010). Medical dominance leaves insufficient space for regulation to be proactive in terms of trying to improve safety. Similarly, it largely overlooks the role which patients themselves may play in terms of securing the safety of their medical care. This book supports a more patient-centred form of professionalism, based on a healthier and more effective form of trust.

Whilst sociologists have long predicted the decline of the traditional sense of professionalism (Haug 1973; Stacey 1992) the medical profession has been reluctant to acknowledge this. This is likely explained by the fear of a loss of control and trust that is associated with a different form of professionalism. It is only during the last decade amidst critical comment about safety problems and the failure of self-regulation that professional bodies have attempted to refashion a modernised form of professionalism. In 2005, a Royal College of Physicians' report advocated a new type of professionalism, stripped of the perceived negative references to autonomy and self-regulation and shifting the focus to patients and partnerships (RCP 2005). The report notes that '[i]n an age where deference is dead and league tables are the norm, doctors must be clearer about what they do, and how and why they do it' (2005: xi), and, we might add, how safely they do it. In a follow up report, the Royal College calls for a new type of medic suited to this age of decreased deference and the rise of the informed consumer. The model professional must now be flexible, emotionally intelligent, patient-centred, and fully engaged with technological innovations and initiatives in patient safety research (2010). The report echoes the de-professionalisation thesis in terms of noting the challenge that increased internet usage poses to traditional notions of authority and expertise. It also correctly predicts that as individuals become more aware of risk, they become more interested in patient safety and patient-centred care (2010: 26).

Other influential organisations have echoed this call for a new form of medical professionalism. A scoping study commissioned by the Health Foundation, an independent healthcare charity, argues for a vision of professionalism which focuses on healthy relationships with patients as partners in healthcare (Christmas and Millward 2011). Similarly, the Society for Cardiothoracic Surgery in GB and Ireland (2011) has criticised professionalism for its misplaced sense of collegiality and a lack of patient-centredness. Instead of being reduced to a list of appropriate traits, professionalism must be recognised as being socially constructed through interaction with patients and other professions (Martimianakis et al. 2009). Modern professionalism must also embrace features of modern healthcare systems, such as the emphasis on evidence-based practice, patient centredness and a commitment to accountability and regulation (Martin et al. 2015). It must also welcome teamwork and be open to the suggestions and scrutiny of others, including those traditionally lower down the power hierarchy. Professionals should be honest about safety, both before treatment in terms of meaningful informed consent, and also after treatment in the sense of being candid with patients and their families when things go wrong in the delivery of treatment. Professionalism should also involve a commitment to engage with the science of patient safety and improvement.

This vision of professionalism disturbs prevailing assumptions about what constitutes a good doctor, which has tended to be associated primarily with technical competence. This book takes the position that being a good professional must mean more than technical competence and extend to a range of other competencies and attributes, especially around communication. There are a number of important strands to this, but it includes having the confidence to raise concerns about the safety of care, being honest with patients when treatment has caused them harm and more generally involving patients with their care and treatment, including engaging them about the safety of care. The argument in this book thus differs from Freidson's ideal type of professionalism, which largely excludes patients from the evaluation of medical work. It will argue that it is necessary and legitimate to look beyond the profession in order to address the challenge of improving levels of safe care. This necessitates insisting on a role for patients, not only in terms of lay representation in formal regulation, but also for patient and carer involvement in the safety of treatment to become the cultural norm within medicine. In some ways, this is reminiscent of Illich's warning that 'Medical nemesis is resistant to medical remedies. It can be reversed only through recovery of the will to self-care among the laity' (1977a: 35). To be fair, Freidson's arguments must be understood in the context of the golden age of medicine in the 1960s. Indeed, in his final major contribution Freidson accepted that the meaning of professional dominance has changed, most notably in terms of increased managerial control of medical work (2001: 182–5).

Much else has changed since the time of Freidson's professional dominance thesis in the 1970s. There is no doubt that professions (of all types) have been under attack over the past twenty years or so. This began as a new right challenge to the authority of professions, and has continued with the rise of managerialism and new public management. The decline of deference and the rise of the informed consumer, first predicted in the 1970s, have continued as choice and competition have become the new watchwords of the health system. In this context, it is undeniable that the concept of professionalism requires rethinking. As Evetts neatly sums up: the 'association of trust, competence and professionalism is now being questioned' (2009: 25). This has led to talk of two different (and competing) types of professionalism: organisational and occupational, the former driven by managerial concerns with accountability, appraisal and bureaucracy, and the latter with traditional sense of self-regulation, discretion and trust (Evetts 2006: 141).

Arguably, attention to the problem of patient safety represents a catalyst for thinking about professionalism and for addressing one aspect of what Illich called the ills of medicalisation. However, it has been questioned whether professional dominance is actually in decline, or if so, whether it is limited to the encroachment of law in medico-legal areas such as the beginning and end of life (Dingwall 2006: 90). And some argue that professionalism is sufficiently flexible and robust to evolve without significantly diminishing professional power. According to Kuhlmann et al. (2013: 4) 'there is no one uniform pattern of transfor-mations and not "a" new professionalism but various different ways of designing and re-designing professionalism and the relationship with organisations and management'. Others such as Furedi have suggested that a strange consequence of medicalisation has been the end of profes-sional dominance by doctors; indeed going as far as to say that the profession has been pushed out of the picture (2006: 18). But the question of whether or not the profession remains dominant is perhaps of less importance. Of more relevance is the question of *how* professionalism can evolve to embrace patient safety – and within this, the primacy of the patient – as its dominant concern? Policy documents and public inquiry reports are now driven by the idea of putting patients first, but how can this be realised? This is a significant challenge which involves issues of culture, regulation and law. But it is also reliant on practitioners being inspired by a new form of professionalism and demonstrating this in practice (Martin et al. 2015).

This book examines a number of key questions which are central to this evolution of medical professionalism. How can relationships based on trust be maintained given greater lay understanding of medical errors and patient safety problems? How can law and regulation help support this new style of professionalism? How can a culture of openness be fostered around patient safety incidents? How can effective mechanisms of accountability, which help deter unsafe practice, be put in place without creating a climate of fear amongst professionals? How can patients play a more active role in terms of securing their own safety and how can professionalism encourage this? The work of patient safety pioneers such as Atul Gawande and Peter Pronovost, discussed in the next chapter, provides a good example of this patient centred professionalism in action.

2

The Problem of Patient Safety

The term 'patient safety' is beguilingly simple, yet in reality is extremely complex. All aspects of the provision of healthcare have implications for the safety of patients. Most obviously, patients are in the hands of the professionals who treat them and have to trust in their individual competence and performance. However, safety is also dependent on bigger system issues such as appropriate levels of staffing, sufficient bed space, the design of buildings, the manufacture of drugs and devices and the organisation and funding of health systems. It even extends to the work of cleaners and porters in terms of ensuring hygiene and the transporting of patients and equipment around hospitals. It thus involves decisions taken by a range of professionals, managers, politicians, regulators and of course patients. Whilst all of these are important, this book focuses on patient safety and the work of the medical profession in terms of decisions, diagnoses and the discharging of duties of care. Despite its obvious significance, the study of error and safety in medicine remains a relatively new area of research. Indeed, it remains something of a poor relation in terms of academic medicine. Nevertheless, there is now ample evidence about the scale of medical errors and more broadly of areas where patient safety is routinely compromised. The subject of safety has been transformed from a private professional problem to an important issue of global public health. It is no longer the preserve of doctors which calls into question the continued relevance of the professional dominance thesis. However, despite the increase of patient safety research and political and public anxiety, questions about measuring, monitoring and improving safety remain difficult. Unfortunately, despite some notable examples in specific specialities and for particular conditions, there is no reliable data to demonstrate that patients are, on the whole, safer. After tracing the history of medical error and patient safety, this chapter will explain this with reference to informational and cultural deficits in relation to safety in medicine.

Medical Error: A Brief History

As the sociologist Everett C. Hughes (1958) explained, mistakes are a predictable property of work. In every occupation there is a calculus of the probability of making mistakes, and a certain amount of error remains normal, routine and thus inevitable. Despite being the stuff of everyday things (Norman 1988), or a type of 'illegal normality' (Vincent 2010: 316), the sociology of mistake has, with a few notable exceptions (Paget 1988; Vaughan 1999), been a neglected field of study. The *formal* and *systematic* study of error and its higher profile in professional, policy making and regulatory environments is a recent development. Yet the safety of patients is hardly a new field of concern; after all, the first principle of medicine is the famous Hippocratic instruction to 'help or at least do no harm' (Sharpe and Faden 1998: 6). At the turn of the twentieth century, the study of error was embraced by a few radical and visionary professionals. These are 'forgotten heroes' of patient safety (and more broadly of public health), who championed a simple science based on monitoring and learning in order to prevent medical failure. It would be remiss not to acknowledge their somewhat overlooked contribution to patient safety and the lessons which can be learnt from such a basic approach which is now advocated by those championing the science of improvement (Marshall et al. 2013).

The formal gathering of hospital records and statistics was advocated in the late nineteenth century by Thomas Percival (1849) and Florence Nightingale (1863). However, arguably the most influential figure in terms of evaluating the quality of medical work was the American surgeon and reformer Ernest Codman. In the early twentieth century Codman developed the 'end-result system', based on the 'common-sense notion that every hospital should follow *every* patient it treats long enough to determine whether or not the treatment has been successful, and then inquire 'if not, why not?', with a view to preventing similar failures in the future' (Codman 1984: xii quoted in Sharpe and Faden 1998: 29). Not only did this represent one of the first systematic attempts to determine the causes and learn from adverse events, but by encouraging *public reporting* of the deficiencies in medical work, it was a considerable challenge to the autonomy of medical professionals. The compiling of a complete patient record, including an assessment of reasons for the failure of the treatment was central to the system. This was based on:

errors due to lack of technical knowledge or skill; errors due to lack of surgical judgment; errors due to lack of care or equipment; errors due to lack of diagnostic skill; the patient's unconquerable disease; the patient's refusal of treatment; the calamities of surgery or those accidents and complications over which we have no control.

This data collection represented an early (and controversial) attempt at medical audit. By replacing individual conscience with documented competence as the basis for clinical evaluation, Codman 'challenged the moral and professional autonomy of the physician' (Sharpe and Faden 1998: 31). Codman was a radical anti-establishment figure and his ideas were considered unorthodox and initially unrealisable (Mallon 2000). However, his work gained credibility in 1916 when the American College of Surgeons incorporated his Committee on Hospital Standardization, and it was Codman's work which ultimately led in 1952 to the introduction of the Joint Commission on Accreditation of Hospitals to oversee hospital quality in the United States.

Codman was not alone in banging the drum about medical error. Harvey Cushing, a former classmate and colleague, was also enthused by the promise of transparency. A pioneering neurosurgeon, he was famous for writing up case notes and publicising his errors in the hope of educating others (Pinkus 2001; Bliss 2005). And most notoriously, there was Ignac Semmelweiss, the eccentric Hungarian doctor who claimed that the unclean hands of his colleagues accounted for the increased mortality for puerperal fever at a Vienna hospital. Although his hypothesis about the cause of puerperal fever was not proven beyond doubt, his relentless efforts in pursuing a clean hands campaign (Wootton 2006: 215–23) was an early example of what is now reflected in World Health Organisation policy (2009). It is regrettable that the work of Codman and others was largely forgotten until the 1980s when the more systematic study of medical error and patient safety began to emerge.

From the 1960s onwards, data started to accrue suggesting that a high proportion of hospital patients experienced potentially preventable iatrogenic harm. This attracted little attention until the 1990s, when the data was converted into estimates of the number of people in America who died each year in from iatrogenic injury (180,000), and (strikingly) of what this equated to in terms of jumbo jet crashes (three every two days) (Leape 1994). Media coverage of these estimates greatly raised public awareness of the scale of the problem (Davies and Shields 1999; Millenson 2002), often via sensationalised stories about blunderers, botchers and butchers. Yet, the 1990s also saw the emergence in the mainstream medical literature of a coherent challenge to the hitherto 'bad apple' theory of medical harm. Most notably, two Boston based physicians, Don Berwick and Lucian Leape, inspired by work in human factors and cognitive psychology (Reason 1990; Rasmussen 1990), argued that insights from research into human error and systems failures could be usefully applied to hospital medicine (Berwick 1989; Leape 1994). These enlightened practitioners recognised that many safety problems in healthcare arose as a result of the complexity of healthcare delivery systems. They recommended that efforts to identify and investigate errors be made routine, and that healthcare delivery systems be redesigned to reduce the likelihood of errors (for example by reducing reliance on human memory and standardising processes) and to increase the chances of intercepting errors before they cause harm (for example by building in multiple checking procedures) (Leape 1997).

These ideas moved into mainstream thinking about healthcare quality with the publication of the landmark American report 'To Err is Human' (IOM). This report emphasised the scale of error and harm in healthcare and the fact that these problems were for the most part attributable to features of healthcare delivery systems rather than individual health professionals. It attracted significant media publicity, gained the attention of high level policy makers and 'galvanized a dramatically expanded level of conversation and concern about patient injuries in healthcare both in the United States and abroad' (Leape and Berwick 2005). It was quickly followed by another report setting out recommendations for systems improvement and patient centred care (IOM 2001). In the United Kingdom, the publication by the Chief Medical Officer of 'An Organisation with a Memory' (Department of Health 2000) repeated this call for focusing on system problems and had a similarly energising effect.

These two major reports have inspired what is now a busy research area. There is no longer, as Charles Vincent opined in 1989, a 'negligent' lack of research into errors and safety (Vincent 1989). Reflecting the multi-disciplinary nature of healthcare safety, a body of work has evolved in psychology (Vincent 1993, 2010), medical sociology (Bosk 1979; Bogner 1994; Dixon-Woods 2010), policy studies (Rosenthal et al. 1999), health services research (Davies et al. 2007; Rowley and Waring 2011) and medico-legal studies (Sharpe and Faden 1998; Merry and McCall Smith 2001; Mulcahy 2003; Runciman et al. 2007; Tingle and Bark 2011; Healy 2011). Encouragingly, the foundational work of Don Berwick, Lucian Leape and Charles Vincent has been continued by an enthusiastic new generation of patient safety heroes, physician and policy activists such as Atul Gawande (2003, 2007, 2009), Alan Merry (2001, 2007), Jerome Groopman (2007), Peter Pronovost (2010) and Tim Draycott (2015). Submissions to specialist journals such as the *BMJ Quality and Safety* and the *International Journal of Quality in Health Care* have increased as an evidence base is established. The level of interest in patient safety is reflected in the number of Google searches, which have increased enormously from 500,000 in February 2004 (Emslie 2005) to 113,000,000 as of January 2016.

This has prompted governments to establish national agencies to collate evidence in an attempt to improve quality and safety. In the United Kingdom, a National Patient Safety Agency was established in 2001, describing itself as the most ambitious patient safety data collection system worldwide (NPSA 2004: 6). Its main task was to collect and disseminate information, for example the 'Seven steps to patient safety checklist' and issue patient safety alerts. It focused on 'never events', that is, serious and entirely preventable errors that should not occur, such as wrong site surgery and leaving surgical instruments inside patients (NPSA 2004). It also coordinated the National Clinical Assessment Service, which deals with concerns about the performance of practitioners referred by health-care professionals or managers (it does not respond to complaints by patients), dealing with 4,748 cased during its first eight years of operation (NPSA 2009: 50). Whilst receiving criticism for being 'simply an information collection system' (NAO 2005: 6) and for failing to ensure compliance with its safety alerts (*The Guardian*, 15 February 2010) it is regrettable that the NPSA was abolished in 2012 as part of Government cost cutting of public services. Whilst its functions have been transferred to the NHS Commissioning Board, the profile and momentum gained by the NPSA have been lost somewhat. However, the case for a single independent agency to investigating patient safety incidents (Macrae and Vincent 2014) has been accepted by the UK government with its proposal to establish a new Healthcare Safety Investigation Branch (DOH 2016).

Internationally, other notable agencies include the Australian Commission on Safety and Quality in Health Care, the Veterans' Affairs National Center for Patient Safety and the Joint Commission on the Accreditation of Healthcare Organisations in America. Patient safety is also on the agenda of the World Health Organisation, which hitherto has largely focused its efforts on managing the response to infectious disease outbreaks, but has expanded under the World Alliance for Patient

Safety (Pittet and Donaldson 2006). Its second patient safety challenge was the 'safer surgery saves lives' initiative which has culminated in the safe surgery checklist that is now being mandated across the world. Nevertheless, despite its higher profile, it remains a poor relation within academic medicine. The perception that patient safety research is 'not real science' is problematic yet misconceived, given the reality that it holds as much life-saving potential, for example, as cancer vaccine research (Gawande 2007). The campaign to inspire medics to engage with the science of improvement has begun, but has a long way to go (Marshall et al. 2013). Before examining such work, this chapter will explore efforts to define the subject of medical error and patient safety.

Error and Safety

The term 'medical error' has been used alongside terms such as mistakes, mishaps, failures, accidents, deficient or substandard care, adverse or untoward events, iatrogenic harm, as well as more pejorative terms such as negligence and incompetence. Whilst some have preferred to focus on understanding the complexity of the system as opposed to agonising over conceptual distinctions (Phillips 1999), others have attempted to carefully define key terms. One of the most important conceptual advances in the literature has been the separation of errors from violations (Merry and McCall Smith, 2001; Runciman et al. 2007). Error is defined as 'unintentionally being wrong in conduct or judgement' (Runciman et al. 2007: 296) or as 'the failure of a planned action to be completed as intended, or the use of a wrong plan to achieve an aim' (IOM 1999: 54). Errors are unintentional and involuntary, whereas violations are deliberate deviations from accepted rules or standards. They usually involve choice, whereas errors are almost always exceptional. Violations may be classified as 'routine' (not hand washing), 'corporate' (working long hours and associated fatigue) or as 'exceptional' (not record keeping or completing checklists in emergencies) (Runciman et al. 2007: 132).

James Reason has famously unpacked error into knowledge based, ruled based and skill based events. He offers a working definition of error as a 'a generic term to encompass all those occasions in which a planned sequence of mental or physical activities fails to achieve its intended outcome, and when these failures cannot be attributed to the intervention of some chance agency' (1990: 9). More specifically, Reason labels slips as 'execution failures' and mistakes as 'planning failures'

(1990: 8). Mistakes may be further distinguished into 'rule-based' and 'knowledge-based' types (1990: 53). The quest for detailed definition and the drawing of distinctions can lead to the identification of many different error types. For example, Runciman et al. (2007: 115) have developed a comprehensive tenfold classification of error:

- errors in information (handovers are a particular problem)
- errors in acquisition of knowledge (information in the individual's mind)
- errors in perception (e.g. seeing what you expect to see – drug labels)
- errors in matching (confirmation bias or fixation error)
- errors in knowledge stored as schemata (absent or incorrect knowledge)
- errors in knowledge stored as rules (not knowing/forgetting a rule, error in interpretation)
- skill-based errors – slips and lapses (being distracted)
- errors in choice of rule – (good rule, wrong context)
- technical errors (mismatch between skill/ability of individual and what is required)
- deliberative errors (the use of judgment and discretion when rules run out)

This detailed approach recognises the complexity of error and reminds us of the human dimension reflected in the expression that 'to err is human', or as Runciman et al. put it, 'error is the downside of having a brain' (2007: 124). However, the subject of medical error has been subsumed within the broader concern for patient safety. This is a positive development given the greater promise of focusing on risk and harm rather than just error reduction. This shift from error to safety is partly explained by concern about the problems of hospital acquired infections. Media attention to deaths caused by bacterial infections such as Methicillin-Resistant Staphylococcus Aureus (MRSA) and Clostridium Difficile, playing on fears of dirty and dangerous hospitals, has led to urgent (and successful) action which has resulted in a decreased infection rates (see Vincent 2008). The language of safety, as opposed to error, is also significant in terms of the professional dominance thesis. Whereas medical error is a professionally owned term, patient safety puts patients in the centre and signals that they ought to have a more prominent role in terms of securing safety.

The term safety is increasingly used in modern society without sufficient understanding of what it means. Safety is generally defined as 'freedom from hazard' which increases as risk is reduced (Runciman et al. 2007: 2). It can also be defined as the capacity for being resilient to risk (Macrae 2014). Ensuring safety requires planning the design of systems, products, processes and influencing the behaviour of individuals in order to prevent harm. Whilst medical error is a contested term, safety is an elastic term with potentially broad boundaries (Vincent and Amalberti 2015). Little in healthcare is irrelevant to safety, based as it is on the input and interactions of a plurality of professionals in a large and increasingly specialised health system. Thus, a comprehensive examination of patient safety would encompass the work of all health professionals, the design of buildings, the manufacture of drugs and devices, the effect of policy and management and the effect of resource allocation decisions. It even extends appropriately to the work of cleaners and porters. Whilst all are worthy of close attention, doing so would risk losing the focus of this book, which is limited to the role of healthcare professionals (mainly medical professionals) and their contribution to safety through everyday medical work, in other words, by decisions, diagnoses, procedures, performance and attitudes. It does not extend to the safety of drugs and devices, which have been expertly examined elsewhere (see Light 2011; Jackson 2012; Goldberg 2013). The focus here, then, is on the human dimension of everyday medical encounters involving healthcare professions and patients.

There are many different possible measures of safety – in relation to different actors (individuals, wards/departments, hospitals), into outcomes of care or compliance with processes and in relation to different things (e.g. infection rates, mortality and morbidity rates after heart surgery). Whilst such measurement must include the raw data of outcomes, complication rates and mortality statistics, it also extends to patient satisfaction surveys and other indicators of safety culture such as teamwork, policies about raising concerns and open disclosure, and the prevalence of complaints or litigation involving safety failures. There is no one single measure of safety which renders the task of measuring and demonstrating safety a complex one (Vincent et al. 2013). It is demonstrated by reference to evidence, for example surgical outcomes, yet is also deeply psychological in terms of perceived safety – we commonly feel safe when confronted by familiar and reassuring images and brands. Beyond evidence, safety is also based on feel and perception – we would not (and should not) feel safe on an airplane or in a hospital with insufficient numbers of staff or staff without appropriate qualifications. We tend to feel safe when we believe that those entrusted with our safety have this as their absolute priority. However, the word safety is often misused. For example, reviews of healthcare services often reveal disturbing findings about staff shortages or insufficient bed space yet wrongly conclude that the system remains perfectly safe.

Patient safety has been broadly defined as 'any unintended or unexpected incident which could have harmed or did lead to harm for one or more patients being cared for by the NHS' (NPSA 2004: 6) or as 'freedom, as far as possible, from harm, or risk of harm, caused by medical management' (as opposed to harm caused by the natural course of the patient's original illness or condition) (HCHC 2009: 9). Vincent phrases it more eloquently as '[t]he avoidance, prevention and amelioration of adverse outcomes or injuries stemming from the process of healthcare' (Vincent 2010: 31). The World Health Organisation has identified 48 concepts in this area and expresses a preference for 'patient safety incident', which it defines broadly as something which could or did result in unnecessary harm to the patient (Runciman et al. 2009). Viewed in line with the World Health Organisation's broad definition of health, then, safety is about much more than reducing error and harm (Runciman et al. 2007: 2). And, similar to the holistic vision of health, this pursuit of safety is complex, challenging and ambitious.

However, the term 'patient safety' is not warmly welcomed by all – Professor Sir Ian Kennedy, for example, disliking not only its grammatical inelegance but the subtle sidelining of patients. Kennedy regards it as a 'managerial concept: something to be included on an agenda and be ticked' and, thus, always at risk of bureaucratic hijacking. He prefers the more patient centred 'safety of patients', which he argues is a significant shift in terms of changing 'control of the discourse of care' (Kennedy 2006: 29). Kennedy is correct to remind us about the person at the heart of patient safety, and the need for attention to the personal preferences of patients. Forgetting about the patient as a person is part of a wider problem – modern medicine, with all its tests and treatments, tends to treat diseases rather than people with diseases (Leape, personal communication, 8 June 2010); the individual, with his or her preferences, can get lost amidst this. In particular, the potential of patients to contribute to safety has been somewhat overlooked. This book argues that efforts to improve safety must engage with patients and their carers, and their potential role in improving safety is explored in Chapter 9.

As Mary Dixon-Woods (2010) reminds us, patient safety is difficult. It raises issues beyond competency and attitude and is also a site of organisational and professional politics. It is also, perversely, something of a 'hard sell' to professionals. Safety has connotations of behaving conservatively, avoiding risks and abiding by rules. This might make it unattractive for independent-minded practitioners who resist restrictions on their discretion and autonomy. A further objection professionals may have is that compliance with safety protocols may be labour and resource intensive in terms of the greater care and time required. Furthermore, the reality is that safety is not the overriding priority in healthcare, competing as it does with other objectives such as efficiency and effective use of resources (Vincent 2010: 31). Yet, engaging with the science of safety requires imagination, dedication, implementation of scientific findings and effective interpersonal skills. Whilst regulation has an important role to play here, it is essential that engagement with the science of safety is embraced as an essential part of a revised form of professionalism (Martin et al. 2015).

Given the breadth of safety, in order to tackle specific problems and demonstrate improvement, research activity has focused on specific areas. A good example is 'never events' such as wrong site surgery or leaving surgical instruments inside patients, which are seen as entirely preventable. Despite efforts to try and eliminate such events by following safety protocols, according to NHS statistics, there were over 1100 such events between 2012 and 2015 (Patients Association 2016). For some, this focus on egregious error is disproportionate given that they represent less than 1 in 1,000 of all things that can go wrong and result in death or serious injury; it would be more rational to build a uniform database of all the things that *can* go wrong (Runciman et al. 2007: 49). Yet it is undeniable that patient safety success stories have started with specific interventions, such as decreasing the infection rate with the use of venous catheters and the simple yet significant promise of checklists for encouraging cultural change (Pronovost 2010; Gawande 2009). However, apart from specific success stories, overall, there is a worrying information deficit in relation to demonstrating levels of safety. This is particularly marked in primary care where no case review studies have been carried out (HCHC 2009: 20) and where there is a dearth of information on quality (Dawda et al. 2010). In short, whilst it is hoped that safety and quality has improved, and despite progress in certain specialities, there remains a lack of hard evidence to demonstrate overall improved safety as well as explaining the reasons for such improvement (Pronovost et al. 2011).

Informational Deficit

The work of pioneers such as Ernest Codman remains the exception to the norm in medicine. Efforts to monitor and evaluate errors and safety have been met with resistance by practitioners and organisations. Ultimately, for a variety of reasons, engaging healthcare professionals with safety and quality initiatives is tougher than it should be (Davies 2007; Vincent et al. 2008 and 2013). Frustratingly, frequent calls for action have fallen on deaf ears. In 1990, the then editor of the *British Medical Journal* called for an epidemiology of malpractice (Smith 1990). However, despite the attention which has followed the high-profile safety failings outlined in Chapter 1, numerous regulatory initiatives and an increase of patient safety research, we know relatively little about the safety of healthcare. The questions 'how safe is my doctor?' and 'how safe is my hospital?' lack clear evidenced responses. In 2000, a report chaired by the UK Chief Medical Officer (DOH 2000) concluded that NHS reporting and information systems only provided a 'patchy and incomplete picture of the scale and nature of the problem of serious failures in health care'. Just under a decade later, the House of Commons Health Committee lamented the inability of the Department of Health and its National Patient Safety Agency to collect adequate data in order to evaluate the success of patient safety policy (2009: 95). And, in his review of the Bristol inquiry, Sir Ian Kennedy lamented that whilst Bristol was awash with data, it lacked information (2006: 37).

A number of US studies first suggested that the true toll of medical error was substantial. In 1964, Schimmel found that 20 per cent of patients admitted to a university hospital medical service suffered iatrogenic illness (Schimmel 1964). Steel et al. (1981) found a higher figure of 36 per cent. Larger scale population studies provided a better assessment of the nature and frequency of error. The first of these, the California Medical Association's Medical Insurance Feasibility Study, estimated that 4.7 per cent of hospital admissions led to injury, with 0.8 per cent being due to negligence (Mills 1978). The Harvard Medical Practice study, by far the most comprehensive and sophisticated study of the incidence of adverse events and negligence to date, found similar results. The study analysed a random sample of over 30,121 patient records from

New York State hospitals in 1984. It identified 1,133 (3.7 per cent) adverse events caused by medical treatment. The authors calculated that of the 2,671,863 discharged patients from acute-care hospitals in New York State in 1984, there were 98,609 adverse events. In 27.6 per cent of these adverse events the injury was due to negligence (i.e. it was considered preventable). The study thus concluded that there was a substantial amount of injury to patients from medical mismanagement and that many of these resulted from substandard care (Brennan et al. 1991). It has been estimated that medical error accounts annually for more deaths than motor vehicle accidents, breast cancer or AIDS (IOM 1999: 1). Unsurprisingly, such statistics have been effective in attracting headline attention to this pre-viously ignored public health problem.

Until recently, only one major UK study had investigated the incidence of medical errors. The Brighton study reviewed over 15,000 patient admissions to a hospital between 1990 and 1992 in 12 specialities. Of incidents subject to peer review, 21 per cent were judged to be avoidable (Walshe and Buttery 1995). The most notable British (pilot) study by Vincent et al. (2001) found that 10.8 per cent of hospitalised patients experienced an adverse event, with half of these judged to be preventable with ordinary standards of care. International studies have estimated a rate of 8–12 per cent of hospital admissions are associated with an adverse event (Vincent 2010: 54). Extrapolated to the NHS in England, based on the 8.5 million in-patient episodes per annum, it is estimated that there are 850,000 adverse events each year in hospitals, with 70,000 being fatal. It is not entirely clear how many adverse events are preventable, although a study of the medical records of 1,000 people who died in 10 acute hospitals in England in 2009 estimated that around 5 per cent of these deaths were likely to be preventable (Hogan et al. 2012). The financial cost of adverse events to the NHS has been estimated at anything between 1 to 2.5 billion pounds per year (Frontier Economics 2014). The fact that not all incidents lead to adverse outcomes, and the documented reluctance of healthcare professionals to report each other's mistakes (Vincent and Davis 2012) suggests that these figures under-estimate the size of the problem.

Historically, the profession has been reluctant to embrace attempts to evaluate the quality of medical work, reflecting a weak commitment to patient safety. The approach of the UK medical profession to medical audit, the oldest and least threatening form of evaluation, is revealing. In short, there has been a grudging reluctance to accept that audit is necessary. The earliest form of professional audit in the UK was the

Confidential Enquiry into Maternal Deaths (CEMD), formally established by the Royal College of Obstetricians and the Department of Health and Social Services in 1952, but originating in the mid-nineteenth century (Shennan and Bewley 2012). Information is confidential, anonymous, and participation is voluntary. A report is published every three years which identifies avoidable and preventable factors contributing to maternal deaths. Similarly, in 1987, the Royal College of Surgeons and the Royal College Anaesthetists jointly established the National Confidential Enquiry into Peri-operative Deaths (NCEPOD). This is a study of all deaths within 30 days of surgical procedures. Similar to CEMD, it is based on the principles of case collection and peer review, and questionnaires are returned on a voluntary basis, which perhaps explains the high number not taking part. This is now called the National Confidential Enquiry into Patient Outcome and Death, with an extended remit to cover all specialities and also near misses. These confidential inquiries are now under the umbrella of the Healthcare Quality Improvement Partnership (HQIP) which has been contracted by NHS England to deliver outcome focused quality improvement mechanisms (www.hqip.org.uk).

The profession's previous hostility towards audit was reflected in the BMA (British Medical Association's) evidence to the Royal Commission on the National Health Service in 1977. The BMA considered that 'the place of "medical audit" in health care is still controversial', and rejected 'any suggestion that there should be "medical audit" by the state' (BMJ 1977: 301). In fact, the BMA felt confident enough to declare that it was 'not convinced of the need for further supervision of a qualified doctor's standard of care' (1977: 303). It was not until 1981 that the policy of medical audit was accepted by the BMA membership, and this was conditional on its being voluntary, confidential, unconditional and non-directive (BMJ 1981: 253), a position which it has since maintained. The rise of the 'audit society' (Power 1997) was not purely motivated by the concern to improve quality, but also had economic and political motivations. It is best understood against the backdrop of the Conservative government's drive to control public expenditure and the 'new right' assault on professions as inefficient (Perkin 1990). The concern with value for money was reflected by the introduction of the Audit Commission and National Audit Office in the early 1980s to monitor the efficiency and effectiveness of public bodies. The former's remit was extended to cover health service bodies by the

National Health Service Community Care Act 1990, consolidated in the Audit Commission Act 1998.

However, audit has largely operated on an unsystematic and voluntary basis with the guarantee of anonymity. There has been a lack of time, skill, interest and the information systems necessary for audit, and many within the profession have remained unconvinced about its value. As Power neatly explained, without a 'tradition of knowing what to "do" with audit results, there has been a tendency to be content with the fact that an audit was done rather than with knowing what exactly was done' (1997: 106). In 1995, Klein noted that the 'full potential of [the NHS's] ability to identify poor performers – individual consultants as well as institutions – remains to be exploited' (1995: 235). This largely remains true today, with official NHS websites containing unhelpful references to data being unavailable (Boyce et al. 2010: 35). This informational deficit is partly explained by a reluctance (by both individuals and institutions) to collect data on the quality and safety of care. This is likely explained by a lack of time, interest and familiarity with such work. Given that the subject of quality improvement or patient safety science is largely absent from medical curricula and training (NPSF 2010), the low level of professional engagement with such work is unsurprising. There are also understandable concerns about the uses of such information and the implications for accountability and trust. There are undoubtedly challenges in how to collect and present data which is reliable with professionals and can be trusted by patients. However, credible evidence based information about the safety of healthcare has the potential to function as a 'bridge' between doubt and trust (Kuhlmann 2006a: 192).

Modest progress towards providing publicly accessible data on safety has been made, in the context of greater attention on patient safety and choice. Since 1998, there have been various attempts to rate the safety and quality of NHS care, mainly through aggregate ratings of hospitals and NHS trusts. This began with the introduction of a Performance Assessment Framework in 1998 (DOH 1999) and was followed by a system of star ratings (by the Commission for Healthcare Improvement between 2001 and 2004), an annual health check (by the Healthcare Commission between 2004 and 2009) and to compliance with fundamental standards of quality and safety by the Care Quality Commission. This information has generally been about organisations, rather than being broken down into different areas or specialities, and it would appear that its main use has been in terms of helping providers improve their care as opposed to aiding patient choice. It contains information of a general nature and is thus of limited use to patients who want information about specific areas (Nuffield Trust 2013). Overall, efforts at measuring quality have tended to focus on compliance with processes rather than on the outcomes of care (Porter et al. 2016).

Private companies have been quick to identify gaps in the market and in our knowledge here. For example, since 2001, Dr Foster has provided an annual hospital guide which includes data on comparative adjusted death rates called Hospital Standardised Mortality Ratios (HSMRs), which is a measure of deaths of patients whilst in hospital care. A similar measure, in the form of Summary Hospital-level Mortality Indicators (SHMI), has been adopted by the Department of Health. Summary Hospital-level Mortality Indicators monitors all deaths within English hospital trusts and within 30 days of discharge. This is basic surveillance which the DOH has commissioned the Health and Social Care Information Centre (HSCIC) to undertake. Essentially, this tracks whether mortality rates at individual hospitals are within the expected range and may trigger more detailed investigations by regulators. To be precise, The SHMI is the ratio between the actual number of patients who die following treatment at the trust and the number that would be expected to die on the basis of the national average, given the characteristics of the patients treated there. It results in mortality rates being described as 'expected', 'lower than expected' or 'higher than expected'. Given the traditional dearth of information on outcomes and quality of care, the use of the SHMI represents some progress. However it is limited as its focus is general rather than specific and is seen as a 'poor diagnostic test for quality' (Lilford and Pronovost 2010). Some argue that the use of such mortality statistics are a weak and misleading signal of quality and should be abandoned (Black 2010; Hogan et al. 2015). Such indicators are best viewed as one source of data on the quality of care, alongside more specific indicators and patient experience data, for example. But they are likely to remain popular given that collecting and disseminating mortality data is far easier than measuring quality by observing clinical processes.

Progress has also been made in terms of information about the performance of individual clinicians. Cardiac surgeons have long led the way here. In collaboration with the Society of Cardiothoracic Surgery, the Care Quality Commission produces comparative survival rates for all cardiac surgery combined and also for coronary artery bypass graft and aortic valve replacement surgery, assessing both hospital units and individual surgeons. The data covers procedures carried out by around 3,500 consultants, showing the number of times a consultant has carried out a procedure, mortality rates and whether clinical outcomes for each consultant are within expected limits. Whilst participation is voluntary, the number of surgeons refusing to participate is small. This appears to have been a success, with evidence of decreased death rates since the start of this work. A report by Keogh et al., found that death rates in coronary artery surgery fell by 21 per cent and in aortic valve replacement operations by one-third, despite older patients and increased complexity of their conditions (*The Guardian* 29 July 2009). This has been hailed as vindicating the bold step of publishing individual surgeon survival rates and is an example to other specialities.

Until recently, cardiac surgery remained the exception to the norm, but consultants from nine other specialities: vascular, bariatric, interventional cardiology, orthopaedics, endocrine and thyroid, urology, head and neck, bowel cancer and upper GI, have now followed the lead of cardiac surgeons. Most of this information is accessible via the NHS choices webpage. Whilst this represents significant progress, there are limitations of such data. It is limited to 30- or 90-day mortality statistics and thus there is little on overall quality – which is harder to measure. From the patient's perspective, this data is somewhat limited. Aside from identifying any outliers with mortality data and revealing how many procedures a surgeon carries out, such data does not and perhaps cannot capture important aspects of quality such as pre- and post- operative care and commitment to ethical ideals such as honesty and dignity. Also, even with ten specialities now committed to the principle of public reporting, this still only covers 20 procedures. Overall, healthcare providers and professionals have a limited understanding about the safety of care provided. Measuring improvement is clearly difficult given the lack of rigorous and comprehensive data with which to compare against. However, data collection and measurement is itself no guarantor of better safety. It requires professionals to engage with the process and demonstrate a commitment to improve outcomes and other indicators of safety.

Cultural Deficit

Culture is a complex concept, especially in healthcare where different specialities mean different and competing cultures and subcultures. Large multi-disciplinary organisations such as hospitals host numerous competing subcultures, which are complex, deeply rooted and difficult to measure or change (Jacobs et al. 2013; Rowley and Waring 2011: 14). Regrettably, healthcare has no established culture of safety. Reflecting the belated systematic interest in safety, it was only in February 2010 that the Royal Society of Medicine launched its Patient Safety section, as its 58th section stream. Numerous aspects of culture in medicine explain this ignorance of safety, but the most important are: the myth of infallibility; a closed hierarchical system; the fear of blame and punishment; the normalisation of errors, a reluctance to speak up about safety, and a pragmatic 'mend and make do' mentality, which are, in the words of Sir Ian Kennedy, 'simply inappropriate' (2001: 269) from a safety standpoint.

Traditionally, medical culture has perpetuated a myth of perfection or infallibility in relation to error. Gorovitz and MacIntyre (1976: 51) began an important paper in 1976 by stating that 'No species of fallibility is more important or less understood than fallibility in medical practice.' Challenging the position that error arises from ignorance or ineptitude, they sought to develop a theory of medical fallibility. Some pioneers bravely confronted their mistakes with moving accounts of the pain felt by physicians as the second victims of medical harm (Hilfiker 1984). In his seminal paper, Leape (1994) explained how the culture of medicine mitigated against the development of effective error prevention systems and attacked the damaging myth of perfection. Medical training emphasised the need for doctors to strive for perfection and regard themselves as solely responsible for patient outcomes. Doctors, thus, got the message that mistakes were unacceptable and that they should be infallible. This, combined with the perceived threat of damaging malpractice litigation, led to the closeting of mistakes, and with it the opportunities for shared learning. In this climate, learning is motivated by the fear of making mistakes or looking stupid; seeking help is regarded as sign of weakness and a source of embarrassment. Mistakes threaten the perception of infallibility the profession is socialised into holding of itself, and create an unwanted image of vulnerability. In short, infallibility is intellectually dishonest, hypocritical and prevents appropriate lessons being learned from adverse events (McIntyre and Popper 1983).

Old school professionalism and its emphasis on professional autonomy, as discussed in Chapter 1, is ill suited to the pursuit of safety. Closed hierarchical systems vesting authority with the 'top dog' discourages the necessary inter-professional vigilance, checking and questioning vital for safe systems. As Leape et al. (2009: 424) note, safety 'depends on achieving a culture of trust, reporting, transparency and discipline' which despite its descriptive brevity, represents a considerable challenge. This requires reform of medical education to encompass human factors, safety science, leadership and teamwork (2009: 427). The toughest task is in creating a safe space to talk openly about safety (or lack of safety) and ensuring that safety improvements can be sustained. A culture of safety is one where, for example, nurses and patients feel comfortable asking surgeons whether they have washed their hands. The US National Patient Safety Foundation has noted the unmet need of reforming health professional education in order to teach safety by educating medics in terms of 'systems thinking, problem analysis, application of human factors science, communication skills, patient-centered care, teaming concepts and skills, and dealing with feelings of doubt, fear, and uncertainty with respect to medical errors' (2010: 1). A major part of this involves moving away from an egocentric to a team-ethic way of working. This must begin by encouraging medical schools to integrate patient safety learning within their medical curricula, which the WHO has started with its patient safety curriculum guide for medical schools (Walton et al. 2010). Until safety sits above personality, power and politics, any gains will always be limited to the few safety champions and their teams.

For some, the desired cultural change risks individual responsibility evaporating within the murky talk of systems responsibility, or as Sharpe notes (2004: 12), of the system providing an excuse for 'moral shirkers'. But this is somewhat misguided given the need to focus on the responsibility of individuals *and* the organisations where they work (Pellegrino 2004; Aveling et al. 2016). Whilst there is a need to design, build and manage for safety, there is also a need to focus on how individuals can perform better, and to understand which attitudes and characteristics are associated with safety and danger (Lloyd-Bostock 2010). Empirical evidence from the United States underlines that medical errors are explained by a complex web of individual and systems factors, and the same may be said about safety lapses more generally. Mello and Studdert's (2008) large study of closed malpractice claims found that individual and systems factors combined in over two-thirds of cases in their sample. Furthermore, those associated with systems errors tended to be more serious in terms of having a stronger relationship to causing death. Perhaps most importantly, systems factors are more amenable to prevention through design, in that whilst the human mind will always forget, systems are more amenable to building in safeguards, and thus deserve special attention.

Despite the fashionable talk of systems and organisations, this is unlikely to completely replace the well-established psychological need to hold people responsible. Patients are psychologically predisposed to focus on individual, rather than system responsibility, given the difficulties of making any human connection or emotional attachment with an abstract system. Doctors also tend to think in terms of individual, rather than systems responsibility, thus raising doubts about the likelihood of a no-blame culture given the professional need for control and responsibility (Collins et al. 2009). This partly explains the attraction of legal mechanisms of accountability, mainly through civil and criminal obligations. It has been argued that a medico-legal environment whereby patients complain, claim and even pursue criminal charges against healthcare professionals is completely at odds with a culture of safety. However, the potential role of legal mechanisms for contributing towards a culture which prioritises patient safety is explored further in Chapters 5–7.

Conclusion

The subject of patient safety is potentially extremely broad. As interest in patient safety has grown, so has the tendency to regard everything as an issue of safety. Historically, studies have tended to focus on a fairly narrow range of adverse events committed by those working in secondary care specialties. The work of healthcare professionals is clearly of central importance to the study of safety. But it also extends to the role of healthcare managers, researchers as well as policy and lawmakers. Whilst interest in medical error and the wider problem of patient safety is not new, the systematic study of this problem is a recent phenomenon. Unfortunately, an information deficit still surrounds safety. Despite notable exceptions such as anaesthesia and cardiac surgery, there is little evidence to substantiate claims of improved safety. Greater interest in patient safety is highly significant from a professional dominance perspective. The shift from medical error being a private professional problem to an issue of public health challenges traditional notions of professional autonomy and responsibility. Attention to safety problems has shifted beyond the privacy of medical confessions, with parliament, regulators, the media, and most importantly, patients becoming increasingly involved. It is unclear whether such interventions are always welcomed by healthcare professionals. But, such resistance must be confronted: it is both legitimate and necessary to involve patients in efforts to improve safety in healthcare. This offers the best hope of embedding safety within individual and institutional norms of behaviour. The danger of medical dominance is that it provides an environment ill-equipped to ensuring other professions (and patients) play an effective role in terms of safety. A climate in which expert authority is not questioned, and where teamwork and the voice of patients is undervalued is ill-suited to the needs of safety (Vincent 2010: 18). It seems odd to regard patients as outsiders here, as in reality no one is more on the inside, but the potential role of patients has generally been overlooked. Ivan Illich's fierce but farsighted attack on medicalisation (outlined in Chapter 1) is particularly prescient here. Whilst engaging professional interest in the science of improvement is key to improving patient safety, there is a danger in only focusing on this. The overmedicalisation of safety risks diminishing the importance of patient involvement and to the insights from research in other relevant disciplines, especially the social sciences.

3

Regulation and Trust

This chapter will introduce the key concepts of regulation and trust, focusing on their inter-relationship in the context of the medical profession and patient safety. Whilst most scholarship in this area has explored the general regulation of the medical profession, the regulation of patient safety is a much more recent focus of inquiry. The ability to define and deal with error and safety incidents is one of the most jealously guarded aspects of professional autonomy. However, a combination of the series of high-profile disasters described in Chapter 1, together with prevailing social and political conditions, has left the profession unable to resist the erosion of traditional self-regulation. This has led to the emergence of a state led bureaucratic regulatory model, (Davies 2000; Dixon-Woods et al. 2011) which is discussed in Chapter 4. Self-regulation and professional autonomy are challenged by an apparent decline of trust. The concept of trust is central to this changing face of regulation; put simply, high trust usually translates into minimal regulation and low trust encourages more regulation and monitoring. As Francis Fukuyama claims (1995: 27):

> [P]eople who do not trust one another will end up co-operating only under a system of formal rules and regulations, which have to be negotiated, agreed to, litigated and enforced, sometimes by coercive means. This legal apparatus, serving as a substitute for trust, entails what economists call 'transaction costs'. Widespread distrust in a society, in other words, imposes a kind of tax on all forms of economic activity, a tax that high trust societies do not have to pay.

Adam Seligman makes the same point:

> Our increasing inability to negotiate the boundaries of interaction without involving hard and fast rules and regulations is but another manifestation of the replacement of the open-ended negotiation of trust with the rule-bound behavior of system confidence (1997: 174).

An important preliminary question is about whether safety and trust are amenable to being regulated in the same way that people, products, processes and places are. The short answer is that we regulate *for* safety and trust rather *than* regulating safety and trust. That is, people, processes and places are regulated in order to improve safety and ensure trust. However, there is arguably much more to be gained by moving beyond the idea of regulating professions towards the more challenging task of regulating for safety and trust. Regulating both safety in medicine and maintaining trust in the profession is a difficult balancing act. One of the likely explanations for the professional silence over safety is the perceived damage to trust if patients knew the truth about safety. It might be tempting to view trust and regulation as opposing ways of managing important human interactions: we can either rely on trust or regulation. Whilst this is a somewhat crude analysis, nevertheless, mechanisms of control and accountability clearly have the potential for damaging trust (O'Neill 2002; Kuhlmann 2006a).

This chapter will explore ways of striking a balance between blind trust and regulatory overkill around patient safety. It will unpack the key concept of trust, which has only recently attracted sustained scholarly scrutiny (O'Neill 2002). In particular, there have been relatively few investigations into the relationship between trust and patient safety. A nuanced and positive conception of trust is proposed which is important in terms of improving patient safety and maintaining healthy levels of trust. Which type of regulation is most compatible with improved safety and higher levels of trust? This is a difficult question to answer given the dearth of empirical evidence on the effect of regulation on professional behaviour. This book will argue that safety should be the priority for regulation. Focusing squarely on safety also means it is legitimate, and even necessary, to consider how legal mechanisms may be used in order to help secure safety. Similarly, patients and patient groups may also play a role in helping to regulate safety. This chapter thus adopts a positive view of regulation as a collaborative enterprise (Prosser 2010), simultaneously protecting safety rights, encouraging solidarity between professions and patients, and allowing space for patients and their carers to contribute to safety.

Defining Regulation

Regulation has become an important concept within the social sciences. Although originally explored with reference to the economy, it is now a familiar concept in areas such as health and safety, the environment and consumer protection. As Tony Prosser points out, utility regulators no longer represent the paradigm (2010: 3). Whilst regulation is not a 'term of art' and has acquired a number of different meanings, it has been described broadly as any form of behavioural control (Ogus 1994: 1). Julia Black offers a more detailed definition of regulation as the 'sustained and focused attempt to alter the behaviour of others according to defined standards or purposes with the intention of producing a broadly identified outcome or outcomes, which may involve mechanisms of standard-setting, information-gathering and behaviour-modification' (2002: 20). In the context of medicine, the term regulation is generally used to describe formal attempts by statutory bodies to shape the behaviour of practitioners, primarily through education, ethics and discipline. We can trace its origins to the creation of the General Medical Council under the 1858 Medical Act. However, a broader vision of regulation would encompass the work of numerous organisations operating at local, national and international levels. These would include the medical Royal Colleges, defence unions, trade unions such as the British Medical Association, and the numerous guidelines and protocols issued by national and international bodies. Indeed, the last decade or so has witnessed the growth of a 'pluralistic regulatory landscape' (Trubek et al. 2008: 6) where numerous organisations with overlapping responsibilities attempt to implement rules and shape behaviour. And regulation can also take place on a more informal level in terms of the effect of cultural norms and peer pressure.

Such complexity risks the term regulation becoming unwieldy (Brownsword 2008: 7) and perhaps even meaningless (Walshe 2003: 10). This is undoubtedly true. However, to focus only on the work of formal institutions of regulation, which is done in Chapter 4, would be to miss the increasingly important role played by law (Chapters 5–7), and the potential role of honesty and transparency through professional duties to be candid and report their safety concerns (Chapter 8). This book will argue that patients also have an important yet largely overlooked role to play in contributing to regulating safety (Chapter 9). At bottom, regulation is thus about seeking to control and change behaviour in order to realise important goals, in this case ensuring and improving the safety of care. But it is not the only way to try and achieve these objectives. Broadly speaking, we can observe a distinction between internal and external mechanisms for improving quality and safety. An example of an internal mechanism would be strategies and policies which emerge from within a healthcare organisation, and an external mechanism might be the use of hard law, such as civil obligations or criminal offences. Yet as Walshe wisely points out, regulation has the capacity to bridge the divide between internal and external mechanisms and, given that it is carefully designed, is able to draw on the strengths of both approaches (2003: 9).

Regulating Medical Work

Regulating medical work raises a number of special problems. First, it is complex; as Fox notes, 'It is one thing to regulate the quality and price of drinking water; quite another to regulate what hundreds of thousands of doctors say and do to millions of patients on any particular day' (1994: 1220). Secondly, it is a dynamic environment with numerous regulatory actors exercising related responsibilities and subject to frequent reform. Mulcahy and Allsop's warning that researching the regulation of the NHS in the 1990s was 'like shooting at a moving target' (1996: 1) remains true, with Prosser noting that health and social care is the fastest changing regulatory arena (2010: 134). Given that regulation in healthcare is increasingly multi-layered and complex (Field: 2007) it is important to be clear on the precise focus of regulation in this book – in other words, are we dealing with regulation of the medical profession, the health system (in this case the NHS), or the issue of patient safety? Inevitably there will be some overlap between these foci for regulation; the regulation of patient safety, for example, relates to general professional regulation and vice versa.

Shifting the focus to regulating *patient safety*, as opposed to the traditional focus on regulating the *medical profession*, is important. Regulating patient safety means that it is both necessary and legitimate to involve patients, and this requires regulation to be seen as a collaborative enterprise between patients and professionals. The shared interest is safety – patients in receiving, and doctors in delivering – high quality and safe healthcare. Regulating the safety and performance of medical work has to contend with entrenched cultural attitudes about autonomy and discretion, which are part of the professional dominance thesis outlined in Chapter 1. The safety of patients is an important public health issue that justifies looking beyond the profession for solutions. Adopting Bilton and Cayton's observation that regulation is mainly concerned with products, prices, processes, places and people (2013), this book focuses on the processes, places and people. The discussion will therefore not extend to regulating the safety of products such as drugs and devices, which have been subject to searching critique elsewhere (see Jackson 2012 and Goldberg 2013). Nor will it consider the regulation of prices and the issue of allocating scare resources (Syrett 2007), which is primarily about economic regulation, albeit with clear implications for safety.

As with the subject of patient safety, the regulatory environment in healthcare is certainly complex. No one surveying the plethora of different regulators and the production of so many rules and guidelines could deny this. Indeed, some have gone so far as to condemn such regulatory complexity as being a threat to patient safety (Carthey et al. 2011). Regulation has also tended to be viewed negatively by healthcare professionals, regarding it as a burden which limits professional autonomy. Thus rules, regulations, guidelines and checklists, whilst written in the name of patient safety, may also be seen as intruding on jealously guarded professional judgment and discretion. On this view, regulation is a 'hard sell' to doctors as it implies the imposition of external control and compliance with rules or approaches which may lack professional legitimacy.

This has also led to calls for less reliance on regulation and more emphasis on professionalism and personal responsibility (Cayton 2014). Whilst this begs the question about defining what we mean by appropriate professionalism, it also underplays the possible connection between regulation and professionalism. There is a tendency to see professionalism and regulation as somehow two different models of ensuring the quality of healthcare, whereas good regulation should surely have a positive impact on appropriate professionalism. The problem is that this is something which is difficult (if not impossible) to evidence. The same lack of proof applies to the relationship between regulation and safety. However, the lack of evidence about the impact of regulation on improving safety does not mean that there is no such connection.

An important question arises about the aims of regulation. What is the principal aim of regulation in the context of healthcare? Is it, as some would contend, to try and encourage basic standards of care rather than concern itself with responsibility for quality improvement? (PSA 2015). This pragmatic view holds that regulation can only realistically try and ensure that care is 'just good enough' and that improving levels of safety and quality is a matter for others at a more local level. There are, according to this view, clear limits on what regulation can achieve. Whilst there is an element of truth in this (after all, regulation sets rules or guidance in the hope of influencing behaviour) we should arguably be more optimistic and ambitious about the potential of regulation. Thus, Ian Kennedy, in a trenchant essay in the aftermath of the Bristol Royal Infirmary inquiry, conceives of regulation as encouraging improvement (a task for the regulator) and ensuring improvement (a task for managers and professionals). For Kennedy, '[r]egulation . . . can be at the forefront of ushering in a patient-centred system of healthcare, which is safe and of good quality' (2006: 71). He adopts an optimistic approach to regulation as 'the totality of processes and systems for assuring and improving safety and quality of healthcare, including the regulation of healthcare professionals and the regulation of the institutions in which they work' (2006: 261) and focuses on enforcing standards and disseminating information on performance (2006: 315). Regulation is thus primarily about setting standards rather than being about performance management. However, this is not to deny a role for regulation in contributing towards improving the quality of healthcare.

It is unfortunate that the benefits of regulation receive less attention than its burdens. As Kennedy points out, whilst it is easier to measure the time invested in complying with regulatory requirements, it is less easy to calculate the gains (or losses avoided) by complying. For example, there are the costs 'saved by not having to respond to as many complaints, or the threat of litigation, or the readmission of a patient because of avoidable error . . . or the reduction in bullying of staff which has in turn led to absenteeism' (Kennedy 2006: 65). In theory, the benefits of such regulation could be demonstrated through a cost-benefit analysis (Glaeser and Sunstein 2014), though doing this would be difficult given the complex range of factors which are relevant to ensuring patient safety. It would also be controversial in terms of putting a monetary value on the issue of saving lives and avoiding harm.

This positive vision of regulation recognises its potential for both improving safety and for involving patients in the delivery of care. Regulation is here seen as a collaborative enterprise (Prosser 2010). However, this positive view of regulation is not necessarily shared by professionals who tend to associate it with discipline and sanction. Professional regulation thus faces a challenge in terms of its legitimacy with practitioners: excessive regulation risks alienating practitioners who have long preferred to rely on individual discretion and judgement. A number of studies confirm that professionals prefer their own judgements and those of colleagues over regulation and governance imposed by 'outsiders'. For example, Currie et al. (2009) examined the narrow question of how anaesthetists dealt with attempts to regulate the use of single-use devices (SUDs) in terms of compliance with a guideline of the Medicines and Healthcare Products Regulatory Agency (MHRA). Informed by a survey, they collected data via semi-structured interviews with anaesthetists, nurses and theatre managers, and found that medical devices were subject to reuse, and that this was rationalised with reference to clinical judgement rather than regulation. The study authors concluded that 'Regulatory and surveillance mechanisms will only be effective where their intent converges with the behaviours of healthcare professionals as they exercise clinical judgement' (2009: 132–3). This clearly creates a problem for regulators seeking to implement rules that do not alienate practitioners but nevertheless win public confidence in terms of ensuring safety and accountability.

Understandably, regulators would prefer to see a positive correlation between their interventions and the safety and quality of care. Yet it would be naïve to expect total compliance with regulations. It is here that the concept of 'relational regulation' is useful, in other words, the pragmatic realisation that regulators should abandon the pursuit of perfection in favour of keeping behaviour within a 'band of variation' and focus on 'governing rather than erasing' the gap between expectations and performance (Huising and Silbey 2011). In other words, regulation should be seen as the art of the possible. Thus various visions of regulation have been suggested as best suited to improving the safety and quality of medical work, such as 'responsive regulation' (Ayres and Braithwaite 1992; Healy 2011) 'smart regulation' (Gunningham and Grabosky 1998), 'right touch regulation' (PSA 2010a) and 'risk regulation' (Hutter 2001). These all share a similar vision for what regulation can achieve and how it can do so.

The best known of these, the responsive regulation model set out by Ayres and Braithwaite (1992), argues that regulation needs to respond to the context and culture of the regulated, should begin with soft supportive nudges and be slow to utilise command and control measures such as legal penalties. The spirit of responsive regulation thus strikes a chord with patient safety leaders, who have long stressed the need to try and understand a little more and blame a little less (Berwick 1989; Leape 1997). And as Healy explains, it also relies on the concept of 'networked governance' whereby multiple regulators adopt multiple strategies (2011: 59–61). The benefits of so-called co-regulation seem self-evident. A number of studies suggest that behavioural change is more likely when a *combination* of factors conspire to convince practitioners to alter their practice (Quick 2011). Thus, regulatory goals fare better when a number of sources of influence (for example, professional regulation, clinical guidelines, legal obligations, terms of employment contracts, professional leadership and even financial incentives) steer practitioners in the same direction. Some suggest that this means there is some method in the madness of overly complex and duplicate regulation (Field 2007) but this seems an overly generous interpretation of the regulatory environment.

The term 'right-touch' regulation was coined by the Council for Healthcare Regulatory Excellence, now called the Professional Standards Authority for Health and Social Care, which supervises the work of professional regulators such as the GMC. This term has been used to refer to regulation which is proportionate, consistent, targeted, transparent, accountable and agile (CHRE 2009: 3). This aims to strike an appropriate balance between regulation and professionalism by only having as much regulation as is required. This is similar to the idea of 'risk regulation' whereby regulators channel their energies on individuals or institutions that appear to be at higher risk for causing harm. The idea of responsive and risk regulation is explored further in Chapter 4. Others suggest promise in the idea of 'design based regulation', for example designing medical devices with technical specifications that prevent errors or safety breaches before any harm is done (Yeung and Dixon-Woods 2010). Clearly, this is based on looking beyond professional agency for solutions to the problem of patient safety, which is consistent with the systems analysis explanation for most safety problems. Yeung and Dixon-Woods are right to note the failure of professional norms and law to ensure safety and that 'Leaving safety as purely a matter of professional responsibility is no more a utopia than design-based systems are a dystopia' (2010: 508). The challenge is to design regulation that prioritises patient safety, yet leaves sufficient room for professional discretion.

Möllering pins down the broader challenge of the relationship between trust and regulation: 'trust-building is about finding ways of positively accepting agency and limiting it without destroying it' (2008: ix). Design may be extended further in terms of the design of medical education, training and culture which is not currently designed for safety (Leape 2010). Also, it is somewhat artificial to view design-based regulation as somehow valueless and being in conflict with professionalism. Yeung and Dixon Woods are surely correct to note that design based regulation implies a commitment to certain values (minimise risk of harm, involve patients in their care) and is not necessarily about restricting clinical autonomy but about helping ensure that best practise is followed. Ultimately, all these attempts are united in the pursuit of what we can call 'safety first' regulation. We thus confront a considerable challenge.

how to redesign a system of regulation, including a range of legal mechanisms, which unashamedly prioritises patient safety but maintains public and professional trust. This will be explored further in the chapters to follow, after the concept of trust is examined.

Trust

Trust is the basis of social interaction and is necessary for daily life. Few, if any, situations function without trust: it pervades many and diverse situations, 'from marriage to economic development, from buying a second-hand car to international affairs, from the minutiae of social life to the continuation of life on earth' (Gambetta 1988). As Möllering reminds us, trust is no modern 'faddish' issue, but rather a classic human and social problem (2008: x). Although interesting to philosophers, psychologists, sociologists and economists, leading theorists have noted the 'strange silence' on this topic (Baier 1994: 98) especially compared to the vast literature surrounding the related concept of autonomy. However, a significant general literature has emerged to analyse what is, by common consensus, a complex and multi-layered concept (Barber 1983; Earle and Cvetkovich 1995; Fukuyama 1995; Seligman 1997; O'Neill 2002; Möllering 2006; Seldon 2010). Yet despite its higher profile within a number of disciplines, it is often used generically and uncritically without careful unpacking of its different layers, and also hampered by a lack of empirical evidence to test out various hypotheses.

Broadly speaking, psychologists define trust in terms of personality traits, while sociologists and anthropologists perceive trust as culturally determined by place and through time. Gambetta has defined trust as the 'subjective probability with which an agent assesses that another agent or group of agents will perform a particular action, both *before* he can monitor such action ... *and* in a context in which it affects *his own* action' (1988: 217). According to Mechanic, 'to say we trust is to say we believe that individuals and institutions will act appropriately and perform competently, responsibly, and in a manner considerate of our interests' (1996: 173). The concept of trust may be distinguished from confidence. Trust presupposes a state of risk and uncertainty. Whilst we may have *confidence* in the medical professional's ability, *trust* only arises in periods of risk and uncertainty. In a familiar environment one exercises confidence, while in a risky environment one relies on trust (Luhmman 1988: 97). For example, after surviving brain surgery an individual may have *confidence* in his neurosurgeon's skills for any future procedures. Before the procedure however, he can only *trust* his judgment and skills. Thus we normally invest trust in some future occasion outside our control, often without any prior investigation. To trust represents a risk judgment that others will not harm us, yet also accepting that our expectations may be disappointed.

A useful philosophical review by Jones (1998) identified four generally accepted observations about trust (1–4) and three further claims about which there was widespread agreement (5–7) that accounts of trust should accommodate: 1. trust involves risk (those who trust run the risk of letting those they trust near things that they care about); 2. those who trust give those whom they trust some discretion as to how their trust should be fulfilled and are willing to forgo an immediate accounting of whether and how this has been done; 3. trust facilitates cooperation and allows people to inhabit a less threatening world in which they need not plan for every contingency; 4. trust and distrust are self-confirming (those who trust tend to interpret favourably the behaviours of those they trust and may also encourage trustworthy behaviour); 5. the absence of trust does not imply distrust (there can be a neutral stance of neither trusting nor distrusting); 6. trust cannot be willed (although people can sometimes make themselves act as though they trust); and 7. the value of trust is not exhausted by its instrumentality for cooperative relations (Jones 1998).

The placing of trust may involve a 'leap of faith' and suspension of belief (Möllering 2001), but those who trust make an active decision to do so. People who trust render themselves vulnerable to those they trust; thus it has generally been conceptualised in terms of asymmetrical relationships such as the power imbalances between doctors and patients. This has led to what may be regarded as the 'traditional' position that trust releases individuals from the need for checking (Power 1997: 2) or is only necessary for those lacking knowledge and who are dependant on others (Gambetta 1988: 218). It is arguable that pure trust exists in state of relative ignorance and powerlessness, with patients relying on instinct and emotion in trusting in the absence of evidence whether it is well placed. Such a view of trust is not well suited to ensuring the safety of care. Consequently, this book argues for an understanding of trust which extends beyond the weak and ignorant and accommodates the knowledgeable and vigilant patient. This more nuanced understanding of trust is more appropriate in the context of improving patient safety.

This relationship between trust and safety requires a little more explanation. Whilst trust is generally viewed as a good thing essential for effective relationships, it is also recognised that blind trust may be dangerous in exposing overly trusting individuals to harm. Baier (1986) has proposed a number of ways for distinguishing proper from improper or healthy from unhealthy trust. As a test for the moral decency of trust relationships, she suggested consideration of the ability of these relationships 'to survive awareness by each party to the relationship of what the other relies on in the first to ensure their continued trustworthiness or trustingness' (1986: 259). A trust relationship is morally bad if 'either party relies on qualities in the other which would be weakened by the knowledge that the other relies on them' (1986: 256). Pathologies of trust include the misuse of discretionary powers by the trusted (either by being too adventurous or by failing to use discretion at all) and either excessive checking of the actions of the trusted by the truster or a failure on the part of the truster to check at all because of an exaggerated fear that any checking would insult the trusted. Threats to trust include a failure to forgive on the part of the truster and undue sensitivity to criticism on the part of the trusted (1986: 238).

O'Neill has suggested that 'Well placed trust grows out of active enquiry rather than blind acceptance' (2002: 76), and that is placed when 'we can trace *specific* bits of information and *specific* understanding to *particular* sources on whose veracity and reliability we can run some checks'. There is an increased interest in the notion of informed, conditional or earned trust (Calnan and Rowe 2008), which emphasises the distinction between trust and both enforced dependency and vague hope. O'Neill argues that in order to tell the difference between trustworthy and untrustworthy individuals (for example, healthcare providers) people need to be able to distinguish between trustworthy and untrustworthy sources of information about these (2002: 88). As Kuhlmann points out, information can function as the 'bridge' between different actors and doubt and trust (2006b: 616). The question of what makes people trust is still poorly understood, though there is some small scale empirical work which suggests that trust is still based on emotional personal interaction as opposed to 'abstract disembodied data' such as that included in performance ratings (Calnan and Rowe 2008: 102). But this presupposes that there has been a general decline of trust in society, an oft-asserted claim that requires analysis.

Decline of Trust?

The debate about trust, both in the academic literature and newspaper commentary, tends to assume that trust is in decline. But are we really less trusting today? This is a difficult question to answer in general terms given the relevance of different contexts and aspects of trust. A number of social theorists point to waning trust in the late modern period. Although US theorists have led the debate, their arguments are applicable to UK society and its professions. In his treatise on trust, Francis Fukuyama notes its importance in allowing for successful economic society. Although distinguishing between so-called 'high-trust' societies such as the United States, Germany and Japan, and 'low-trust' societies such as Hong Kong, France and Italy, he notes the decline of trust and sociability, and the rise of individualism in the former (Fukuyama 1995). Adam Seligman claims that at the end of the twentieth century, western societies are losing their ability to establish trust as a mode of social interaction (1997: 192). He relates this to changes to the individual in 'postmodern' societies, in particular the dissolving of individual agency so that we are less capable trusting one and other. Giddens (1990) and Beck (1992) have written about the increasing scepticism towards experts, expert knowledge and expert institutions in a 'risk society'. Despite different theories, there is something of a consensus that there has been a shift in attitudes to and perceptions of experts, the system they work within, and the institutions which regulate them. This is connected to related processes of societal change, in particular, a decline of deference and an increasing tendency for consumers to challenge traditional forms of authority.

Available empirical data on trust tends to be based on crude questions which oversimplify a complex question. For example, most public attitude surveys tend to focus on one aspect of trust: trust in truth telling (Ipsos MORI 2013). Evidence of high levels of trust here, whilst clearly important, do not equate with high levels of trust in relation to safety. In other words, trust in honesty is not the same as trust in safety. Measuring such levels of trust is a difficult task, not the least given the lack of empirical evidence on which to draw from. Yet there are other indicators of distrust – for example, increased regulation and levels of complaints and litigation arguably reflects declining trust. Carole Smith argues that the decline of trust is partly explained by fact that policy makers have focused on attempts to increase confidence in institutions (at the expense of trust in individuals). She further argues that the lack of 'operational boundaries' of trust mean that it remains a difficult concept to pin down, and renders talk of declining trust difficult to measure (2005: 307). Reforms aimed at bolstering the institutions of regulation, discussed in Chapter 4, would tend to support this analysis.

Trust and the Medical Profession

The notion of trust is particularly important in medical settings. Permitting others to see and touch our bodies as well as revealing personal information involves the investment of a large amount of trust. However, the significance of trust extends beyond its role in the millions of everyday doctor-patient interactions. It represents an essential feature of professionalism. Chapter 1 demonstrated how the growth of public trust in the profession allowed it to define the scope of medical work, increase its power and legitimise its autonomy. In particular, the professional dominance thesis defended by Eliot Freidson is reliant on a high degree of trust. Diminishing trust thus alters the nature of professionalism and gives credence to arguments predicting the decline of professional autonomy. Discussion of health and trust are important for examining the changing role of professions and what we mean by professionalism (see Kuhlmann 2006a)

As with regulation, trust has meaning on a number of different levels. As Möllering (2008: vii) reminds us, we need to be 'extra careful' when discussing trust in the context of health. He explains that trust is about competent and benevolent efforts to cure people and may be broken by individual, organisational or institutional weaknesses, or of a combination of these. First is the trust of patients and the wider public in the profession. This operates at both micro and macro level – in other words, the interpersonal trust found within the individual doctor-patient relationship and the social trust manifest in public attitudes to the collegial body of the profession. There are many aspects to this type of trust:

(i) Trust in knowledge (impersonal trust in authority);
(ii) trust to do no harm and trust in safety;
(iii) trust to act in our best interests;
(iv) trust in honesty, particularly in relation to information disclosure, and trust not to conceal errors;
(v) trust in responsible and effective regulation.

Although reciprocal trust is not essential in the medical setting, there are circumstances whereby the *profession* must trust patients (for example, to accept advice and take medication). In addition, there is public trust in medicine, and since 1948, in the institution of the NHS. There is also the trust between profession and the state which forms the basis of self-regulation. Although these notions of trust are separate and distinct, they are by no means unrelated: as Baier explains 'trust comes in webs, not in single strands, and disrupting one strand often rips apart whole webs' (1994: 149). Within medical settings, there is a connection, albeit somewhat difficult to pin down, between our attitudes towards individual doctors and how we feel towards the collective notion of the medical profession, the institutions of self-regulation, the NHS, and scientific medicine as a whole. In other words, these notions of trust, although different, may be connected. High trust in an institution may transfer to unknown individuals. Likewise trust in individuals may generalise to organisations. Professionals are regarded as representatives of the system therefore individual failures are more likely to be seen as general failures in expert systems, thus reinforcing a loss of trust in the system. Similarly, failures of the general system may translate to generating a loss of trust in individuals.

Trust and Patient Safety

There has been little coherent thinking in relation to trust and patient safety. As a preliminary point, it is unclear whether there is a causal relationship between greater knowledge about safety lapses and levels of trust. It is widely assumed that that awareness of healthcare safety problems might make patients less inclined to trust (Quick 2006), but this has not yet been investigated empirically. And not all patient safety episodes raise question marks about misplaced trust. For example, incidents outside the control of those who might be trusted (i.e. system design flaws or resource constraints leading to a shortage of staff or bed space for example) should not necessarily lead to feelings of distrust in those individuals. However, this is not to deny that such flaws can affect levels of trust in the system, in the sense of distrusting particular hospitals. But key messages from patient safety research might suggest that investing too much trust in individuals is of limited relevance given the more significant role played by failing systems in explaining safety lapses, or that we need to think more carefully about how individuals trust systems (see Smith 2005). And of course, even when patients think they are placing trust in one particular individual, that patient and her doctor are 'embedded in a network of interpersonal, institutional and system relations' (Brownlie et al. 2008: 4). For most people, these different types of trust are likely to be interrelated. Given the reality that all doctors will commit medical errors at some point in their careers, focusing on competence as the cornerstone of trust is likely to be insufficient. So our understanding of what we mean by a trustworthy doctor in relation to our safety must mean more than just technical competence. Arguably, there are four key elements to what we might justifiably expect from professionals we can trust:

(i) Participation in patient safety efforts

Doctors deserving of trust should display awareness of safety problems and understand and apply the latest research on how to minimise risks. Doctors seeking trust in relation to patient safety should at the very least demonstrate an engagement with the science of safety, as opposed to just promising to do their best. A good example of this is the use of evidence-based safety protocols for minimising central line infections (Pronovost and Vohr 2010). This entails strong leadership and efforts to instil a safety culture. This commitment to what has been called the science of improvement (Marshall, Pronovost and Dixon-Woods 2013) requires engagement with patient safety research and a willingness to amend practice where appropriate.

(ii) Honesty about safety

Secrecy or deception about safety clearly fail Baier's test for the moral decency of trust relationships. Patients feel the strongest sense of betrayal (and thus distrust) on discovering that they have been denied the truth. Honesty about safety should take place both before treatment, in terms of accurate data about individual success or complication rates, and afterwards in terms of candour if things go wrong. A healthy view of trust thus involves the profession embracing standards of open disclosure about safety lapses leading to harm. This can be strengthened by imposing a legal duty on providers of care to be honest with patients about medical harm, as discussed in Chapter 8. This is likely to be the most contentious criteria for this new form of trust argued for here. Agreeing how far one should go in divulging 'suboptimal' conditions to patients is a contentious point, and this covers a range of possible factors such as admitting staff shortages and management failures, or the various types of errors unpacked in Chapter 2. The hardest type of case would involve doctors acknowledging that they failed to follow certain safety protocols in relation to a particular procedure. It is here that professionals understandably fear that such admissions are fatal to trust. This raises the difficult question: how can patients trust those they know have committed harmful mistakes? Arguably, this type of situation is salvageable, especially as patients begin to be better educated on the risks which they face and the reality that errors will occur. The loss of trust caused by secrecy and deception is, arguably, gone forever in patient-professional relationships.

(iii)   Helping patients contribute to their own safety

It is a reasonable assumption that patients might trust those who involve them in the task of keeping them safe. Clearly, the question of whether it is ethically desirable for policies to encourage patients to be vigilant for their safety is contentious. Some argue that it is unfair and inappropriate in the context of therapeutic relationships, and connected to this, perhaps uncomfortable for professionals. Examples that have been implemented include asking patients to double check the correct dosage of their medications and encouraging them to ask whether those treating them have observed hand-washing protocols. Professionals are likely to be sensitive to what may be interpreted as hostile questions that are at odds with the notion of professional dominance. However, a short answer is to say that if we are to take safety seriously, then the overriding concern must be with avoiding bruising patients as opposed to bruising professional egos. The role of patients and their carers in contributing towards ensuring safety is examined in more detail in Chapter 9.

(iv)   Caring in the aftermath of safety incidents

This is connected to point (ii) in relation to being honest and providing support in the aftermath of harm. Patients who suffer harm in the aftermath of errors, whether physical and or emotional, deserve the support of the professionals treating them. Caring responsibilities should extend beyond the performance of technical work to encompass emotional care in the aftermath of medical harm. This calls for greater attention to the ethics of care or what some have called 'intelligent kindness' (Ballatt and Campling 2011).

This is essentially trust in the 'moral competence' of others, that is, that they will be caring and sensitive (Jones 1998).

Failure to comply with these (especially (ii) and (iv) are likely to lead to feelings of betrayal and thus a loss of trust, in the sense of being deceived or not told the whole truth. This book takes the position that it is important to develop a vision of trust which is better placed to encourage safety and honesty, but also able to withstand the reality that is (and always will be) a degree of error and complication.

What about patients? It is commonly assumed that trusting patients are ignorant and passive participants in the process, but this need not necessarily follow, and is arguably undesirable from a safety perspective.

(i) Trusting patients are not necessarily ignorant and may also be vigilant

If we accept that trust is possible in the light of awareness of patient safety problems, then the placing of trust by a patient in a healthcare provider does not necessarily depend on the patient being ignorant of healthcare safety problems. The traditional view of trust has associated it with feelings of security, a tendency to interpret the actions of those trusted in a positive light and a lack of checking. Yet this need not necessarily be so. Trusting patients can also be vigilant for their safety and thus undertake a number of checks about the individual and institution providing their treatment. Trust should not be equated with dependency, and it is not necessarily placed once and for ever (patients who place trust may continue to monitor their situation and reassess the grounds for and nature of their trust). Patients who trust healthcare providers will not necessarily be unwilling or unable to be safety conscious and to contribute to their own safety as they use health services. Although they entrust aspects of their health and care to health professionals, they need not be regarded as relinquishing their own roles in contributing to their care. Trust can serve to facilitate cooperation and can and does occur between cooperating partners in an enterprise. There is no reason in principle why trusting patients should not make active contributions to their safety – and indeed it is plausible that well-placed trust may enable patients to work effectively with healthcare providers to support their own safety. For example, patients whose trust in their healthcare providers includes an expectation that those providers will take any concerns they express about their care seriously may be more likely to raise any concerns they have about their safety and have these addressed in good time. We must acknowledge, however, that such potential may not be achieved in practice, if, for example, health professionals exert their power to (directly or indirectly) exclude patients or frustrate their desire to be involved.

Richard Horton has argued that what may be regarded as a *loss* of trust to professional eyes may be celebrated as an opportunity to involve patients as partners and enhance the therapeutic relationship (Horton 2005). Arguably, if health professionals place a high value on patients' trust, it may be appropriate to encourage them to think not in terms of a loss of trust but rather a shift in the nature of the patient professional relationship in which trust might occur. If patients' trust is seen less in the context of a dependency relationship and more in the context of a partnership relationship (in what is mutually acknowledged to be a somewhat risky enterprise), patients' potential contributions to their safety can be regarded as compatible with, rather than indicative of a lack of, trust. Shared values and cooperation have been identified as being conducive to trust (Smith 2005). There will, of course, still be important questions to be asked about which forms of patient vigilance, including those advocated with a view to preserving safety, are compatible with trust. Although trust involves the granting of some discretion to the person trusted and thus is not compatible with a continuous and suspicious checking of their every action, some checking is likely to be appropriate, particularly when honest mistakes are clearly possible and may be easily spotted and corrected. Even if harmed, if treated with care and respect, patients may not lose trust, or may regain it. Clearly this will depend on the circumstances and require skills of care and communication from healthcare professionals. Given the reality that errors will occur in medicine, it is arguably desirable that trust is able to survive such setbacks and enable relationships to be maintained and even strengthened. These aspects of how patients may be vigilant yet also trusting are explored further in Chapter 9.

Conclusion

This chapter has unpacked two central concepts at the heart of this book: regulation and trust. Regulation is viewed broadly as any form of control over behaviour and also positively in terms of its potential for improving the safety of patients. However, it is fair to say that regulation has generally attracted a bad press from those subject to regulation, who tend to resent the perceived restriction on clinical autonomy and the threat of sanctions. Regulation is best thought of as a collaborative enterprise, especially for matters of public health, and thus should embrace professionals and patients, though efforts to allow patients to participate run counter to the professional dominance thesis which places undue trust in professions. Trust is a complex multi-layered concept that requires careful analysis. A high degree of trust is central to the professional dominance thesis discussed in Chapter 1, and indeed is essential to professionalism. This chapter has presented a nuanced and positive conception of trust to inform the discussion in the chapters that follow. This is different from conventional understandings of trust in being robust enough to accept the reality of patient safety failures and allow for patients to be vigilant about whether their trust is well placed. Whilst claims of a decline of trust are difficult to evidence, it is arguably manifested in significant changes to the tripartite relationship between the profession, state and society. A more robust system of regulation delivered by independent regulators such as the Care Quality Commission and the Professional Standards Authority, as explored in the next chapter, reflected a need to restore trust in a damaged system. It also provided an opportunity for redesigning trust in order to better ensure patient safety.

4

Professional Regulation and Patient Safety

Chapter 3 noted that medical professional regulation may be interpreted narrowly or broadly. In its narrow sense it has traditionally been confined to the work of state sanctioned professional regulators such as the General Medical Council (GMC) and Nursing Midwifery Council (NMC). These professional regulators are now supervised by a meso-regulator in the form of the Professional Standards Authority for Health and Social Care and operate alongside an ambitious systems regulator called the Care Quality Commission. But if regulation is conceived more broadly as 'any form of influence on behaviour', this encompasses a wider array of institutions beyond these formal regulators such as the Medical Royal Colleges, the Medical Defence Unions and the British Medical Association. Indeed, this broader vision of regulation would extend to local regulations and protocols adopted within particular hospitals. Whilst such a broad conception of regulation recognises the potential of various factors for influencing behaviour, ultimately it stretches the true meaning of regulation too far and renders it unworkable. However, this book will look beyond the narrower definition of regulation by also considering the role of law, via civil obligations, criminal offences and coroners' inquests, in shaping the regulatory environment. These are discussed in Chapters 5, 6 and 7. The roles of professional responsibility, peer pressure and patient engagement, as forms of informal regulation, are considered in the final two chapters. Before exploring these less formal types of regulation, this chapter begins by exploring the role of three institutions with major responsibility for regulating patient safety in England: (i) The General Medical Council (GMC), (ii) The Professional Standards Authority for Health and Social Care (PSA) and (iii) The Care Quality Commission (CQC). It does not consider the work of Monitor, which focuses more on economic regulation.

This chapter will evaluate the changing roles of these regulators in dealing with the problem of patient safety. A crisis of trust, partly connected to the high profile regulatory failures exposed by the Bristol,

Shipman and Mid Staffordshire stories described in Chapter 1, has led to significant changes to the structure and remit of professional regulators. Cracks in the commitment to self-regulation became apparent with reforms introduced by the Health Act 1999, which signalled a departure from state-sanctioned self-regulation to managerial interventionism by government (Davies 2000; Waring et al. 2010). Further reforms have significantly altered, if not quite abolished, self-regulation, leading to what Kaye has neatly called 'regulated self-regulation' (2006). The creation of both a meso-regulator, in the form of the PSA, and a system regulator, in the form of the CQC, has meant that professional regulation now operates within a broader environment of healthcare regulation. This chapter will consider the significance of changes to the regulatory landscape for the notion of professional dominance. Does the shift from self-regulation towards greater state intervention, via the work of regulators accountable to Parliament, further diminish professional dominance? It also considers whether (and in what ways) regulation impacts the behaviour of health professionals and organisations, especially in terms of encouraging safer care.

The General Medical Council

Formal regulation of the medical profession began with the creation of the General Medical Council in 1858. As part of the state-sanctioned model of self-regulation, the Medical Act 1858 granted the GMC three responsibilities: 1. maintaining the medical register, 2. acting as the legal guardian of medical education and 3. disciplining those guilty of misconduct. It would take some time before its jurisdiction was extended to deal with the health (1978) and performance of practitioners (1995). Initially, the council was composed of 24 members, 17 chosen from within the profession, 6 nominated by the crown, and the president chosen by the council as a whole (Corfield 1995: 147). This medical dominance led to George Bernard Shaw's infamous blast that the GMC constituted a 'conspiracy against the laity' (Shaw 1931: 117), a charge which it has struggled to refute. Criticisms have gone beyond its alleged bias in favour of practitioners, to include disquiet about a reactive model of regulation, a lack of transparency, and for only investigating a fraction of the cases referred to it.

The criticism about under investigation was connected to the fact that for most of its history, the GMC has been limited by the single charge of 'serious professional conduct', a vague term which was interpreted narrowly to include only the most extreme cases of misconduct (Smith 1994: 36). Significantly, this term was largely interpreted to exclude consideration of medical errors. Indeed, in 1979, the Council's code of conduct, known colloquially as the 'Blue Book', stated that 'The General Medical Council is not concerned with errors of diagnosis or treatment' (GMC 1979). By 1985 this had modified somewhat so that:

> The Council is concerned with errors in diagnosis or treatment and with the kind of matters which give rise to action in the Civil Courts for negligence, only when the doctor's conduct in the case has involved such a disregard of his professional responsibility to patients or such a neglect of his professional duties as to raise a question of professional misconduct (GMC 1985: 10 para. 38).

This reflects the somewhat surprising reality that professional regulation has historically been insufficiently focused on the subject of safety. Despite its stated statutory goal 'to protect, promote and maintain the health and safety of the public' (Section 1A Medical Act 1983), the GMC has tended to focus on problems of misconduct rather than the problems of safety. Historically, the GMC has demonstrated a weak commitment to patient safety. What may have sounded like a hackneyed charge that it was more concerned with the so-called five A's (alcohol, addiction, adultery, advertising and abortion) rather than the quality and safety of medical work did not lack substance. Statistical evidence corroborates the claim that the GMC has had a weak grip on patient safety for most of its existence. Empirical studies into the workings of the GMC, albeit conducted some time ago, have suggested that the real reasons for under-investigation and leniency by the GMC are its fear of losing legitimacy with the profession (Stacey 1992), and under-resourcing which limits its workload (Rosenthal 1987). Striking a balance between providing adequate accountability for medical misconduct and ensuring public confidence, in addition to retaining the support of the profession is undoubtedly a tough task for the GMC. Smith's magisterial study of all cases dealt with by the Professional Conduct Committee (PCC) (as it was then called) illustrates the low priority given to cases of patient safety. In his empirical study of the Professional Conduct Committee's disciplinary proceedings from 23 November 1858 to 31 December 1990, Smith (1994: 103) noted that 2,015 individual practitioners were involved in public proceedings before the PCC which he categorised into 15 types of misconduct in the following rank order.

Table 4.1 *Type of Cases Dealt with by the PCC, 1858–1990*

Type of case	Rank order	Cases (per cent)
Alcohol offences	1	13.44
Sexual offences	2	12.14
Financial offences	3	11.58
Certification	4	9.62
Drug offences	5	9.90
Neglect	6	7.79
Attracting patients	7	8.70
Unregistered practice	8	6.74
Covering/delegation	9	5.41
Abortion	10	3.55
Drug prescription	11	3.12
Offences against the person	12	3.33
Unstated/other	13	2.81
False registration	14	1.02
Breach confidence/consent	15	0.85

Much has changed at the GMC since Smith's research. Most striking is the number of complaints received, which have increased markedly from 1500 in 1995 (GMC 2001: 5) to a high of 10,305 in 2012 (GMC 2013a: 45). The number of complaints received in 2012 increased by 24 per cent since 2011 and by 104 per cent since 2007 (GMC 2013a: 45). In terms of the source of complaints, 62 per cent originated from members of the public, although only 20 per cent met the threshold for a full investigation. The explanation for this is that many of these complaints are based on a single incident and therefore are less likely to raise questions about an individual's fitness to practice. The number of complaints originating from other doctors has increased marginally from 7 per cent in 2000 to 10 per cent in 2012 (GMC 2013a: 47). Given that colleagues will observe the majority of conduct which could merit a GMC investigation, this remains a relatively low percentage which likely reflects professional norms of non-criticism and loyalty. The remainder of complaints originate from employers, police and the GMC itself.

Significant, in view of previous criticisms, are changes to the *type* of complaints investigated by the GMC. Smith's research found that it tended to focus on investigating cases involving alcohol, addiction, adultery, advertising and abortion. Whilst some of these cases will no doubt have raised questions about the safety of the care delivered, this was not the dominant concern. In 2011, the main type of allegation investigated concerned 'investigations or treatment'. Most of the subcategories cover patient safety issues such as substandard treatment, lack of further investigation, inappropriate prescribing or failure to diagnose. The other two main categories of complaint were communication and respect for patients. This is also seen in the 2012 report, where 54 per cent of complaints were about clinical care, although interestingly these constituted only 44 per cent of complaints that the GMC investigated fully (GMC 2013a: 48). A further analysis conducted by the GMC of all cases investigated between 2010 and 2013 found that out of 16,769 cases investigated during this period, 1,367 involved professional performance and 2,576 involved clinical competence (GMC 2014a: 97). Its reformed guidance to practitioners also underlines the importance of ensuring the safety of patients, noting that the duty to protect patients overrides any personal or professional loyalties. The most recent guidance encourages practitioners to be proactive where patient safety is compromised by 'the practice of colleagues or the systems, policies and procedures in the organisations where they work' (GMC 2012: 5). This marks a welcome change from the previous reluctance to engage with issues in terms of the performance of colleagues and systems factors which impact on patient safety. The important question of whether this actually impacts on the behaviour of practitioners, by making them more safety conscious, is examined below.

The GMC has also undergone significant reform to its structure and complaint handling processes. Indeed, the Council has undergone more change between 1997 and 2014 than in its previous 150-year history. This began in July 1997 when its jurisdiction expanded to deal with the performance of registered practitioners. The Medical (Professional Performance) Act 1995 amended the Medical Act 1983 by extending the Council's jurisdiction into the territory of 'Seriously Deficient Performance'. This included matters such as the use of appropriate techniques, hygiene arrangements, referral rates, record keeping and the exercise of clinical judgement. The momentum for change gathered pace under the stewardship of its progressive president, Sir Donald Irvine (Irvine 2003), and was hastened by criticisms contained in the inquiry reports into events at the Bristol Royal Infirmary (Kennedy 2001) and the killings of Harold Shipman (Smith 2004) outlined in Chapter 1. In particular, the reports of Dame Janet Smith into the Shipman Inquiry were highly critical and influential in prompting radical restructuring of its functions. In short, the fallout from the Bristol and Shipman inquiries has led to a very different GMC not only in terms of its structure, jurisdiction and procedures, but also in terms of its focus on patient safety.

In terms of its structure, it is now composed of 12 medical and 12 lay members, with the latter being independently appointed as opposed to being elected by the profession. This is a notable change from the previous dominance of medical members. In terms of its jurisdiction, the charge of serious professional misconduct has been replaced with one of 'impaired fitness to practice' which also now captures conduct which was previously referred to as 'seriously deficient performance'. Whilst 'impairment' is not statutorily defined, it is accepted that its meaning is wider than serious professional misconduct, thus giving the GMC a wider discretion to investigate. Furthermore, it is also now equipped with broad powers to order the interim suspension of practitioners for the 'protection of the public' or in 'public interest' of up to 18 months, under the Medical Act 1983 (Amendment) Order 2000 No 1803, which inserted s41A into the 1983 Act. The number of interim panel hearings has increased most years to a number of 634 in 2013 (GMC 2014b: 8). A study of 294 interim order panel cases considered between July and September 2009 reveals that in a significant proportion of cases (32 per cent) the interim sanction outweighed the final sanction (Case 2011), offering some evidence that the Council is taking its commitment to protect patients and upholding public confidence seriously. Case also concludes that there is more to interim sanctions than meets the statutory eye: it maintains public confidence in self-regulation, it facilitates professional redemption in allowing doctors to reflect on their wrongdoing and it enhances regulatory stealth and efficiency in strengthening its hand in negotiating with deviant practitioners. The broad brush nature of these powers appears to sacrifice due process safeguards in relation to individual practitioners for the supposedly greater good of attempting to ensure public confidence in the medical profession and its regulation.

The culmination of the medico-political process following the publication of the Shipman public inquiry report led to the lowering of the standard of proof in GMC cases from the criminal to the civil one (s.112 of the Health and Social Care Act 2008 amending s.60 of the Health Act 1999). It was also proposed that the council would be stripped of its adjudicative functions, merely being prosecutor, and not judge and jury as it had traditionally been. Yet the proposed Office of the Health

Professions Adjudicator (OHPA) was not taken forward by the Government, purportedly on grounds of cost, and instead it asked the GMC to separate its investigative and adjudicatory functions. The result is the Medical Practitioners Tribunal Service (MPTS) which began work in June 2012. Whilst it remains funded by and accountable to the GMC, it is managed separately and so has a degree of distance (if not complete independence) from the council's investigative process. It remains a creation of the GMC, although there are proposals to establish it as a statutory committee under the Medical Act 1983, as well as providing the GMC with a right of appeal against its decisions (GMC 2015). At the time of writing, only practitioners have a right of appeal. A degree of transparency is provided in that it publishes a record of its determinations on its website, as well as listing upcoming hearings against doctors.

Arguably the most important development at the GMC dates back to February 1999, when it approved the most significant change to its regulatory responsibility – the principle of revalidation. The lack of requirement for doctors to undergo regular competency checks has always compared unfavourably with more stringent requirements for other experts, for example, airline pilots to continually evidence their flying skills. Essentially, revalidation entails the regular demonstration by doctors that they remain fit to practise safely and so remain on the register. This was, in part, a response to the criticisms levelled at the profession and the GMC for high profile failings such as the paediatric heart surgery failings at Bristol and the killing of Harold Shipman. It heralds a shift from reactive to proactive regulation, and reflects the fact that trust is no longer assumed, and must be earned. As the consultation document explained, revalidation allows doctors to 'demonstrate publicly that they are worthy of their patients' trust' (GMC 2000: 4). However, the process of introducing revalidation has been painfully and shamefully slow. Eventually, on 3rd December 2012, revalidation regulations were introduced via The General Medical Council (Licence to Practise and Revalidation) Regulations Order of Council 2012 (No 2685). The stated aim of the GMC is that the majority of registered practitioners in the UK will have been revalidated by March 2018.

Revalidation requires that all registered medical practitioners demonstrate their competence in relation to four areas: (1) knowledge, skills, and performance; (2) safety and quality; (3) communication, partnership, and teamwork; and (4) maintaining trust (GMC 2013b: 1). Doctors are expected to maintain a portfolio of information about their work, including audits, complaints and positive or negative feedback from colleagues and patients. Prior to the introduction of GMC led revalidation there had been a system of medical appraisal within the NHS, whereby doctors were appraised by a medical colleague. This has been a requirement for hospital consultants since 2001 and for GPs since 2002 (NHS England 2013). GMC revalidation formalises this by requiring practitioners to collect and reflect on supporting documentation in relation to the key areas highlighted above, in order to demonstrate their continued competence and retain their registration. After five years, a Responsible Officer, usually the medical director of the primary care or hospital trust, can either recommend that a doctor is up-to-date and fit to practise, defer revalidation (based on lack of evidence) or refer the practitioner to the fitness to practice mechanism at the GMC. Given that revalidation is in its early stages, there is no data on its regulatory impacts, although the GMC has commissioned research by a collaborative research group called Umbrella (www.umbrella-revalidation.org.uk/). Some early findings based on interviews with key stakeholders suggests there is some confusion about what precisely revalidation is intended to achieve (Archer et al. 2013). However, it is clear that these developments reflect significant changes to the traditional model of self-regulation. Not only has the GMC undergone significant reforms to its structure, jurisdiction and investigatory procedures, but its regulatory activities are now under the watchful eye of the Professional Standards Authority for Health and Social Care.

Professional Standards Authority for Health and Social Care

Reflecting the lack of public confidence in self-regulation, the work of professional regulators such as the GMC is now supervised by the Professional Standards Authority for Health and Social Care (PSA). The PSA was created by the NHS Reform and Health Care Professions Act 2002, and operated first as the Council for the Regulation of Health Care Professionals, and then the Council for Healthcare Regulatory Excellence (CHRE) before changing its name to the PSA in December 2012. It functions as a meso-regulator by overseeing the work of the following nine health regulators: General Medical Council, General Chiropractic Council, General Dental Council, General Optical Council, General Osteopathic Council, General Pharmaceutical Council, Pharmaceutical Society of Northern Ireland, Nursing and Midwifery Council, and the Health and Care Professions Council. The PSA aims to 'promote the health, safety and well-being of patients and other members of the public and to be a strong, independent voice for patients in the regulation of health professionals throughout the UK' (CHRE 2010). It is committed to what it calls 'right touch regulation' which it defines as the minimum regulatory force required to achieve a desired result, and which is proportionate, consistent, targeted, transparent, accountable and agile (CHRE 2010). It further defines this as being 'based on a proper evaluation of risk, is proportionate and outcome focused; it creates a framework in which professionalism can flourish and organisations can be excellent' (CHRE 2010: 8). This approach shares much in common with more established ideas of 'smart regulation' and 'risk regulation' described in Chapter 3. According to these models, regulation should be carefully designed with reference to known risks and be sensitive to the relevant working context of those being regulated.

The PSA regulates the regulators in two main ways. First, it undertakes an annual performance review of individual professional regulators. This provides a degree of accountability by checking whether regulators are performing well against what it calls 'standards of good regulation'. These standards of good regulation cover the four main functions of professional regulators in relation to: setting and promoting guidance and standards for the profession(s), setting standards for and quality assuring the provision of education and training, maintaining a register of professionals and taking action where a professional's fitness to practise may be impaired. The Authority has a detailed and demanding set of criteria for standards of good regulation which it expects individual regulators to comply with. For example, in relation to fitness to practise, the PSA regards good regulation as including the following: that anyone can raise a concern about fitness to practice, information about concerns is shared with employers, cases are dealt with efficiently, the process is transparent, fair, proportionate and focused on public protection, and that decisions are well reasoned, consistent, protect the public and maintain confidence in the profession (PSA 2010b: 6.1) In 2013, the General Medical Council was found to have met all of these standards of good regulation (PSA 2013).

Second, the PSA examines a sample of the initial decisions by regulators not to investigate and also examines final decisions made by regulators' fitness to practice panels. In line with the general increase of complaints in healthcare, its workload has increased markedly. The Authority reviewed 590 fitness to practice decisions in 2004/2005 and 4,043 in 2014/2015 (PSA 2015: 5) Significantly it has the power, under Section 29 of the 2002 Act, to refer 'unduly lenient' fitness to practise cases for review by the courts. It has used this power on 114 occasions up to November 2016. The courts have upheld 33 of those referrals, dismissing five with 58 being settled by agreement and the remainder withdrawn (www.professionalstandards.org.uk/what-we -do/our-work-with-regulators/decisions-about-practitioners/cases-appealed). The notes of all the Section 29 case meetings for the previous two years are accessible from the Authority's website, offering a degree of transparency. It is also empowered, under Section 27 of the Act, to direct that regulators make or change its rules in the name of public protection. Section 28 makes provision for the PSA to respond to complaints made against a regulator, providing a form of ombudsman style investigation into complaints. This has not been implemented via any specific regulations, although doing so would arguably benefit public protection and further enhance the accountability of profes- sional regulators (CHRE 2012). The ability of the PSA to investigate complaints about healthcare regulators appears to be an inevitable next step in the erosion of trust in self-regulation. However, despite gaining approval from the Law Commission (2012) as part of its review of the statutory framework for health and social care professional regulation, it has not been acted upon by the Government, which, at the time of writing, has not yet implemented the Commission's recommendations (DOH 2015b).

The presence of the PSA is clearly an important alteration to the traditional structure for regulating healthcare professionals. The creation of an organisation that supervises the work of individual regulators reflects a growing distrust of those regulators and a greater emphasis on accountability, external scrutiny, public protec- tion and consistency of decision making. Beyond its specific role of overseeing regulators and encouraging good practice, it also plays an important role in reflecting on the role of regulation and encouraging research into the impact and effectiveness of regulation which is discussed in more detail below. The Authority also raises a fundamental point about the appropriate remit of regulation. It argues that the increase of regulation has also seen unrealistic demands placed upon it. Instead of regarding regulation as a means of setting standards and encouraging compliance, we have inap- propriate expectations that it is also responsible for ensuring improvement, which, according to the PSA, is the responsibility of healthcare professionals, managers and organisations. According to this view, it is the job of regulation to encourage improvement, but not to be responsible for such improvement, which risks regulators losing their objectivity (2015: 16).

The Care Quality Commission

The Health Act 1999 created two important regulatory agencies: the National Institute for Health and Care Excellence (NICE) responsible for producing guidelines on the use of approved drugs and treatments, and the Commission for Health Improvement (CHI) to monitor the quality of hospital care. The work of NICE in recommending and approving various treatments on the NHS has some significance for safety, and it has made some safety specific recommendations in terms of safe levels of staffing (2015). However, its primary role is about the effectiveness and efficiency of care, and so it is not discussed here. Of more significance is the institution which began life as the Commission for Health Improvement and has undergone various transformations since. The first involves its frequent change of name, beginning as the Commission for Health Improvement (2001–2003), becoming the Commission for Healthcare Audit and Inspection (2003–2004), and then the Healthcare Commission (2004–2009). The latter was absorbed into the Care Quality Commission (CQC) in 2009, which is a very large organisation with a wide remit for monitoring and inspecting a variety of health and social care services in terms of their compliance with fundamental standards of care.

In short, the CQC aims to be the independent regulator of the safety of health and social care services. Its jurisdiction is for England, with different agencies operating in Wales, Scotland and Northern Ireland. The creation of this agency fills an important gap in the regulation of patient safety; whilst doctors have long been subject to regulation by the GMC, healthcare organisations have not been subject to special regulation until the creation of the CQC (and its predecessors). Given that, as discussed in Chapter 2, most safety failures are caused by organisational rather than individual failings, the formal regulation of healthcare organisations and the system of delivering care is essential to improving quality and safety. The CQC's stated legislative purpose is 'to protect and promote the health, safety and welfare of people who use health and social care services' and to encourage improvement of services 'in a way that focuses on the needs and experiences of people who use these services' (Health and Social Care Act 2008, s.3(1)-(2)). Its reach is very wide in extending beyond hospitals to include GP surgeries, care homes, ambulance services and a proportion of dental services. It aims to regulate these services in a variety of ways. First, it sets out standards below which care should not fall. These were previously called 'essential standards of care' but have been bolstered and renamed as 'fundamental standards of care' following a recommendation from the Francis Inquiry into Mid Staffordshire (Francis 2013: 87). There are 13 fundamental standards which cover the following: person-centred care, dignity and respect, consent, safety, safeguarding from abuse, nutritional and hydration needs, premises and equipment, acting on complaints, good governance, staffing, fit and proper staff, a duty of candour and a display of ratings (Health and Social Care Act 2008 (Regulated Activities) Regulations 2014). These cover an impressively wide array of matters, which makes the work of the CQC incredibly important yet presents challenges in terms of implementation and enforcement.

The CQC also has responsibility for registering, monitoring and inspecting care services in terms of their compliance with these fundamental standards, and publishes its findings on its website. Given the breadth of the services it covers, this is a formidable task. It has also presented the CQC and its predecessors with a difficult choice in terms of its regulatory approach, namely whether to adopt a light touch or a heavy-handed approach to inspection and monitoring. This places the regulator in an invidious position of trying to reduce the regulatory burden on organisations, but nevertheless aiming to reliably measure quality, provide accountability and maintain public confidence. The ethos behind the creation of the Commission for Health improvement, the original agency established in 2001, was very much based on the idea of light-touch regulation and trying to stimulate learning and regulation from within healthcare organisations. This approach of encouraging improvement and relying on a degree of self-assessment, rather than policing and penalising, was championed by the Healthcare Commission under the leadership of Sir Ian Kennedy (Healthcare Commission 2009: 10). Such an approach was consistent with the approach to quality improvement advocated by leading figures in the patient safety movement, who have stressed the importance of culture that tries to understand and learn rather than blame and punish (Berwick 1989; Leape 1997).

However, this light touch approach to regulation is always vulnerable to criticism, especially in the wake of major problems such as the neglect and mismanagement at the Mid Staffordshire NHS Foundation Trust, which was noted in Chapter 1. The fact that this Trust had not been identified as problematic by the Healthcare Commission did not inspire confidence in its inspection system. It would be wrong to simply blame the regulator here, given that it operated within the confines of rules and regulations dictated by the Department of Health, and regretted its lack of complete independence (Francis 2013: 785). However, such criticisms have continued to be made against the CQC. In particular the National Audit Office expressed concern at the relatively low number of compliance reviews completed (NAO 2011). Unsurprisingly given the public criticism and political pressure, it has responded by increasing its number of inspections from 1,405 in 2012/13 to 39,567 in 2013/14 (CQC 2014: 9).

The CQC and its predecessors have utilised various different systems for monitoring and inspection. Its system of 'intelligent monitoring', which was introduced in 2013, is essentially a form of risk regulation that uses various sources of data and intelligence to decide where, when and what to inspect. This builds on the previous work of the Healthcare Commission in pioneering an information-led risk-based approach to the task of regulating (2009). The CQC has greatly expanded the range of information it uses, and now draws on 150 separate indictors, which are used to give hospitals a risk banding between 1 (the highest risk) and 6 (the lowest risk) (CQC 2014: 14). Informed by these risk bandings, the CQC carries out inspections of care providers which are led by three chief inspectors of General Practice, Hospitals and Adult Social Care who manage teams of specialist inspectors in these settings. Whilst the CQC has previously been criticised for its approach to identifying high-risk organisations, most notably in relation to problems at Mid Staffordshire (Francis 2013), the National Audit Office has found that it is now using this data more effectively to plan its inspections (2015). The CQC has also attempted to better capture the patient experience by recruiting 500 'experts by experience' who are individuals with experience of using care services and who participate in inspections. It has also expressed its intention to monitor social media pages for adverse comments about the quality of care, which may trigger its decision to investigate (*The Telegraph* 12 February 2016). This approach of involving patients is an important aspect of the Commission's approach to regulation and is more than merely symbolic. The issue of patient involvement in seeking to ensure the safety of care is discussed in more detail in Chapter 9.

A large inspection team carry out both announced and unannounced inspections on care providers and issue detailed reports. These lead to ratings, displayed prominently inside hospitals, as to whether a trust is safe, effective, caring, responsive and well-led. There is also an overall rating based on these key criteria. This mirrors the approach of the education sector regulator (OFSTED) in rating services as 'outstanding', 'good', 'requires improvement' or 'inadequate'. Inspection reports are detailed and demonstrate the wide array of safety issues with which the CQC is concerned, including systems issues such as staffing, bed capacity, waiting times, patient flow through hospitals, the accuracy of medical records and infection control. Reports also comment on aspects of culture such as commitment to teamwork and an ethic of care and compassion. In October 2015, it was revealed that 76 per cent of NHS hospital trusts were given a rating of 'inadequate' or 'requiring improvement' by the CQC (*The Telegraph* 15 October 2015), perhaps reflecting the lack of a safety culture as discussed in Chapter 2. The question about the impact of its regulatory efforts remains unclear, but it cannot be denied that the CQC evaluates a wide range of issues that are central to patient safety and for which organisations were previously largely unaccountable for.

Unlike its predecessors, the CQC is equipped with direct enforcement powers. This includes issuing warning notices, fixed penalty notices, suspending registration or prosecuting care providers. It took enforcement action on 1,523 occasions in 2013/14, with the majority of these being the issuing of warning notices (CQC 2014: 9). Its powers have been strengthened following the implementation of recommendations from the Francis Inquiry into Mid Staffordshire. These were based on a zero-tolerance approach to poor care backed up by the creation of a criminal offence of breaching fundamental standards (regulation 22 of The Health and Social Care Act 2008 (Regulated Activities) Regulations 2014). Significantly, the requirement that the CQC issues a warning notice prior to every prosecution has been removed. Under Section 50 of the Health and Social Care Act 2008, it may also recommend to the Secretary of State for Health that special measures be taken against a provider for failing to comply with standards of quality and safety. These enforcement powers are clearly designed to respond to public concern following failures such as those at Mid Staffordshire and bolster the accountability of healthcare organisations. However, this tougher approach is also potentially counterproductive to the aim of encouraging an open culture where staff feel safe to speak up about safety problems.

This raises the issue of which *type* of regulation and method of enforcement is likely to be most effective? This depends on the objectives of regulation, which in this context should be dominated by ensuring safe and effective medical care. Regulation scholars have distinguished *formal deterrence* from *compliance*-based approaches, the former relying on penal responses and the latter on negotiation. According to Ayres and Braithwaite, most successful regulatory agencies find an appropriate balance and the 'trick of successful regulation is to establish a synergy between punishment and persuasion' (1992: 25). The traditional deterrence-based 'command and control' regulation, which devotes resources towards litigation and inspection, has been criticised as being counterproductive (Grabosky 1995). This point has been embraced by patient safety researchers who generally agree that too much and punitive regulation risks being counterproductive in terms of discouraging a culture of openness and honesty about safety. Donald Berwick has described two approaches to this problem of quality enhancement: the theory of bad apples, and the theory of continuous improvement. Proponents of the bad apple theory search for better methods of inspection, 'publish mortality data, invest heavily in systems of case-mix adjustment, and fund vigilant regulators' (Berwick 1989: 53). Advocates of this approach are typically supportive of disciplinary and legal mechanisms for punishing individual failings. The theory of continuous improvement, on the other hand, encourages an environment of learning from experiences and focuses on organisational rather than individual responsibility. The current regulatory regime is a somewhat uneasy combination of both of these approaches.

Evaluating the Regulatory Environment

According to Light (1995: 35)

> The end of professional dominance involves the state and other major players entering the governance structure of the profession to monitor its work and restrain its economic and clinical activities. The state's development of highly professional agencies that analyse health care practitioners more systematically than the practitioners themselves changes the balance of power fundamentally.

To what extent have changes to the GMC and the creation of two new regulatory bodies discussed above had this effect? On the face of it, the quote from Light appears to be an accurate description in relation to the regulation of the medical profession in the United Kingdom. Reforms to the GMC and the creation of two significant regulatory actors in the form of the PSA and the CQC reflect an interventionist approach by the state. It also reflects a loss of trust in the ability of self-regulation to ensure sufficient accountability and safety. The era of professional dominance through a pure system of self-regulation has arguably gone forever.

The changes discussed in this chapter represent more than what had previously been described as 'uncomfortable adjustments' to professional self-regulation (Elston 1991). The regulatory landscape has changed considerably. However, while these changes appear to signal the end of professional dominance through pure self-regulation, it is less clear what the implications are for improving the quality and safety of care.

Whilst the regulation literature, as discussed in Chapter 3, is well established, there is a dearth of empirical evidence in relation to the question of whether, and in what ways, regulation impacts the behaviour of the regulated. Considerable effort has been devoted to designing and enforcing regulation, yet there is little understanding of whether it works, or if so, in what ways. It is surprising that few studies have *directly* addressed the question of how regulation affects the behaviour of health-care professionals or healthcare organisations. The regulation of indivi-dual professionals has a much longer history than that of healthcare organisations, yet we know relatively little about the impact of regulation on both. Amongst many explanations for this is a methodological one: trying to isolate the impact of professional regulation amidst the myriad other sources of influence on professional behaviour is difficult, if not impossible. Understanding how *one* type of regulation affects behaviour is sufficiently challenging, and when we factor in the messy interaction of different types of regulatory influences (guidelines, law, employment contracts, peer support/pressure) we encounter a far more complex problem. Many recognised sources of influence are connected to profes-sional regulation, for example, medical education (including continuing professional education) and codes of conduct, practice guidelines, pro-tocols and checklists. This dearth of material may also reflect the reality that *clinical practice* (as opposed to non-clinical misconduct) remains a relatively recent focus for regulation and governance. After all, it is only during the last decade that professional regulation has moved away from its ineffective past (Stacey 1992) with attempts to foster a new style of professionalism (Irvine 2003; Kennedy 2006; Royal College of Physicians 2005, 2010).

This gap in the literature is striking given the consensus that the main goal of regulation is to encourage or discourage certain beha-viour. Whilst there has been detailed discussion about principles of good regulation (Prosser 2010), there has been little attention to evaluating the *practical impact* of regulation on individuals and orga-nisations. Furthermore, most ethnographic studies about regulation (from other settings) have focused on *regulators* rather than the *regulated*, or assessed its impact on firms or organisations rather than individuals. This major gap in our state of knowledge has long been noted. Horder et al. (1986: 521) remarked that 'Given the interest in reaching and convincing the widely dispersed and varied body of general practitioners, it is surprising that so little work has been done in this area. Considerable time and money is spent in attempting to bring about change and some effort in evaluating which approaches are successful would seem to be a wise investment.' And in his magisterial study of the professional conduct jurisdiction of the GMC (1858–1990), Smith observed that 'it would be instructive to conduct a follow-up survey of practitioners dealt with by the GMC to determine whether they continue to practise medicine during the period of their erasure, and also after their names have been restored to the Register, *and, if so, what changes take place with respect to their professional conduct*' (my emphasis) (1994: 202). Yet, few have taken up the challenge. As Healy (2011: 12) remarks in her international review of healthcare regulation, 'while regulatory actors have scattered many seeds they have had little time so far to walk over the terrain to check which plants have grown, flourished and borne fruit'.

Chapter 3 notes the promise of so-called responsive or smart regulation. This is based on the belief that regulators should be sensitive to the relevant context and prefer softer rather than more punitive forms of encouraging compliance and dealing with non-compliance. Regulators should thus begin with soft supporting nudges and be slow to utilise command and control measures such as legal penalties (Gunningham and Grabosky 1998). The spirit of responsive regulation is welcomed by patient safety champions who have consistently called for more empathy and less blame directed to those at the sharp end of patient safety incidents. Responsive regulation is also reliant on the idea of 'networked governance' whereby multiple regulators adopt multiple strategies and communicate with each other (Healy 2011: 59–61). There has been some progress here. For example, the General Medical Council now shares intelligence with the Care Quality Commission (PSA 2015: 15), and there is a Memorandum of Understanding between the later and the Health and Safety Executive (CQC 2015b). However, it is less clear whether such responsive regulation has actually improved quality and safety (Healy 2011; PSA 2015).

The Professional Standards Authority has drawn on a range of scholarship in order to reflect on the progress of regulation and to provide some guidance on its appropriate role. It concludes that the current approach to healthcare regulation is failing, stating that 'if regulation was going to improve care, it would have done so by now' (PSA 2015: 21). The Authority explains this failure with reference to two key factors. First, there has been no overarching design to the system of regulation described in this chapter, nor a shared vision amongst the main regulators for ensuring standards are met and safety improved. Rather, the regulatory landscape has emerged largely in response to the relevant context of various healthcare scandals, with the creation of new regulators and laws in an attempt to bolster accountability and regain public confidence. During this busy period of regulatory reform in the healthcare sector, there has been little thought devoted to identifying and agreeing a shared set of values of safe care on which all regulators can agree and communicate consistently (Bilton and Cayton 2013). Achieving regulatory objectives – in this case ensuring the quality and safety of healthcare – is more likely if a combination of methods all repeat the same key message (Quick 2011). When different sources of influence (for example, professional regulation, clinical guidelines, employment contracts, law and even financial incentives), all nudge practitioners in the same direction, then regulatory goals stand a greater chance of being realised. However, the current regulatory environment, occupied as it is with multiple regulators working in different ways, lacks cohesion and is unfortunately unable to demonstrate its effectiveness.

Second, is what we might call regulatory overkill, with far too many regulators overburdening healthcare organisations, causing confusion and inefficiency. Beyond the main regulators examined in this chapter, there are more than 20 agencies that have responsibility for monitoring health and care (PSA 2015: 5). Having so many regulators with heavy workloads has a large financial cost – the PSA estimates that the annual operating costs of regulation of healthcare professionals and organisations is around £600 million. This does not include the operational costs to the organisations regulated, therefore the true cost is in excess of this (PSA 2015: 14). Organisations are thus stretched in trying to pay attention and comply with a variety of rules and sets of guidance from different regulators. Heimer (2009: 31) offers an interesting analysis of the problem of 'paying attention' in this world of regulatory pluralism. She suggests that "If the core problem for decision making is the limited capacity of people and organizations to collect and process information, it is their limited capacity to pay attention that poses the challenge for regulation." Whilst this reflection is in relation to a study from a different context (how rules are used in five clinics for treating patients with HIV) nevertheless, her point that in order to "understand the effect of rules, we need to look not just at what they do to people's actions but what they do to people's attention" is pertinent to the problem of regulating safety in healthcare more generally. Having an ever increasing number of rules and regulations, implemented by a range of different regulators, increases the risk that busy individuals and institutions become over-loaded and unable to pay attention to what really matters – delivering safe patient-centred care.

The PSA has provided a fairly detailed diagnosis of the problem with the current system of regulation. It also offers a prescription for improve-ment. Regulation should be proactive instead of reactive by seeking to prevent specific problems, for example aiming to reduce risk and the incidence of well-known safety problems. It also needs to encourage professionals to engage with regulation and regulators, rather than regarding regulation as something negative and punitive. Perhaps the biggest challenge here for regulation is to encourage a culture that prioritises safety, as described in Chapter 2. This means a culture where professionals are able to speak up about safety concerns without fear of reprisals, and where staff and organisations listen to the concerns of patients and their carers. Unfortunately, such a culture has been slow to develop. Regulators are placed in a difficult position in terms of seeking to help foster such a culture. The increase of regulators and a strengthening of their enforcement powers, mainly as a response to scandals such as Bristol and Mid Staffordshire, is unlikely to set the right climate for encouraging staff to speak up. Regulation faces a tough task here in trying to change well established norms of non-criticism and also a tolerance of unsafe conditions which are entrenched in healthcare. Chapter 8 explores the need for honesty and transparency around safety, and in particular, considers the potential of a duty of candour in relation to medical harm and an associated duty on professionals to speak up about safety problems.

Conclusion

Despite the thin state of knowledge on the impact of regulation, few would argue for a system without regulation, given its role in seeking to ensure safety. Whilst regulation will have both positive and negative consequences, we do not (as yet) fully understand the impact that it has in practice. No system of regulation will be perfect – mistakes and misconduct will occur even in the best designed and appropriately implemented systems. This book considers important alternative sources of regulation, from formal legal mechanisms, to the more informal role of professional and patient engagement with safety. As with mechanisms of formal regulation explored in this chapter, legal mechanisms should also be approached in terms of what they might offer for improving safety. Legal mechanisms for providing accountability have been perceived negatively in terms of their ability to improve safety. Indeed, many have argued that the fear of being sued or prosecuted is counterproductive to the pursuit of a culture of safety, on the basis that professionals will be reluctant to admit and report mistakes for fear of damaging legal repercussions. However, there is a danger of generalising that all legal mechanisms will have the same effect, whereas it is possible that different types of laws will have different effects. As Brownsword reminds us, 'the relationship between law and regulation is unclear. Is law to be understood as a broader enterprise than regulation, or is it narrower?' (2008: 6). Given that regulation is fundamentally about shaping behaviour, then law certainly qualifies as a form of regulation. But whether it operates in a way to help or hinder the regulatory objective of safer care is somewhat less clear. This important question will be explored in the next three chapters.

5

Complaining and Claiming

The next three chapters consider whether law helps or hinders patient safety. This is a difficult question to address, not least because it depends on how patient safety and law are defined. As Chapter 2 noted, patient safety is potentially extremely broad. Arguably, everything that takes place in healthcare, from the competency of professionals to decisions about the funding and provision of services, even to the work of porters and cleaners, has implications for the safety of patients. The focus of this book is on patient safety and the work of the medical profession, that is, the human dimension of everyday encounters, decisions and procedures in healthcare. We might think that law is fairly well defined, but again, at its broadest it includes a wide variety of laws, regulations and guidance that have some connection to the aim of improving safety in healthcare. These are too various and numerous to explore within the next three chapters, which will instead focus on established legal mechanisms for responding to patient safety failures through civil, criminal and coronial law. It is important to acknowledge that these legal mechanisms are not designed primarily with patient safety in mind; at best, safety is an indirect side effect to the dominant issues of accountability, compensation and punishment in the case of civil and criminal law, and fact-finding in the case of coronial law. Furthermore, these legal actions do not operate in isolation and are best understood alongside systems for dealing with complaints about NHS care. This chapter will thus include a brief outline of the NHS complaints system and explain its relationship with the litigation system. Whilst it is difficult to separate the effect of law from these other mechanisms, this chapter will nevertheless try to understand whether there is (or could be) a connection between liability systems, legal rules and the safety of patients.

It is frequently asserted that tort law is unhelpful in terms of patient safety. This is based on the belief that the fear of litigation leads to secrecy around safety rather than the openness required for learning and prevention (Kennedy 2001, recommendations 33 and 35).

For the same reasons, the severe option of criminalising medical mistakes (discussed in the next chapter) has also been viewed negatively from a safety culture perspective (Quick 2010). However, these chapters will move beyond pessimistic accounts of law and the legal system to consider their *potential* for improving patient safety. It is important to remember that the law of tort is not the only way of responding to cases of harm caused by medical treatment. This chapter will thus consider the merits of no-fault systems for dealing with medical error, especially those operating in New Zealand and the Nordic countries. However, given the unlikely abolition of the fault-based system of liability in the United Kingdom, this chapter will conclude by considering alternative ways within the fault system that may be better suited to improving safety. This includes the underused option of the direct liability of healthcare organisations for failing to ensure a safe healthcare environment, or more onerously for breach of a non-delegable duty of care. Finally, the radical option of creating specially designed 'Health Courts' will also be considered, before exploring the potential for supporting safety through closer collaboration between medical insurers and providers of care.

A Culture of Complaining and Litigating?

One of the characteristics of contemporary British society has been an increased culture of complaining (Institute of Customer Service 2010). The most treasured institution of the welfare state, the National Health Service, and its traditionally dominant force, the medical profession, have not been immune from this. At the beginning of the 1970s there were around 9,000 written complaints per year about hospitals (Klein 1974: 366). In 2012/13 the number of complaints made about NHS care had grown to 162,000 (Clwyd and Hart 2013: 9). Despite this dramatic increase, this number remains relatively small in proportion to the number of possible complaints that could be made. People are generally reluctant to complain about their experience of the NHS, whether through a lack of confidence in achieving a satisfactory outcome or by the fear of being labelled as troublemakers and the effect this may have on their ongoing care (HCHC 2011: 33).

The constant reform and reorganisation of the NHS has also been reflected in its system for handling complaints, which has undergone considerable change and evaluation during the past two decades (Wallace and Mulcahy 1999; Clwyd and Hart 2013). In short, there are two stages to the complaints system: local resolution and recourse to the ombudsman. The vast majority of complaints are handled via the local resolution stage where providers have the opportunity to respond to the complaint. Those dissatisfied with the response are able to complain to the Parliamentary and Health Service Ombudsman. Consistent with other parts of the NHS complaints system, the workload of the ombudsman has increased significantly. Its first full year of operation in 1974–5 witnessed 493 complaints. This has increased to around 16,000 complaints in 2012–13. However, only around 10 per cent of these are investigated. In terms of remedies, the ombudsman can ask for organisations to make apologies, pay limited compensation, or recommend management action. In 2013–14, the ombudsman requested the following remedies: 752 apologies, 628 compensation payments, (£595,861 from health organisations, £152,053 from government organisations), 631 recommendations for management action (which can include action plans and changes to policy and procedures), and 197 other actions to put things right (for example reinstating patients on GP lists and reviewing care and treatment provided) (PHSO 2014a: 13).

Complaints in the NHS relate to a wide variety of things, from aspects of clinical work, including errors and safety incidents, to non-clinical matters such as delays and rudeness. Complaints about medical errors or the safety of care are the most relevant to the core technical aspect of professional autonomy and most pertinent to professional dominance. Research suggests that the majority of complainants about healthcare are seeking an explanation, apology and assurances that the same fate will not befall others (Mulcahy 2003: 94). Effective complaints systems hold professionals and organisations to account and may also offer some redress for complainants (Lloyd Bostock and Mulcahy 1994). In terms of improving patient safety, complaints have potential for offering learning opportunities about the safety and quality of care. Complaints provide valuable information or 'market research' enabling professionals and managers to assess and improve quality. In addition, they may allow the early identification of potential negligence claims, trigger disciplinary action, and function as a dispute resolution tool. The story of poor standards of care at the Mid Staffordshire NHS Foundation Trust, summarised in Chapter 1, is a prime example where complaints were not taken sufficiently seriously and acted upon in order to prevent further harm.

However, complainants may also turn to law in terms of seeking redress for unresolved grievances. Indeed, as Mulcahy and Allsop explain, complaints resemble negligence claims in being an individualistic form of regulation, reliant on service users voicing their grievances (1996: 7). Complaints may well proceed into legal actions and the relationship between complaints and litigation is interesting. Previously, the complaints system allowed NHS organisations to decide against investigating where legal proceedings were pending. However, since 1 April 2009, even if a complainant has expressed an intention to commence legal proceedings, NHS organisations are expected to work towards resolving the complaint promptly unless there are compelling legal reasons not to do so (The Local Authority Social Services and National Health Service Complaints (England) Regulations 2009). In the United Kingdom, most actions in the tort of negligence proceed against NHS trusts as vicariously liable for the conduct of their employees. Actions can also be brought against General Practitioners or hospital doctors working privately. In practical terms, the NHS has provided indemnity for hospital doctors for allegations arising out of contracted NHS duties since 1990 under the Hospital and Community Health Services indemnity scheme. General Practitioners and dentists are compelled to have private medical insurance, usually with the Medical Defence Union or the Medical Protection Society, as are hospital doctors working privately. Since 1995, claims brought in England have been managed by the NHS Litigation Authority, which administers the Clinical Negligence Scheme for Trusts. In Wales, similar functions are performed by the Welsh Risk Pool, a mutual self-assurance scheme, and Legal and Risk Services, which acts for all trusts and health boards in Wales (Ferguson and Braithwaite 2012). The Central Legal Office in Scotland administers a Clinical Negligence and Other Risks Indemnity Scheme (CNORIS) (Stephen et al. 2012).

Historically, whilst the number of claims increased with the introduction of the National Health Service, compared with other areas of litigation, they remained low. In 1978, the Royal Commission on Personal Injury Compensation estimated that there were about 500 claims against medical services (doctors, dentists and pharmacists) per year (1978: 2). The 1980s witnessed a growth in the number of claims (up by approximately 500 per cent) and an increase in the costs of settling claims (up by about 250 per cent) (Walshe 1999: 69). Research by Fenn et al. (2000) suggested that the volume of litigation in 1998 was more than twice the level at the beginning of the 1990s. In the period between 1978 and 2006, the level of claims increased dramatically by 1,200 per cent (Harpwood 2007: 2). In 2014–15, 11,497 claims of clinical negligence and 4,806 claims of non-clinical negligence against NHS bodies were received by the NHS Litigation Authority in England. In terms of financial cost,

£1.16 billion was paid in connection with clinical negligence claims during 2014–15 (NHSLA 2015).

In England, only around 2 per cent of claims end up being tried in court, with the vast majority being settled or mediated out of court. From 2002 to 2012 the NHSLA received 65,944 negligence actions with 47 per cent being settled out of court, 35 per cent abandoned by the claimant, and 16 per cent remaining unresolved (NHSLA 2012). Beyond noting the number and cost of claims, the NHSLA provides little information about why certain cases are settled and others defended (Mulcahy 2014: 284). A likely factor in explaining why cases do end up in court is that the parties estimation of the strength of the claim, or the amount of damages potentially payable, are widely divergent. In terms of its remit, the NHSLA aims to 'ensure that claims made against the NHS are handled fairly and consistently, with due regard to the interests of both patients and the NHS' (NHSLA 2013a). Clearly, balancing the interests of patients (particularly those bringing claims) with the interests of the NHS is challenging, but it is perhaps understandable that the Authority ultimately prioritises the financial interests of the NHS, in terms of trying to settle claims efficiently and influencing case precedents by deciding which actions to litigate in court (Mulcahy 2014). This reference to financial savings has been underlined by a recent Department of Health review of the NHSLA, noting that it 'ultimately act in the interests of fairness to patients, staff and the public, whilst having regard to protecting the public purse' (DOH 2015c: 5).

However, whilst the NHSLA primarily focuses on reducing the cost of defending legal actions, which could instead be used for patient care, it is well placed to facilitate improved safety. Previously, it sought to incentivise safety by offering subscription discounts of up to 30 per cent to trusts complying with its risk management standards on governance, learning from experience, competent and capable workforce and safe environment (NHSLA 2013b). However, a review of the NHSLA concluded that it was unclear whether the agency made maximum use of its extensive claims database in order to arrive at more accurate risk profiles and thus more appropriate discounts or penalties to individual trusts. The same review was unable to find a 'conclusive correlation between improved patient safety and adoption of risk management' (MARSH 2011: 46), although it is expected that trusts who comply with risk management standards are well led and thus likely to be engaged with efforts to improve safety. As a result, the NHSLA no longer offers such discounts to NHS Trusts. This decision, whilst based on the absence of conclusive evidence supporting a correlation between insurance premium discounts and patient safety, is regrettable in the absence of further research exploring a fuller safety profile of those trusts who were previously eligible for discounts. The Authority also attempts to support a learning culture by sharing claims data with trusts and also analysing and disseminating data in relation to high risk areas such as obstetrics. However, it is unclear whether it has maximised its potential for facilitating improvements to safety, and the Department of Health has called for a rethink of its approach to reducing the number of claims and thus improving safety (DOH 2015: 5).

The increased number and cost of claims has fuelled fears of a 'compensation culture' or a 'claims crisis', which is perceived negatively given the suggestion of unmeritorious claims and a decline of individual responsibility (Furedi 1999). However, research evidence from both the United Kingdom and the United States suggests that such claims are exaggerated, if not wholly misleading. In 1991, the Harvard medical practice study found that there were eight times as many adverse events as claims (Brennan et al. 1991). This has subsequently led to claims from the United States that there is actually an epidemic of malpractice rather than of malpractice litigation (Baker 2005). In the United Kingdom, numerous scholarly reviews have exposed the compensation culture claim for a lack of evidence (Dingwall 1994; Lewis et al. 2006; Morris 2011), leading Williams to conclude that the British are a nation of 'lumpers rather than litigators' (2005: 499). The presence of a so-called compensation culture is thus dubious at best, and the extent to which it has any foundation, is limited to road traffic accident claims, with no evidence in the United Kingdom suggesting there is a flood of meritless claims in the clinical negligence context. This is supported by research evidence from the United States, which suggests that the tort system is effective at separating meritorious from unmeritorious cases (Studdert et al. 2006). In short, there is little evidence of a compensation culture, and in fact, substantial evidence that only a minority of potential claimants turn to law. This is not to deny the rising costs of claims, but rather to acknowledge the lack of safety culture, which arguably warrants much greater attention. Unfortunately, this lack of evidence has not stopped the UK government from peddling this myth of a compensation culture. It is thus regrettable that the Young (2010) report commissioned by the UK government is based on the assumption of an 'over the top' safety culture when the prevailing culture of safety in healthcare, as explored in Chapter 8, is relatively weak.

Negligence and Patient Safety

The relationship between the system of medical negligence and levels of patient safety is unclear. Many would question a strong linkage between the tort system and the quality and safety of patient care. For some, they are culturally incompatible: the name and shame aspect of liability encourages secrecy rather than the candour essential for patient safety (Kennedy 2001: recommendations 33 and 35). The threat of being sued is often identified by professionals as a barrier to the open culture necessary for greater patient safety (Van Dijck 2015). Whilst this may be true, it should be remembered that improving patient safety through deterring bad practice is somewhat secondary to tort's principal aim of compensation. Whilst the corrective justice rationale might work for the minority who are compensated, it does nothing for the broader (and much bigger) problem of tackling unsafe cultures. In short, tort law is not designed to address issues of patient safety. As Miola (2011) reminds us, it remains a retrospective remedy to compensate the relatively few who bring legal actions. In a similar vein, Jackson (2006) has argued that tort law offers limited protection for patient autonomy despite appearing to offer professional accountability for the failure to disclose information to patients.

Important common-law decisions about medical negligence reveal no consistent approach in favour of respecting patient safety. The well-known direction of Mr Justice McNair in *Bolam v. Friern Hospital Management Committee* [1957] 2 All ER 118, at 122 that "A doctor is not guilty of negligence if he has acted in accordance with a practice accepted as proper by a responsible body of medical men skilled in that particular art" set the scene for the medicalisation of the standard of care. Tort-law scholars have long noted that this direction was misinterpreted so that evidence of common professional practice appeared to be determinative rather than suggestive of the issue of negligence (Grubb 1993). Over a 30-year period, decisions in this area favoured the former approach, probably reflecting a deliberate policy of judicial paternalism towards the medical profession and fuelled by the (unfounded) fear of a litigation crisis. This led to significant criticisms about the professionalisation and 'Bolamisation' of medical law (Montgomery 1989; Brazier and Miola 2000). In particular, the Bolam approach was inappropriate as a way of evaluating the standard of care in cases about the disclosure of risks, on the basis that patients, rather than 'a responsible body of medical men', should decide what information is relevant to their decision to consent to treatment. Nevertheless, for 30 years, the leading case of *Sidaway v Board of Governors of the Bethlem Royal Hospital and the Maudsley Hospital* [1985] AC 871 essentially defended such a position.

However, the 1990s signalled the beginning of increased judicial interventionism in relation to the standard of care. Prior to this, there were only sporadic instances of judicial unease with *Bolam*. The House of Lords decision in *Bolitho And Others v. City and Hackney Health Authority* [1997] 3 WLR 1151 at 1160 restored the conventional position in tort law, that common professional practice can only be evidence rather than determinative of negligence, and thus has paved the way for courts to reclaim the issue of evaluating the standard of care:

> ... in cases of diagnosis and treatment there are cases where, despite a body of professional opinion sanctioning the defendant's conduct, the defendant can properly be held liable for negligence... In my judgment that is because, in some cases, it cannot be demonstrated to the judge's satisfaction that the body of opinion relied upon is reasonable or responsible.

This approach has also been applied to information disclosure cases. Indeed, the tendency for judges to favour patient autonomy, and by association, patient safety, has been a prominent feature of recent landmark decisions of the Appeal Courts in England and Wales. The best example was the willingness of the majority of the House of Lords in *Chester v Afshar* [2004] UKHL 41 to bend the rules of causation in the name of patient autonomy and in order to recognise informed consent in English law. Ms Carole Chester brought an action in negligence against Mr Afshar, a consultant neurosurgeon, after suffering complications following a spinal operation he performed on her. Whilst the procedure was carried out competently, Ms Chester suffered a known side effect, called cauda equina syndrome, which resulted in partial paralysis. She claimed, successfully, that Mr Afshar failed to warn her of the 1–2 per cent risk of this complication materialising, and that had she known, she would not have consented to the procedure at that time, although might have gone ahead in the future. The case hinged on the significance of this latter fact, given that the complication was an unavoidable risk which had the same probability of materialising had Ms Chester had proceeded with surgery in the future. In short, according to conventional principles of tort law, the failure to warn could not be said to have caused the harm. This divided the House of Lords, but the three majority judges were prepared to establish a causal link in order to respect Ms Chester's autonomy and so give effect to the concept of informed consent. As Lord Steyn explained [at para 24]:

> as a result of the surgeon's failure to warn the patient, she cannot be said to have given informed consent to the surgery in the full legal sense. Her right of autonomy and dignity can and ought to be vindicated by a narrow and modest departure from traditional causation principles.

This prioritisation of patient autonomy and choice was also evident in the decision of the Supreme Court in *Montgomery v Lanarkshire Health Board* [2015] UKSC 11. Nadine Montgomery gave birth to a baby son in 1999 who suffered serious birth injuries. This was due to a complication called shoulder dystocia, where the baby's shoulders are too large to pass through the mother's pelvis, causing the baby to become stuck, and thus representing a medical emergency. She was at greater risk of this complication given that she suffered from diabetes which is associated with larger babies. She was also of small stature. She was concerned about whether her baby could be safely delivered naturally, especially as the baby was larger than average. She alleged negligence in two ways: first, in failing to disclose the risk of shoulder dystocia, and the possibility of an alternative delivery by caesarean section to avoid that risk, and secondly that the management of labour itself had been negligent, in that the obstetrician had failed to perform a caesarean section when there were indications that this would have been advisable. Despite losing her case in the Scottish courts, Mrs Montgomery's argument found unanimous favour with the UK Supreme Court, which overruled the majority approach in *Sidaway* which had held that the standard of care in relation to treatment risks should be determined by the *Bolam* test. In *Montgomery*, Lord Kerr and Lord Reed were clear that the courts, and not the medical profession, are the ultimate arbiters of the appropriate standard of care:

> what risks of injury are involved in an operation, for example, is a matter falling within the expertise of members of the medical profession. But it is a non sequitur to conclude that the question whether a risk of injury, or the availability of an alternative form of treatment, ought to be discussed with the patient is also a matter of purely professional judgment. The doctor's advisory role cannot be regarded as solely an exercise of medical skill without leaving out of account the patient's entitlement to decide on the risks to her health which she is willing to run (a decision which may be influenced by non-medical considerations). Responsibility for determining the nature and extent of a person's rights rests with the courts, not with the medical professions (para. 83).

However, despite these high profile victories for patients, the current medical negligence system is not designed in order to improve patient safety. The main aim of the system is to interpret the evidence appropriately in order to determine whether the elements of the tort of negligence have been established on the balance of probabilities. The question of what is in the best interests of the safety of patients is, at best, a background consideration. The most promising rationale for a connection between tort law and patient safety is that the *threat* of litigation deters dangerous practice. This is the so-called 'defensive medicine' thesis, which suggests that professionals might make decisions about the care of patients with some concern about the potential for legal actions if things go wrong, especially in terms of missed diagnoses. It is important to note that this is not necessarily conducive to safety in that caution and conservatism may be unsafe in certain situations (for example, not doing something for fear of being sued). A 'safer medicine' thesis is arguably a more appropriate term to consider the possible incentive effects of liability rules on the exercise of reasonable care. Clearly, deterrence theory has intuitive appeal in the hope that rational actors and systems will want to minimise harms and thus implement error learning and prevention strategies. It is also inspired by an optimistic belief in the ability to train individuals and design systems in a way which discourages unsafe practices.

Nevertheless, there is no clear evidence connecting the threat of civil action with safer healthcare. Whilst respected commentators have long noted that litigation is a threat to clinical autonomy (Dingwall 1994), there is scant research interrogating its linkages to safety directly, and any indirect evidence remains inconclusive. This is not to say that complaints and litigation have no effect on medical practice. For example, Mulcahy (2000) found that better note keeping and more detailed consultations were common reactions to the fear of litigation and complaints. Attention to the litigation system also sheds light on the issue of medical harm, which has been a springboard for the study of patient safety. And the fear of litigation is likely to play some role in encouraging institutions to take patient safety seriously. This is partly based on the realist belief that financial penalties and shame are the only strategies that work. For example, George Annas (2006) cites the safety progress made by anaesthetists as an exemplar of what litigation can do in arguing for a legal right to safety. More generally, medical negligence litigation can function as an important 'safety valve' in the regulation of quality in the NHS (Mulcahy 2014: 276).

However, literature reviews in both the US and the UK have found no firm evidence supporting deterrence theory (Mello and Brennan 2002; Fenn 2002). Ultimately, it appears unlikely that the tort system helps improve patient safety. In fact, the best research evidence suggests that the tort liability system isn't associated with better health outcomes. For example, in the context of obstetric cases, a study of 2.35 million births over the course of 12 years in 51 American jurisdictions found no correlation between liability pressure (i.e. the threat of being sued) and adverse outcomes. This longitudinal study concluded that the high cost of the medical negligence system is unjustifiable in terms of its connection with improving outcomes. Similarly, reforms that limited tort liability were not associated with worse outcomes. The authors conclude that tort law, at least in the obstetric context, is hard to justify from a harm-reduction standpoint (Yang et al. 2012.) A more recent systematic review of the empirical evidence has also questioned the defensive medicine thesis. This review found that any such effects are limited to survey research rather than practice research, and therefore concluded that defensive medicine is largely a fear confined to the minds of professionals, rather than affecting their actual behaviour (Van Dijck 2015).

Without sufficient empirical evidence, it is difficult to draw any firm conclusions on the linkages between litigation and patient safety. However, tort law is always likely to be limited in terms of safety. Safety goes beyond concern with errors and harmful outcomes, and extends to the cultural and communication problems that conspire to create unsafe conditions, whether or not they actually cause harm. The cases which navigate the tort system are only the tip of the iceberg, which raises legitimate doubts about the merits of spending a disproportionate amount of time (and money) on a relatively small number of events. The narrow legalistic focus of tort law, beset by the professionally threatening term negligence, is likely to impede rather than improve safety. Given that it is unclear (at best) whether tort law has delivered in terms of compensation and deterrence, it is appropriate to consider alternative options to fault liability, and their suitability for supporting safer care.

No-Fault Systems

Despite frustration with its inefficiency and high-profile calls for its abolition (Lord Pearson 1970; Kennedy 2001. 451) the use of tort law to deal with malpractice remains stable in the Anglo-American world. How does it compare with the no-fault compensation schemes in countries such as Denmark, France, Sweden and New Zealand? Regrettably, in the absence of clear evidence, we are unable to reliably measure the potential 'safety gains' of no-fault systems. It is important to note that statistics on the number of compensation claims might not be an accurate indicator of safety levels given that removing the burden of proving fault might be thought to increase the likelihood of a culture of entitlement regarding compensation. It is thus more realistic to consider whether such systems are more conducive to creating the open and honest climate necessary for a safety culture.

The most well-known scheme is that introduced by the Accident Compensation Act 1972 and administered by the Accident Compensation Corporation (ACC) in New Zealand, under the Accident Compensation Act 2001. As regards medical injuries it only became truly no-fault in 2005 with the replacement of the fault-based term 'medical mis-adventure' with the broader concept of 'treatment injury'. In New Zealand, injuries are potentially compensable unless a 'necessary part of the treatment' or part of the 'ordinary consequences of treatment'. This has benefitted claimants with an increase in accepted claims and a reduction in delay (Oliphant 2007; Todd 2011). In theory, this is also good news for patient safety: the replacement of the fault based term 'medical error' with 'medical mishap', one of the two forms of medical misadventure previously recognised, was accompanied by a renewed attempt by the ACC to focus on safety culture. However, the decision to focus on treatment injury, rather than preventability, and thus on *outcomes* rather than *processes* of care, is a limitation from a safety perspective. Unlike the models in Sweden and Denmark, there is no Chinese wall between compensation cases and disciplinary action, as cases may be referred to the disciplinary bodies where there is a 'risk of harm' to the public, which is interpreted narrowly to mean exceptional cases. For example, in New Zealand, between July 2005 and June 2010, 1,661 of such cases were referred by the ACC (Todd 2011: 1206).

In terms of a connection between no-fault and patient safety, a review of the New Zealand system concluded that this remains an open question (Oliphant 2009). Similarly, Stephen Todd is cautious about the claim that no fault means safer care, and is only able to conclude that 'there is little evidence that barring tort claims has compromised safety standards' (Todd 2011: 1216) Furthermore, studies suggest that the incidence of adverse events in New Zealand hospitals at 11 per cent is very similar to that in the United Kingdom (Davis 2002). However, there is some evidence that information about adverse events appears to be annotated in detail in patient medical records in New Zealand and that this might be connected to the system of no-fault liability (Davis 2003). However, apart from this, there is no clear evidence or even a confident belief from within New Zealand that no-fault has helped improve safety standards.

New Zealand is not alone in rejecting tort law in this context with similar systems operating in Scandinavia, Belgium and France. In theory, the Scandinavian approach appears to take safety more seriously. For example, all the Nordic systems adopt the 'experienced specialist standard', which is clearly a much higher standard than the 'reasonable doctor' test for the tort of negligence in England and Wales. If liability or compensation systems do actually have a 'safer medicine' effect, then we might legitimately expect that raising expectations to an experienced specialist standard encourages enhanced safety. In addition, the Danish and Swedish systems place healthcare professionals and providers under an obligation to report adverse events to the public authorities. As with New Zealand there is a lack of evidence to enable firm conclusions on the positive safety enhancing effect of Scandinavian no-fault schemes. For example, a review published in 2012, whilst noting successes in terms of compensating patients, was unable to make the same claim in relation to safety (Ulfbeck et al. 2012). However, there is evidence of greater openness and improved outcomes in maternity care. For example, Swedish obstetricians appear to be candid in their reported management of shoulder dystocia which leads to brachial plexus injury (nerve damage which results in damage to the arm) (Mollberg et al. 2008). Whilst further research is needed, it is plausible that the absence of a fault-based liability system has contributed to a climate of openness around such injuries and thus a greater possibility for learning and prevention (Draycott et al. 2015).

In France, a medical accident scheme compensates victims for serious injuries irrespective of fault, although professional liability insurers pick up the bill for cases where individuals are at fault. Thus whilst legislation seeks to encourage open dialogue about medical errors between doctors, patients and public health bodies, this is tempered somewhat by the retention of liability for fault, and the additional possibility of criminal conviction for negligently causing harm. Although there is a lack of reliable statistical data in terms of whether liability rates have increased or decreased, and a lack of research interest into the linkage between the system and safety, a recent review concludes that the scheme is unlikely to have had a great impact on accident reporting (Taylor 2011). Another (indirect) measurement would be to compare safety culture surveys from countries with fault and no-fault bases systems. In other words, does the absence of litigation fear lead to greater openness and shared learning around safety episodes? Unfortunately, in the absence of directly relevant research findings, we are left with unreliable anecdotal evidence, which regrettably doubts a connection between no-fault and safer care. Unfortunately, the data does not exist in order to make reliable safety comparisons between fault and no-fault systems. At best, we can only hope that no-fault systems create the environment conducive to openness and safety culture (Mello et al. 2011).

In the United Kingdom, a no-fault system was rejected by a somewhat thin review of the evidence, largely based on fears about the increased cost of such systems (Department of Health 2003). Instead, the report recommended a package of redress measures that included systems for investigating adverse events, offering explanations and apologies, providing remedial treatment and an administrative scheme for awarding financial compensation for low value claims, with a suggested upper limit of £30,000. Whilst not the radical reform proposals that some were hoping for, these recommendations nevertheless met some of the shortcomings of the tort system. However, they were diluted even further in the preferred Government scheme introduced in the NHS Redress Act 2006. Eligibility is limited by the need to establish a 'qualifying liability in tort', as opposed to a less onerous threshold of 'avoidability' for example, and any independence is compromised by the management of the scheme by the NHS Litigation Authority and the lack of an appeals process. It does not apply to primary care practitioners and the Act is vague in terms of the important requirement for providing explanations and apologies. In short, issues of containing costs trumped those of satisfying complainants (Farrell and Devaney 2007). However, such criticisms remain redundant given that the scheme has not yet been implemented in England. The Welsh Government has taken forward the reforms in the NHS Redress Act 2006 by passing regulations as part of its 'Putting Things Right' project (Ferguson and Braithwaite 2012). Whilst it is too early to evaluate this scheme, it should be noted that it suffers from the same weaknesses discussed above in relation to the 2006 Act. In Scotland, the Government has considered introducing a no-fault system since 2009, but has not yet been persuaded to act (Scottish Government 2014). Given the unlikely abolition of the fault based system, it is more realistic to consider existing options within the law of tort, which may be better suited to encouraging a culture of safety.

Direct Liability and Non-Delegable Duties

Because the majority of claims proceed against NHS institutions as vicariously liable for the conduct of their employees, most cases revolve around the acts or omissions of individuals. System factors remain a sideshow to the main event of individual error. This is unfortunate given that the deterrent effect of negligence actions is arguably more promising when applied to systems rather than individuals. Whilst individuals will always make mistakes, systems can be designed to minimise the risks and financial costs of safety lapses. An obvious and modest option involves looking within, rather than beyond, tort law in terms of refocusing negligence actions around systems rather than individuals. Despite judicial endorsement of direct liability for system flaws such as failing to appoint sufficiently skilled or experienced staff (*Wilsher v Essex Area Health Authority* [1987] QB 730) or for communication failures (*Bull v Devon AHA* [1993] 4 Med LR 117, *Robertson v Nottingham Health Authority* [1997] 8 Med LR 1 and *Richards v Swansea NHS Trust* [2007] EWHC 487), such cases are rare. Yet empirical evidence supports the case for realigning tort doctrine in the name of patient safety. Mello and Studdert's study of closed malpractice claims found that two-thirds of cases involved both individual and systems factors, and that systems errors are more serious, in the sense of having a stronger connection with death, and more amenable to redesign (Mello and Studdert 2008). Based on these findings, a more pragmatic option rests in realigning tort doctrine to focus its deterrent effect on systems. It may be that such classification is purely academic and that claims against hospitals proceed on the basis of a *combination* of individual and system factors. But it would sharpen the focus on systems and processes of care and help us move beyond individual blame to frame claims in such a way.

A further option would be to place healthcare providers under a non-delegable duty, a more onerous obligation to *ensure* that reasonable care is taken. It is important to note that this duty does not go as far as ensuring safety, but rather to ensure that reasonable care is taken. The difference with such duties (as opposed to vicarious liability) is that it does not matter whether the person who caused the harm was an employee or an independent contractor. The classic example is the duty of employers to employees, and its relevance to healthcare was long ago envisaged by Lord Denning in *Cassidy v Minister of Health* [1951] 2 KB 343 in declaring that the negligence of employees or independent contractors represents a breach by the employer, on the basis that the duty is non-delegable. Recent support for this can be found in the case of *Farraj v King's Healthcare NHS Trust* [2010] PIQR P7 which involved negligent failure of communication and system flaws for investigating the reliability of genetic testing for a condition called beta thalassaemia major. The Court of Appeal assumed (without deciding) that hospitals generally owe a non-delegable duty to patients to ensure that they are treated with skill and care regardless of the employment status of the person who is treating them. As Heywood explains, on one level, the imposition of such a duty is good news from a patient-safety perspective, raising the relevant expectations and standards against which hospitals are judged, in the sense of *ensuring* that reasonable care is taken. However, the boundaries of such a duty are far from clear, which given the potentially far reaching implications may be a cause for concern for the health system (Heywood 2010). And in practice this may have little effect given that under vicarious liability, hospital trusts will be liable in this way for acts of their employees and for having unsafe systems (Kennedy and Grubb 2000: 313).

Health Courts

A more radical option would see the creation of specially designed Health Courts as an alternative to the traditional tort system. Drawing inspiration from the Nordic no-fault model, Mello et al. claim that this would improve fairness (by compensating more patients) and enhance safety (by maximising the learning opportunities from errors) (Mello et al. 2006). Under this proposed system, patients would be compensated where harm was avoidable (as opposed to negligent) which is defined as falling short of best (rather than reasonable) practice. Raising the bar to optimum (as opposed to reasonable) care is consistent with the aim of encouraging excellent healthcare. In terms of the process, there would be a three-tiered structure. Initially, cases would be considered by an internal hospital/insurance panel, with both the decision and amount of compensation amount reviewable by the Health Court and also recourse to an independent Appeal Court. A centralised claims database would help with learning and prevention functions. Further benefits include greater certainty about standards and consistency of decisions and compensation payments. Compliance would be incentivised by insurance surcharges where a claim has begun without prior disclosure of the adverse event by the clinician to the insurer. Whilst litigation is not the only reason for secrecy about medical errors Mello et al. claim that removing the fear of getting sued should at least improve the environment for transparency.

Despite their promise, Health Courts are unlikely to solve all the problems in this area. Whilst the replacement of the pejorative term 'negligence' is welcomed, for the same reasons the term 'court' might have been replaced with the less threatening 'tribunal' or 'inquiry'. This system would also require specially trained judges and the retraining of experts used to applying negligence standards. It also faces an entrenched legal culture in the United States, which defends adversarialism and the right to trial by jury. The Health Courts model may also struggle to succeed in the United Kingdom given a legal culture that focuses on individual fault and the fears, explored above, that such initiatives may encourage a compensation culture. Such systems would also need to be modelled in terms of cost, specifically whether the savings from increased safety will outweigh the costs of the system.Perhaps most controversially, the proposed system envisages a limited form of openness by protecting any information from the reach of regulators and departments of public health. Such guarantees of immunity are seen as a necessary compromise in the name of patient safety, but are controversial. These so-called 'Chinese walls' undoubtedly weaken the individual's position in terms of seeking redress, yet are arguably necessary in terms of encouraging a culture of safety. However, whilst there maybe sound reasons for protecting practitioners from disciplinary investigation, there is surely no justification for withholding information from patients about their treatment, especially when adverse events have caused them harm. The case for a duty of candour in healthcare is explored in Chapter 8.

Models of Insurer-Clinician Engagement?

A possible alternative, which does not necessarily require the abolition of fault systems, is to rethink the relationship between insurers and providers of care. Insurers are able to incentivise best practice and improved safety outcomes in terms of the financial incentives of decreased premiums. They are also are able to play a vital role in linking up patients, health services and policy in order to improve safety. Specifically, insurers can promote effective interventions and financially support safety research. A leading example of this is the work of the Victorian

Managed Insurance Authority (VMIA) in Australia which was established in 1996 as the insurer and risk management adviser to the Victorian government sector. It has been active in promoting a number of initiatives for reducing clinical risk, for example, a training programme to improve the management of obstetric emergencies. This programme, called Practical Obstetric Multi-Professional Training (PROMPT) was developed by a team of midwives, obstetricians and anaesthetists working in Bristol, where it has been associated with improved outcomes and also a 91 per cent reduction in litigation payments (Draycott et al. 2015). A review of the impact of this programme in Victoria showed that it not only improved clinical outcomes but also improved staff attitudes around safety (Shoushtarian et al. 2014).

Another example of effective engagement between insurance agencies and clinicians can be found in Sweden. The Swedish Patient Injury Act, introduced in 1997, compels care providers to be insured and establishes the right for patients to be compensated for avoidable injury. This is part of a larger tax-funded system of social insurance which has long existed in Sweden, and which results in around a third of all claims being compensated, and within eight months of the injury being reported (LÖF 2015). Claims are handled by a mutual insurance company called The Swedish National Patient Insurance Company (LÖF), which was established in 1995 to insure all County Councils against patient injury claims. Beyond compensating inured patients it has been proactive in providing financial and administrative support for patient safety research and training. Drawing on its database of over 170,000 claims has enabled LÖF to design specific safety initiatives around obstetric care, abdominal surgery, use of medication in primary care, trauma care and prosthesis related infections. It is notable that LÖF collaborates closely with specialist professional organisations and harnesses its knowledge of claims in order to fund patient safety research and then facilitate the implementation of this in practice. An encouraging example of this improvement science is the evaluation of an initiative designed to improve obstetric care (the National Perinatal Patient Safety Programme) which noted a decline in settled claims due to substandard care between 2006 and 2012 (Luthander et al. 2016). This kind of collaboration between insurers and professionals has the potential for incentivising safer care and also enabling greater shared learning. It is hoped that these positive examples from Sweden and Victoria will inspire the Department of Health in England to pilot similar schemes.

Conclusion

The question of which medical liability system is better suited to the aim of improving patient safety remains somewhat difficult to answer. There is a lack of sufficient empirical evidence to allow a confident conclusion about which system of liability and compensation is best suited to the goal of improving safety. In the context of maternity care, the best available evidence from the United States suggests that the prospect of tort liability isn't associated with better health outcomes (Yang et al. 2012). But even without a wealth of evidence, we can predict that the tort system is likely to be unhelpful from a patient safety perspective. Litigation creates fear amongst professionals and managers and discourages the openness which is central to a healthy culture of patient safety. It is also limited: very few cases proceed to trial, and those that do tend to focus exclusively on individual failings rather than system problems. The system is costly, time consuming and encourages conflict. Ultimately, it is more likely that the threat of litigation is counterproductive by discouraging an open and learning culture in healthcare. Whilst liability systems have other legitimate aims, mainly of a compensatory nature, the negligence system is limited in terms of improving safety and should be replaced with one designed for safety and fairer, more efficient compensation.

Administrative alternatives to tort law are better at compensating more patients and providing the data necessary for patient safety learning. However, there is (as yet) scant evidence that no-fault systems help safer healthcare, with reviews in New Zealand, Scandinavia and France unable to claim any connection with improved safety. Nevertheless, no-fault systems compensate more victims of adverse events and offer a more humane way of providing redress, from both patient and professional perspectives. And despite the lack of hard evidence, it is reasonable to assert that no-fault systems stand a better chance of encouraging the open culture that is essential for improving the safety of patients. However, given that governments continue to hesitate over creating systems of no-fault liability, there is a need to handle claims in ways which are better suited to investigating safety. Medical negligence actions could be used to target the system in the form of direct liability which focuses on organisational responsibility for a safe healthcare system. Yet whilst this form of liability is better suited to tackling the bigger problem of unsafe systems, as opposed to errant individuals, such cases are rare. And whilst the more onerous option of enforcing a non-delegable duty retains some superficial attraction, it is likely to be too exacting in practice and is insufficiently focused on systems failures. The option of framing claims in terms of the direct liability of healthcare providers for failing to ensure a reasonably safe environment is attractive in terms of moving away from the narrow focus on individual fault. Finally, the potential for closer collaboration between medical insurers and providers of care, in order to incentivise and support safer care, is an idea which has shown promise elsewhere and which the Department of Health will hopefully consider for England. Whilst the use of civil law mechanisms as a way of responding to patient safety failings is likely to remain, this need not prevent the system from trying to manage claims in a way which offers redress to patients and best supports the safe delivery of care.

6

The Criminalisation of Medical Harm

Whilst the use of tort law is often viewed dimly from a patient safety perspective, recourse to criminal law has been condemned as being disproportionate and damaging to a culture of safety. Apart from instances of deliberate harm, such as the mass murder committed by Harold Shipman, commentators have long doubted the appropriateness of criminalising negligence or substandard care (McCall Smith 1993). Prosecuting professionals for negligence or neglect can be seen as a somewhat draconian response that risks increasing secrecy rather than openness about safety. Whilst the fear of being prosecuted is, akin to the prospect of being sued in the civil courts, undoubtedly exaggerated, it is understandable that criminal law causes concern amongst healthcare professionals (Ferner and McDowell 2013). However, criticisms of the use of criminal laws in this context have been based on a limited view that regards all such laws as the same and fails to recognise that certain offences may have greater potential for helping improve patient safety. This chapter will thus explore whether criminal law might have a useful role to play in terms of regulating patient safety. Admittedly, whilst criminal law is likely to play a minor role as part of the major task of improving safety, nevertheless, it would be wrong to dismiss it completely and better to explore which types of offences and enforcement methods are best suited to the task of improving safety.

Criminal Law

Before unpacking the specific offences that apply in the healthcare context, this chapter begins with a brief introduction to criminal law. A broad conception of criminal law is that it is one of several practices through which a society defines and responds to serious wrongdoing. The criminalisation of conduct is arguably the strongest form of condemnation expressed by society. Criminal laws can thus be seen as reflecting moral standards and allowing punishment for breaching these standards. It thus serves a retributive function of giving offenders their 'just deserts' for their harmful behaviour. In addition to this, criminal laws can perform a regulatory or utilitarian function, for example by prohibiting behaviour on the grounds of public health or safety, such as rules requiring the wearing of seat belts in vehicles (Lacey, Wells and Quick 2010: 6). Criminal laws have traditionally been analysed in terms of their conduct and fault elements, that is, the behaviour which is prohibited and the degree of mental awareness required to commit the offence. Whilst defining both these elements may be contested in specific instances, evidence about the mental fault element tends to cause particular problems for those tasked with interpreting and applying the law. In broad terms, most serious offences require proof that the defendant either intended the particular result, or behaved in a reckless or negligent manner. However, this by no means applies to all criminal offences, with many having different fault elements, or indeed no fault element at all for offences of strict liability. One of the features of recent criminal lawmaking is that, contrary to common perception, the bulk of it is of a 'regulatory' and 'preventive' nature (Ashworth and Zedner 2008; Chalmers and Leverick 2013), for example, offences aimed at environmental protection or the provision of financial services, rather than the violence that dominates the public image of crime. Regulatory offences have also been created in order to protect patient safety and will be discussed below.

Criminal laws may differ not only in their design but also their enforcement. So whilst the most well-known crimes such as homicide and assault are dealt with by the police and the Crown Prosecution Service, certain areas fall under the responsibility of specialist agencies who develop their own approaches for seeking compliance with specific rules and regulations. In terms of the problem of patient safety, this includes the work of two agencies tasked with enforcing safety rules and regulations. First, the Health and Safety Executive, which was created under the Health and Safety at Work Act 1974, and which focuses on preventing death, injury and ill-health in the workplace. Secondly is the work of the Care Quality Commission (CQC) in encouraging compliance with fundamental standards of care in order to help ensure patient safety. This chapter will unpack three different types of criminal offences that apply in this context – (i) manslaughter, (ii) ill treatment or wilful neglect and (iii) regulatory offences enforced by the Health and Safety Executive (H&SE) and the CQC – and consider the relationship between such offences and the problem of patient safety. Whilst the use of criminal law has tended to be viewed negatively in this context, this chapter will argue that such a view is simplistic and overlooks the potential for certain types of offences to reinforce existing regulatory interventions. It will also consider the implications of the increased criminalisation of medical errors and mistreatment in terms of the professional dominance thesis.

Medical Manslaughter

Historically, criminal law has played a limited role in terms of responding to patient safety incidents. This has principally been through occasional manslaughter prosecutions of practitioners following fatal medical errors. Such cases are prosecuted with reference to the controversial and catch all concept of 'gross negligence'. Whilst the term negligence is a familiar civil law concept, the gloss of 'gross' suggests a higher degree of carelessness worthy of punishment in the criminal courts, though as will be explored below, precisely what is meant by gross remains some-what unclear. The first known prosecution of a doctor took place in the fourteenth century where a practitioner was commended to God by a judge sitting in Newcastle (Arlidge 1998). The emergence of gross negligence as a basis for prosecuting unlawful medical killing emerged in the nineteenth century (Horder 1997). As discussed in Chapter 1, this was well before the emergence of the modern and dominant medical profession and in fact at a time when patients as clients were in control (Waddington 1984: 191). Although such cases have traditionally been rare, their tendency to challenge the basis of criminally negligent liability has often led them to the appeal courts and into law reports as leading manslaughter authorities. The first of these reported cases concerned the conviction of a Dr Bateman for the criminally negligent treatment of a patient during the delivery of her child (*R v Bateman* (1925) 19 Cr. App. R. 8.) The baby was in the breech position, and in performing a manual version (to move the baby to the head down position), Dr Bateman mistakenly removed part of his patient's uterus and caused other internal damage resulting in death. Lord Hewart CJ described the essence of criminality in such cases as follows: [at p. 11].

> In explaining to juries the test which they should apply to determine whether the negligence, in the particular case, amounted or did not amount to a crime, judges have used many epithets, such as 'culpable', 'criminal', gross, wicked, clear, complete'. But, whatever epithet be used and whether an epithet be used or not, in order to establish criminal

liability the facts must be such that, in the opinion of the jury, the negligence of the accused went beyond a mere matter of compensation between subjects and showed such disregard for the life and safety of others as to amount to a crime against the state and conduct deserving punishment.

In 1994, this test for assessing criminality was endorsed by the House of Lords in *R v Adomako* [1994] 3 All ER 79 where a locum anaesthetist lost his appeal against conviction after failing to spot a disconnected oxygen tube during a routine eye operation which caused the patient's death. Lord Mackay of Clashfern set out the following test of liability for manslaughter by gross negligence [at p. 86:]

> In my opinion the ordinary principles of the law of negligence apply to ascertain whether or not the defendant has been in breach of a duty of care towards the victim who has died. If such breach of duty is established the next question is whether that breach of duty caused the death of the victim. If so, the jury must go on to consider whether that breach of duty *should be characterised as gross negligence and therefore as a crime.* This will depend on the seriousness of the breach of duty committed by the defendant *in all the circumstances in which the defendant was placed when it occurred.* The jury will have to consider whether the extent to which the defendant's conduct departed from the proper standard of care incumbent upon him, involving as it must have done a risk of death to the patient, was such that *it should be judged criminal.*

> (my emphasis)

Whilst acknowledging the inherent circularity of this test, the House of Lords nevertheless approved it for the purposes of determining criminal liability. This has subsequently been affirmed by the Court of Appeal in the case of *R v Misra and Srivastava* [2004] EWCA Crim 2375. Amit Misra and Rajeev Srivastava were senior house officers at Southampton General Hospital who mismanaged the care of a 31-year-old man who developed toxic shock syndrome after a routine knee operation. This is quite a rare complication (unlike MRSA for example) with a fairly low mortality rate of around 5 per cent. Specifically, they responded inadequately to obvious signs of infection, such as raised temperature and pulse rate, and failed to chase up blood test results that would have prompted the antibiotic care that would probably have prevented the patient's death. The jury convicted and their appeals were rejected by the Court of Appeal. They argued, similarly to Dr Adomako, that the vagueness of gross negligence was incompatible with the requirement of legal certainty, now expressed in Article 7 of the European Convention on Human Rights, which prohibits retrospective criminalisation. In other words, the doctors argued that as only the jury can decide what constitutes gross negligence, and by definition this process takes place after the events in question, that this amounted to retrospective criminalisation. This was rejected on the unconvincing grounds that there is 'an element of uncertainty about the outcome of the decision making process, but not unacceptable certainty about the offence itself' (Lord Justice Judge para. 63).

However, despite such judicial endorsement, gross negligence remains an unduly vague concept that is incapable of objective measurement and consistent interpretation and thus potentially unfair to those prosecuted (Quick 2006). Whilst it is by no means the only vague term of criminal liability, the implications of such uncertainty are particularly serious in the context of homicide. Indeed, the imposition of manslaughter liability based on grossly negligent conduct has long exercised legal philosophers. For example, Jerome Hall found this an 'inordinately troublesome' area (Hall 1972: 959). Hall was responding (and rejecting) H. L. A. Hart's celebrated general theory of guilt in which he defended negligent criminal liability as part of a wider capacity theory of responsibility (Hart 1968: 147). For Hall, the imposition of such liability loses sight of the notion of blame, which should be the proper foundation of criminal law. In terms of contemporary criminal law scholarship, however, Hart's view finds support from leading criminal law commentators (Ashworth and Horder 2013: 181–5) and also the Law Commission, albeit in their proposed formulation of 'killing by gross carelessness' (1996 and 2005). Beyond the debate about the merits of negligent criminal liability, it is clear that the range of conduct and culpability encompassed by involuntary manslaughter is such that 'the crime label has become morally uninformative' (Clarkson 2000: 142). Whilst there has been some debate on appropriate alternatives, whether through raising the bar of liability to recklessness or creating a specific offence (Quick 2008), this offence category has survived and is unlikely to be abolished. However, there is little known about the impact of criminal law on medical practice, in particular whether the threat of criminal prosecution deters unsafe and perhaps encourages safer practice.

There is also a lack of reliable data on the number of medical manslaughter prosecutions. The way that cases are filed and stored makes accurate data on prosecutions hard to locate. For example, it appears that the CPS do not record the occupation of defendants charged with manslaughter by gross negligence, and is thus unable to provide data on the number of doctors charged. Available estimates are thus based on trawling media reporting of such cases, which is not the most reliable methodology. For example, Ferner and McDowell's (2006) review of media sources found 38 prosecutions between 1995 and 2005 compared with just seven between 1945 and 1990. However, the evidence of increased investigations is somewhat stronger, based not only on evidence from media sources (Quick 2006) but also in terms of data from the number police and coronial investigations (Griffiths and Sanders, 2013). The conviction rate for cases prosecuted in court has been estimated at around 35 per cent, which is low in the context of manslaughter cases generally (Quick 2011). More recent figures suggest that the conviction rate has increased to around 55 per cent (White 2015). Sentencing doctors to imprisonment for medical manslaughter has traditionally been very rare indeed, with most guilty verdicts leading to suspended prison sentences. However, changes in sentencing law for homicide has meant that courts focus more on the harm caused than the culpability, and given that the outcome is death in these cases, this has increased the likelihood of sentences of imprisonment (Quirk 2013).

Whilst such cases remain relatively rare, nevertheless, healthcare professionals understandably fear the prospect of criminal prosecution and punishment. The conviction and imprisonment of Dr David Sellu on 5th of November 2013 has intensified such fears. The case against Dr Sellu, the 63-year-old colorectal surgeon, was that he should have ordered a CT scan and operated sooner on a patient with a suspected perforated bowel who later died. The patient was recovering from knee-replacement surgery carried out in a private hospital and began complaining about unrelated abdominal pain. The patient's orthopaedic surgeon asked Dr Sellu to investigate, and on examining the patient on Thursday evening, he suspected a perforated bowel and ordered a CT scan to be performed the following morning. Dr Sellu claimed he asked the resident medical officer, Dr Georgiev, to administer two varieties of antibiotic, though Dr Georgiev denied this. A CT scan was carried out on Friday morning and the result, confirming the suspicion of a bowel perforation, was communicated to Dr Sellu at lunchtime. Believing that the patient was on antibiotics, Dr Sellu decided that surgery could wait until the end of his afternoon clinic. Surgery was performed at 9:30 p.m. on Friday but sadly the patient died the next day of multi-organ failure resulting from sepsis. Mr Justice Nicol noted that a series of failures – to order an immediate CT scan and arrange emergency surgery, to prescribe antibiotics and enter this on the patient's medical records coupled with a 'far too laid back attitude' amounted to gross negligence and sentenced Dr Sellu to two-and-a-half years imprisonment (*R v Sellu* 5 November 2013).

The incarceration of Dr Sellu caused much consternation amongst the medical community, and prompted a group of colleagues to successfully campaign for his appeal. The main grounds of appeal surrounded the evidence about causation, namely the risk of mortality for the patient had Dr Sellu operated immediately on suspicion of the perforated bowel, and also the adequacy of the trial judge's direction on gross negligence. On 15 November 2016 the Court of Appeal allowed the appeal on the grounds that the trial judge's direction did not permit the jury to 'understand how to approach their task of identifying the line that separates even serious or very serious mistakes or lapses, from conduct which … was truly exceptionally bad and was such a departure from that standard [of a reasonably competent doctor] that it consequently amounted to being criminal' (*Sellu v The Crown* (2016) EWCA Crim 1716, paragraph 152). This was tied up with concerns that experts called by the prosecution were potentially usurping the role of the jury in appearing to determine the issue of 'gross negligence', an issue that has previously been identified as problematic in such cases (Quick 2011b).

Supporters of Dr Sellu also argued that insufficient attention was given to the clinical context of care in this case, with the trial judge regarding it as an aggravating factor that treatment took place in a private hospital. Mr Justice Nicol noted that Dr Sellu's negligence was not 'committed in the pressured circumstances of an acute NHS hospital where the stress of dealing with very many patients in an emergency condition can be particularly challenging' (*R v Sellu* 5 November 2013). However, it should be noted that unlike NHS hospitals, private hospitals are not equipped to deal with such emergencies in terms of having appropriate clinicians on call to carry out specialist tests and procedures (CHPI 2014). It was reported that an internal investigation at the hospital found that its procedures for dealing with emergencies that developed after routine operations were not robust enough to prevent a systemic failure, and that this evidence was not disclosed at Dr Sellu's trial (Dyer 2015). Such evidence is not only important in mitigating the culpability of individuals, but also raises the possibility of prosecuting organisations for serious systems failures.

Manslaughter prosecutions against organisations have been possible since 6 April 2008, with the commencement of the Corporate

Manslaughter and Corporate Homicide Act 2007. Criminal law has traditionally struggled with the idea and practicalities of prosecuting corporate entities, especially in terms of attributing responsibility (Wells 2001). However, under Section 1 of the Act, organisation will now commit homicide if the way in which it manages or organises its activities both cause a death and amounts to a gross breach of a relevant duty of care owed by the organisation to the deceased. In the case of healthcare organisations, there is little doubt that they will be under a duty of care towards patients; thus the key questions will, as with individual manslaughter liability, revolve around the grossness of the breach and to causation. Under Section 1(4) (b) a departure from the standard of care is gross if the conduct 'falls far below what can reasonably be expected of the organisation in the circumstances'. This is similar to the common-law formulation from *Adomako* and *Misra*, although the Act specifies factors which the jury should take into account in evaluating grossness. Section 8 states that the jury 'must consider whether the evidence shows that the organisation failed to comply with any health and safety legislation that relates to the alleged breach'. In addition, the jury may consider the extent to which the evidence shows that there were 'attitudes, policies, systems of accepted practices within the organisation' that were likely to have encouraged or tolerated health and safety breaches. The Act says little about causation, beyond that the prosecution must prove that death was caused 'by the way that an organisation managed or organised its activities'. Whilst the offences in the 2007 Act are long overdue, commentators have questioned the extent to which the legislation will be effective given the difficulties in terms of proving fault and establishing causation (Wells 2013; Gooderham 2011.)

However, in December 2015, Sherwood Rise Limited became the first care home to be convicted of corporate manslaughter under the Act in relation to the death of a patient following failures around feeding and hydration. Maidstone and Tunbridge Wells NHS Trust was the first NHS organisation to be prosecuted for the offence of Corporate Manslaughter. This followed the death of a woman at Pembury Hospital, Tunbridge Wells, after undergoing an emergency caesarean section in 2012. The prosecution alleged that the trust caused the patient's death by a gross breach its duty of care by failing to take reasonable care to ensure: 1. the anaesthetists involved held the appropriate qualifications and training and 2. that there was an appropriate level of supervision for the anaesthetic treatment of the deceased. However, two weeks into the trial, the judge ruled that there was no case for the trust or the anaesthetist to answer and directed the jury to return not guilty verdicts (*The Guardian* 28 January 2016). It thus remains to be seen whether this offence can be successfully enforced in the healthcare context.

III Treatment or Wilful Neglect

Whilst the imposition of manslaughter liability has been widely criticised (McCall Smith 1993; Quick 2006) the absence of a lesser offence for conduct causing harm short of death has long been questioned (Smith 1971). The assault offences under the 1861 Offences Against the Person Act, albeit subject to flexible interpretation, have generally not been used in a healthcare context. Whilst extreme cases of deliberate harm could lead to prosecutions for assault, these offences require proof that an individual recklessly or intentionally caused harm, which may be difficult to establish. A rare example involved the prosecution of a breast surgeon in 2016 for unlawfully wounding 11 patients after carrying out allegedly unnecessary treatment between 1997 and 2011 (Dyer 2016). However, in terms negligent treatment causing harm falling short of death, criminal law has been ill-equipped to act. In an era of overcriminalisation (Husak 2008; Chalmers and Leverick 2013) it is surprising to find such a gap in the criminal law, albeit that the gap only applied to the neglect of patients with mental capacity. Ill-treating or wilfully neglecting patients without capacity or of those being treated under the Mental Health Act is criminalised by Section 127 of the Mental Health Act 1983 and Section 44 of the 2005 Mental Capacity Act. Given that all patients are vulnerable in health and social care, the absence of a similar offence to protect patients with capacity was hard to justify. This led to calls for creating a new offence of medical neglect endangering life (Griffiths and Sanders 2013) or a broader welfare offence of conduct causing or likely to cause unnecessary suffering (Allen 2013). Such academic pleas may have fallen on deaf ears but for the fallout from events at the Mid Staffordshire NHS Foundation Trust from 2005 to 2009 noted in Chapter 1, with the revelation of the routine neglect and suffering of hundreds of patients.

The public inquiry report written by Robert Francis QC contained many examples of appalling care, such as patients left dehydrated or to suffer in soiled bed sheets (Francis 2013). Amidst the 290 recommendations in the report, it was perhaps inevitable that bolstering accountability through criminal law would feature prominently. The report, in favouring a zero tolerance approach towards breaches of minimum standards of care, recommended that organisations and individuals face potential prosecution where breaches of fundamental standards led to death or serious harm (Francis 2013: recommendations 13, 28–29). However, the Francis report, followed by a report examining its implications for patient safety (Berwick 2013), led to the creation of two new offences of ill-treatment or wilful neglect contained in Sections 20 and 21 of the Criminal Justice and Courts Act 2015, applying to care workers and care providers, which came into force on 13 April 2015.

The offences are not intended to apply to errors or substandard treatment, but rather the most extreme type of poor care (DOH 2014a: 7). The impact assessment for the new offences states that they aim to 'provide a legal backstop against this in order to ensure that individuals who suffer ill-treatment or wilful neglect have a means to legal redress and those responsible are held to account' (DOH 2014b: 13). The existing offences under the Mental Health and Mental Capacity legislation do not define ill treatment or wilful neglect, which in fact appear to be two separate offences (R v Newington (1990) 91 Cr App R 247). Ill treatment covers deliberate actions such as bullying and intimidation, and neglect includes omissions to feed, hydrate or medically attend (R v Newington (1990) 91 Cr App R 247). Obvious examples of neglect would be cases of severe dehydration and malnutrition, unsanitary conditions, bed falls and pressure sores. Horder and Yeung (2010) argue that neglect or ill-treatment should include a broader range of conduct and circumstances such as lack of hygiene, persistent verbal abuse or intimidation, malevolent denial of visiting rights or discharging sick patients prematurely. It remains to be seen whether its application will be so broad and include cases of emotional or psychological neglect or whether (in practice) it will focus on a narrower range of harms. The Section 21 offence applies to organisations with a form of fault similar to that used for the offence of Corporate Manslaughter and Corporate Homicide 2007 Act. This is defined as a gross breach of the relevant duty of care – falling far below what can be reasonably expected in the circumstances. This is essentially a modified version of the common-law test for gross negligence from the leading cases of Adomako and Misra. Difficult cases are likely to involve ill-treatment associated with poor staff-patient ratios and bed shortages, which are of course bound up with the issue of resource allocation.

Controversially, the offences do not require proof that any harm has been caused. This is different from the recommendation of the Berwick review, which envisaged an offence of ill-treatment or wilful neglect that risked death or severe harm (Berwick 2013: 35). This would have led to an endangerment or risk prevention offence, whereas the offences in

Sections 20 and 21 are conduct crimes not requiring proof of actual harm. It is arguable that neglecting or ill-treating patients is in itself harmful and worthy of potential punishment, irrespective of the actual harm to patients in question. The absence of a harm requirement also has practical advantages in avoiding the problem of proving the fault element in relation to the harm (i.e. that the defendant intended or foresaw the *consequences* of neglect but couldn't care less (*Sheppard, and JD* [2008] EWCA Crim 2360.) Inserting a harm requirement would have also encouraged unedifying arguments about whether the harm caused or risked was serious enough. It might also be said that clinicians and carers are already on notice that their patients are at risk. And the stronger the objective evidence of neglect, the harder it will be for defendants to argue that they didn't foresee this. Despite the absence of a harm requirement, in practice, prosecutions are more likely to follow in cases where ill-treatment or wilful neglect has actually caused tangible physical harm.

However, the fault element is likely to be problematic. In the context of the s.44 and s.127 offences, ill-treatment has been interpreted to require deliberate intention, whereas wilful neglect can also be established with proof of subjective recklessness. On a literal reading of the Section 44 offence and also the Department of Health consultation paper (2014a), wilfulness only precedes neglect and is thus limited to that. However, there is no good reason for any such distinction and the offence should share the same fault element in relation to two ways of committing it. In the leading child neglect case of *R v Sheppard* [1981] AC 394, the House of Lords interpreted wilful to mean intention/knowledge or subjective recklessness, which has been described as a 'couldn't care less' attitude. However, recent prosecutions for the Section 44 offence suggest that the precise meaning of wilful is somewhat less settled. For example, in *R. v Patel (Parulben)* [2013] EWCA Crim 965 it was held that the offence was made out if the medical practitioner in question neglected to do that which ought to have been done in the treatment of the patient – in this case, administer CPR to an elderly patient who had suffered a cardiac arrest. It was no defence to say that the nurse's failure to act had been the result of panic, or that the outcome would have been the same whether or not the treatment had been administered. In *Patel* it was held that neglect was wilful if the carer knew they should administer particular treatment but failed to do so, which resembles a negligence standard.

A different approach was taken in *R. v Turbill (Maxine)* [2013] EWCA Crim 1422, where a patient classed as a 'high-risk faller' fell out of bed.

The patient had not been put to bed and was not monitored during the night. He was taken to hospital although did not suffer any significant injuries. Two carers employed at the care home were convicted of wilful neglect, though their appeals were allowed on the basis of the judge's directions on the fault element. Specifically, it was held that the judge's directions may have led the jury to conflate negligence with wilful neglect. The term 'wilfully' meant deliberately refraining from acting, or refraining from acting because of not caring whether action was required or not. Thus it was held that gross carelessness is not enough, despite being sufficient for the more serious crime of manslaughter. At first look, the terms 'couldn't care less' and 'carelessness' seem indistinguishable. The only explanation is that carelessness, even gross carelessness, can be an objective form of fault (i.e. the risk of harm didn't enter the defendant's mind, which in itself constitutes the carelessness), whilst 'could not care less' includes a reference to foresight of risk, or deliberately ignoring risk. The failure to put a high risk-faller to bed and check on him during the night must come close to evidencing a 'couldn't care less' attitude. Interestingly, unlike *Patel*, the CA in *Turbill* endorsed the test from the child neglect case of *Sheppard* in the context of Section 44. So, the interpretation of the fault element for this offence is by no means settled. However, given its association with deliberate or clearly reckless behaviour, the word 'wilful' sets a high bar for prosecution. This is supported by empirical research in the social work setting, which has also shown that professionals have difficulty interpreting the term 'wilful' and view it narrowly to mean intentional conduct (Manthorpe 2014).

Regulatory Offences

Offences such as manslaughter and ill-treatment or wilful neglect belong to what is regarded as conventional criminal law, or so-called 'real crime'. However, criminal law also contains a large number of offences that have been broadly labelled as regulatory. Many of these are offences of strict liability, that is, where there is no requirement to prove any element of fault. Indeed, the amount of regulatory criminal law has increased as governments have responded to problems by creating new criminal offences, many to be enforced by specialist regulators (Lacey 2004; Chalmers and Leverick 2013). The most relevant in the context of protecting patient safety is the work of the H&SE and more recently the CQC. The H&SE, despite sounding like the obvious regulator for this context, has traditionally only played a peripheral role in terms of patient safety. This is because the Health and Safety at Work etc Act 1974 was originally designed (and has been used) to protect the health and safety of *workers* and not as a response to patient safety incidents. Prosecutions for breaches of duties owed to non-employees under the legislation are therefore uncommon. Nevertheless, parts of the 1974 Act do apply in relation to incidents that affect patients, the most relevant being Section 3(1) which states that:

> It shall be the duty of every employer to conduct his undertaking in such a way as to ensure, so far as is reasonably practicable, that persons not in his employment who may be affected thereby are not thereby exposed to risks to their health or safety.

Whilst prosecutions of healthcare trusts under this section are rare, some notable examples remind us of its potential use in this context. The case of *R v Southampton University Hospitals NHS Trust* [2006] EWCA Crim 2971 arose out of the events that led to the manslaughter convictions of Doctors Misra and Srivastava discussed above. The trust was convicted and fined £100,000 for breaching Section 3 of the Act. The initial indictment in this case included allegations that the trust employed one of the doctors without taking up references or conducting a face-to-face interview, failed to organise ward rounds properly and failed to encourage nurses to report concerns about colleagues. Although these particular allegations were not substantiated, it indicates the potential of Health and Safety investigations to probe wider aspects of the system and its responsibility for safety lapses. It is possible to envisage a range of problems stemming from failing systems as opposed to flawed individuals, and the potential greater use of Health and Safety Law here. For example, the case transcript in *Misra* refers to misunderstandings about the correct procedures for obtaining blood results – one of the doctors relied on the laboratory to flag up abnormalities – whilst the prosecution maintained that the onus was on the doctors to chase up the results.

Similarly, Great Western Hospitals NHS Trust was convicted and fined £100,000 following the death of Mayra Cabrera who was mistakenly given an epidural drug instead of saline solution. The two drugs had almost identical packaging and were stored in same racking system (*The Guardian* 17 May 2010). The H&SE also successfully prosecuted Mid Staffordshire Foundation NHS Trust due to the lack of safety procedures in relation to the deaths of four patients. The trust was fined £200,000 in relation to the death of a diabetic patient after nurses forgot to administer her insulin. Staff had failed to check the patient's medical notes which stated that she required insulin, and the system of handover between staff on one shift to the next was described as 'inconsistent and sometimes non-existent' (*The Guardian* 28 April 2014). The same trust was also fined a further £500,000 in relation to the deaths of three elderly patients, one of whom was wrongly injected with penicillin despite her family warning that she was allergic to it, and two for suffering fatal falls (*The Guardian* 16 December 2015). These convictions are symbolically important as an official recognition of organisational fault and remind us of the wide scope of Health and Safety offences in the context of patient safety incidents.

However, such cases have been rare. This is largely because events arising from clinical judgment or the quality of care have not been a priority enforcement area for the H&SE, particularly since the creation of the CQC (and its predecessors) as the main regulator in the health sector. A memorandum of understanding between the CQC and H&SE clarifies which agency is responsible for different types of cases and is an example of closer cooperation between regulators. In short, the CQC is responsible for enforcing the regulations designed to ensure the safety and quality of care for patients treated by providers registered with the CQC, whilst the H&SE takes the lead on health and safety matters for bodies not registered with the CQC. Beyond this distinction, the CQC generally focuses on cases involving patients whereas the H&SE deals with incidents affecting employees (CQC 2015b). It is possible that closer working arrangements between these two regulators may bring an increase of referrals of cases from the CQC to H&SE, although it is likely that such cases will be those of managerial as opposed to clinical failure. This hesitancy of the H&SE to police patient safety incidents, whilst understandable given the role of the CQC, left something of a regulatory gap, which was noted in the Francis public inquiry report into Mid Staffordshire (Francis 2013: recommendation 87).

This gap has been closed somewhat by the creation of a number of offences in relation to breaches of various regulations to be enforced by the CQC. These are covered in The Health and Social Care Act 2008 (Regulated Activities) Regulations 2014 and The Health and Social Care Act 2008 (Registration and Regulated Activities) Regulations 2015. Whilst the CQC has generally followed the H&SE approach of seeking compliance, nevertheless, breach of certain regulations may be prosecuted without the CQC first issuing a warning notice. These include

regulations in relation to consent, acting on complaints, good governance, duty of candour and the requirement to display performance
assessments. A defence to these offences exists where registered persons
took all reasonable steps and acted with due diligence. The background
and likely impact of the duty of candour regulation will be discussed in
detail in Chapter 8. An additional three regulations allow for criminal
prosecution, but only where the breach results in exposure to avoidable
harm or significant risk of such harm occurring. These are 'safe care and
treatment', 'safeguarding service users from abuse and improper treatment', and 'meeting nutritional and hydration needs'. Whilst there is no
doubt that the criminalisation of these safety breaches is symbolically
important, it is less clear whether they will be effective in terms protecting
patient safety. The final part of this chapter will consider the likely
relationship between different criminal offences and patient safety and
what this might mean for professional dominance.

Criminalisation, Professional Dominance and Patient Safety

This increased propensity to criminalise medical harm is clearly significant in terms of professional dominance. As Chapter 1 explained, the
idea of professional dominance entails a high degree of trust in the
profession and minimal external evaluation of the quality of medical
work. The increasing involvement of police, prosecutors and specialist
agencies in reviewing the quality of medical care is a world away from
medical professional dominance. The range of criminal offences to prosecute mishaps and misconduct reflects a decrease of trust in self-
regulation, especially in relation to ensuring safety. Whether or not
such interventions actually mean that the profession is less dominant is
difficult to evidence in practice. But the professional reaction to the
increased criminalisation of medical harm suggests that doctors feel
under attack and somewhat less dominant than before (Ferner and
McDowell 2013). Whilst this increased reliance on criminal law is
a general trend (Husak 2008; Chalmers and Leverick 2013), it is unsurprising that its impact is particularly profound on those in caring professions who are, in the overwhelming majority of cases, trying their best to
do good. However, whether the threat of criminal prosecution impacts
on the behaviour of healthcare professionals, and if so in what ways, is
not well understood.

Little is known about the relationship between criminal law and
patient safety. To date, no research has examined how such prosecutions

impact on the medical practice of those affected or on the policies of organisations. Does criminal law deter unsafe practices? Does it have a positive net effect on levels of safe care? These are difficult questions to answer, not least because there are different types of criminal offences that may apply, but also because the medico-legal and regulatory environment includes numerous other mechanisms and influences on behaviour, making the task of isolating any effect of criminal offences difficult if not impossible. Nevertheless, the absence of hard evidence evaluating the actual impact of criminal prosecutions need not prevent discussion about the likely connection between various mechanisms rooted in criminal law and the pursuit of patient safety. Criminal offences are not all the same and differ in terms of their design, implementation and their possible effect, including the effect they may have on efforts to improve patient safety. Whilst the use of criminal offences in this context has been dominated by concerns about accountability rather than deterrence, it would be premature to dismiss the possibility that the presence of criminal offences may help alter individual and organisational behaviour and thus play some role in securing safety. The deterrence argument needs to be carefully unpacked and considered in relation to specific offences. Deterring errors is difficult, given that genuine errors lead to the opposite of what an individual intended. But deterring intentional or reckless behaviour is a more realistic aim for criminal law. Likewise, organisational offences are more likely to lead to changes in policies and practices that can help improve safety.

In terms of manslaughter, the educative role of such prosecutions, on those prosecuted and to the profession generally is not well understood. Nevertheless, such cases do have the capacity to assist with efforts to learn from safety failures. Whilst manslaughter cases essentially focus on individual fault, they can nevertheless allow high profile attention to be given to the context of fatal errors. The extent to which such lessons are learnt, both by the individual concerned and the wider medical community is not well understood. Perhaps the individual in question is less likely to repeat the same mistake again, but the extent to which this alters the behaviour of others is unknown. The fact that manslaughter prosecutions often tend to revolve around the same safety issue, for example, medication errors, might tend to suggest that such prosecutions have little effect in terms of learning and prevention. Whilst there is no direct evidence, some have speculated that criminal law not only fails to deter, but may in fact fuel a culture of secrecy and shame about errors (Ferner and McDowell 2013). However, whilst occasional manslaughter prosecutions are likely to offer little or no promise in terms of improving patient safety, there are reasons to be more optimistic about the other offences explored in this chapter.

The offences of ill-treatment or wilful neglect have been justified principally on the grounds of censure and accountability, as opposed to deterrence (Horder and Yeung 2014). They are good examples of the communicative function of criminal law and the need for legal expression of the wrong which has occurred (Feinberg 1970). Even critics of the use of criminal law in the healthcare context acknowledge its appropriateness for cases of recklessness or wilful neglect (Ferner and McDowell 2013). However, the deterrent potential of these offence should not be dismissed. Griffiths and Sanders are correct to note that the 'prosecution (or threat of prosecution) of a larger number of cases where there has been deliberate disregard or recklessness, as well as gross neglect, promises much more of a deterrent effect than the prosecution of a few cases' (2013: 154). Others have argued that such endangerment offences offer greater potential for a positive deterrent effect (Brazier and Alghrani 2009; Alghrani 2011). Whilst there is a lack of evidence to support this claim, nevertheless, a deterrent effect is more likely in the context of advertent as opposed to inadvertent harm. In particular, the offence in Section 21 of the Criminal Justice and Courts Act 2015, in targeting providers of care, should lead to greater attention to the implementation of policies that decrease the risk of patients being ill-treated or neglected. This could be related to safe levels of staffing and increased monitoring of vulnerable patients for example. The threat of criminal prosecution should increase the pressure on organisations to have systems in place that minimise the risk of harmful outcomes. It remains to be seen how many prosecutions are brought for ill-treatment or wilful neglect. The number of prosecutions of the Section 44 offence appear to have been reasonably modest. It is estimated that 177 such cases received a first hearing in the Magistrates Court between 2011 and 2012 (Manthorpe and Samsi 2014). Criminal Justice Statistics for completed proceedings suggest a lower number of between 70 and 85 cases per year since 2011. The Department of Health Impact assessment for the proposed new offence, based on data from the Section 44 offence, predicts around 240 prosecutions per year (DOH 2014b): 7).

Similarly, the regulatory offences enforced by the H&SE and the CQC offer more promise in terms of the potential for deterrence. The fact that trusts are unable to insure against the payment of criminal fines may be an important factor for incentivising compliance with safety standards.

Unlike compensation payments in related civil actions, such fines cannot be absorbed within insurance policies. The performance of healthcare providers could be rigorously assessed against a series of health and safety standards, with prosecution the last resort for repeated failure to comply (Hawkins 2002). Arguably, if any branch of the law is charged with seeking to enforce safety standards in the health setting, it should be health and safety law with its expertise in risk management and compliance. Health and safety inspectors are experts at investigating and managing risks and given their independence are able to provide a degree of external accountability. And in focusing squarely on safety, and particularly the contribution of flawed systems, such prosecutions offer a more appropriate response as opposed to mechanisms that focus on individual fault.

A health and safety approach may not only be more appropriate but also more effective. The investigatory lens could be broadened to encompass a variety of important organisational issues involving the recruitment and training of staff, as well as planning and communication problems, which are currently relegated to the background context of prosecutions against individual practitioners. As improvement science leads to the greater use of protocols and checklists designed to ensure safety, inspectors will be equipped with more detailed best-practice guidelines to supplement the broadly drafted sections of the 1974 Act. This could give health and safety inspectors increased confidence with which to evaluate a greater variety of safety events in healthcare. However, this would require the H&SE to take on a greater role in terms of investigating patient safety incidents. Whilst it does now acknowledge its role in this context, this is largely limited to non-clinical incidents such as trips and falls (CQC 2015b) as opposed to matters of clinical or managerial judgment.

Arguably, the regulatory offences enforced by the CQC offer the greatest promise in terms of helping improve safety. The presence of criminal offences in relation to breaches of safe care and treatment symbolises the increased importance placed on patient safety. It sends a strong signal to providers of care that the safety of patients is a serious matter that may lead to prosecution. Akin to Health and Safety offences, it represents a good example of the expressive function of criminal law (Feinberg 1970). However, the effectiveness of such regulations will be largely dependent on the approach taken to enforcement. As explored in Chapter 4, the CQC is at risk of being pulled in two different directions here. On the one hand, it will be conscious that a light-touch compliance approach has been advocated as best suited to encouraging a culture of learning and prevention in healthcare (Berwick 1989.; Leape 1994). But on the other hand, the impact of scandals such as Mid Staffordshire, and the emphasis in the Francis inquiry report on a zero-tolerance approach to poor care, calls for a firmer punitive or deterrent approach. This places the regulator in a somewhat invidious position. An approach that is overzealous in terms of prosecution risks losing its legitimacy with providers. However, an approach that tends to avoid prosecution leaves it open to the charge of not doing enough to protect patients. It remains to be seen how active the CQC is in prosecuting its new powers in this context and whether its approach helps create a safer environment.

Prosecution is not the only available option for the CQC, who may also issue cautions or penalty notices. However, reflecting a tougher approach to enforcement in the aftermath of the Francis inquiry report, the Commission states that it 'will generally prosecute providers where there are serious, multiple or persistent breaches of the fundamental standards (those regulations with prosecutable clauses that specifically relate to harm or the risk of harm) without issuing a Warning Notice first' (CQC 2015a): 29). The CQC's prosecution criteria (2015a): 27) contains a number of factors. However, the most important are the gravity of the incident, the general record and approach of the provider, repeated or multiple breaches, which give rise to significant risk, or persistent and significant poor compliance, and that the service is breaching fundamentals standards of care. Interestingly, it also notes two other factors that may be taken into account in terms of deciding whether to prosecute: that not holding the provider to account could undermine public confidence in regulation and that it may prioritise a single case so that enforcement sends a broader message and encourages other providers to improve their standards. This suggests that the CQC is confident that prosecuting such safety breaches may function to deter unsafe practices and encourage better care.

Conclusion

Until recently, criminal law seemed largely irrelevant as a mechanism for responding to patient safety incidents. In the main, criminal cases were confined to extremely rare instances of murder, such as those carried out by Harold Shipman, or for occasional manslaughter prosecutions following fatal gross negligence. Whilst offences under the Health and Safety at Work Act 1974 have long had potential for greater use in the context of patient safety, they have rarely been used. However, in an era where governments have relied on creating new criminal offences as an additional means of regulation, especially as a response to events such as the Mid Staffordshire scandal, the range of potential offences has increased. Notably, the offence of ill treatment or wilful neglect has filled the gap beneath manslaughter for cases of neglect that don't cause death. Similarly, the reliance on regulators has seen the creation of yet more 'regulatory crime'. It is unclear what this means for the safety of patients, but it may not be entirely negative.

Prosecuting individuals for errors is largely driven by notions of accountability and blame as opposed to having any connection with improving patient safety. Such cases share the same safety blindspots as civil actions: punishing a few errant clinicians in criminal courts is unlikely to help foster an open and learning safety culture. Whilst occasional manslaughter prosecutions are unlikely to make any meaningful contribution to patient safety, the same should not be assumed for the other offence categories, which are arguably better suited to encouraging safer healthcare. Criminal law is able to play a more constructive role in terms of offences which are directed at organisations rather than individuals. Whilst criminal law has traditionally been rooted in the mindset of individual responsibility, a number of offences now explicitly target organisations: corporate manslaughter, ill-treatment or wilful neglect, and the regulatory offences enforced by the H&SE and CQC are all able to appropriately target organisations for causing harm. Whilst such offences are likely to make a limited contribution to the task of improving safety, nevertheless, it would be wrong to overlook their potential for reinforcing other regulatory interventions that seek to protect patients from harm. Rather than assume, as some have done, that all criminal law is counterproductive to the pursuit of safer care, this chapter has argued that regulatory offences do have potential for making a positive contribution for prioritising safety. Ultimately, whether such offences actually have such an effect will depend on effective enforcement by the CQC and research that attempts to better understand the response of providers and professionals to such offences.

7

Coronial Investigations and Inquests

The previous two chapters considered the role that civil law and criminal law may play in terms of patient safety. A less obvious, but increasingly important role is that of coroners for investigating sudden, unnatural or unexplained deaths. Whilst the coroner is an ancient judicial role dating back to 1194, relatively little research has been conducted into how coroners discharge their duties (Slapper 1999; Mclean 2015), and even less in the context of deaths associated with substandard medical care (Griffiths and Sanders 2013). Historically, the role of the coroner was closely connected to the Criminal Justice System, with the power to commit individuals for criminal trial being abolished by Sections 56 and 65 of the Criminal Law Act 1977. But despite the formal attempts to separate coronial and criminal jurisdictions, the perception of it as a mechanism for offering accountability and attributing responsibility largely remains. This is despite the fact that coroners have consistently stated that their task, as set out in Section 5 of the Coroners and Justice Act 2009, is limited to establishing the cause of death and to stating who the deceased was, and when, where and how they died. The last of these questions about 'how' an individual died has always had the potential for broadening out coronial investigations to consider the contribution of system or organisational failings. This has been bolstered by the application of human rights law, namely Article 2 of the European Convention on Human Rights (ECHR), which imposes an obligation on States to have robust mechanisms for investigating deaths where they bear some responsibility, for example deaths occurring in police custody or in NHS hospitals. This ability of coroners to probe wider circumstances is important given the research discussed in Chapter 2, which noted the prevalence of systems rather than individual failings behind most patient safety events.

This chapter will argue that coroners have an important role in encouraging that lessons are learned from tragedies, and that patient safety is improved. In particular, the ability of coroners to make 'prevention of death reports' and to communicate these to those with the capacity to implement changes, is an important function carried out in the name of public health. This includes commenting not only on failures at local level, for example at a particular hospital, but also on failures of regulation and of delivering safe healthcare services nationally. The work of coroners in this context can also be understood as part of the challenge to professional dominance as it represents a further opportunity for external and often adverse comment on the quality of medical care. Whilst coroners are primarily interested in pursuing facts rather than fault, those called to give evidence at inquests experience similar cross examination, scrutiny and the possibility for public shame which is central to criminal trials. Professionals who give evidence at inquests are essentially accounting for their conduct and are aware that coroners have powers to refer cases to regulators or prosecutors.

The Coronial System

Despite being one of the oldest judicial offices in the English legal system, dating back to the Articles of Eyre in 1194, relatively little research has been conducted into the coronial system. This is partly attributed to the fact that coroners provide a local service, have lacked a sense of coherence and consistency and suffered from a lack of funding (Mclean 2015). Coroners are independent judicial officers and their investigations are governed by the Coroners and Justice Act 2009 and The Coroners (Inquest) Rules 2013 and The Coroners (Investigations) Regulations 2013. These replaced most of the Coroners Act 1988 and Coroners Rules 1984, though it seems that reference to key rules under the old system have survived in practice. Under Section 1 of the 2009 Act Coroners have a duty to investigate deaths if they suspect that a violent or unnatural death has occurred, the cause of the death is unknown or the deceased died while in custody or state detention. There are 110 coroner jurisdictions which are served by 97 coroners, the vast majority having legal backgrounds, which is now compulsory under the 2009 Act for those appointed after 25 July 2013. They are helped by 280 assistant coroners (MOJ 2015b: 1). Responsibility for the service is shared between the Ministry of Justice, the Lord Chancellor's Department and Local Authorities. The Coroner's Court is an inferior court of record and inquest hearings sit in public. There are no parties, such as defence and prosecution, only 'interested persons', and consequently there exists no burden of proof between them. It resembles inquisitorial criminal justice systems in its emphasis on the search for truth, illustrated by the admissibility of hearsay evidence (*R v Attorney General for Northern Ireland ex parte Devine and Breslin* [1992] 1 WLR 262).

Coroners retain wide-ranging powers and discretion in terms of conducting investigations (*R on the application of Sreedharan v HM Coroner for the County of Greater Manchester and others* [2013] EWCA Civ 181. Unlike the judge in a criminal trial, the coroner decides which witnesses to call and who can give relevant evidence. This has led to criticism about inconsistency of coronial practice and the outcomes of inquests (Thornton 2012: 2). Coroners conduct the vast majority of inquests alone, and only sit with juries in 2 per cent of cases (MOJ 2013a: 19). The majority of jury cases arise because of Section 7(4) since the circumstances of the death are notifiable. Thus, deaths at work usually lead to a jury inquest as they are notifiable to the Health and Safety Executive. Jury inquests also include cases involving unnatural deaths in custody or connected with the conduct of the police. A good example of the latter is the decision in 2012 to open fresh inquests into the 96 football supporters who died at the Hillsborough stadium in 1989 (*The Guardian*, 19 December 2012). The coroner's historic role in the criminal justice system has largely diminished with the removal of the power to commit a person for murder, manslaughter or infanticide (Criminal Law Act 1977, ss. 56 and 65). However, the perception that it functions to attribute blame largely remains. A clear tension persists between its main function of determining the cause of death – a *medical* matter, and the public misperception as its duty to comment on responsibility – a *judicial* concern. The question of establishing the cause of death can thus sometimes merge into issues of blame allocation, at least in the eyes of the bereaved searching for accountability (Wells 1991).

As noted in Chapter 6, deaths associated with medical error only occasionally end up as criminal trials, although a trend of increased investigation is apparent. A far greater number of such cases are reported to coroners, and a significant number that should be reported are not. The vast majority of cases referred to coroners are either those which end up being classed as natural deaths, a term which has not been interpreted consistently by different coroners (Roberts et al. 2000) or those associated in some way with medical treatment (Start et al. 1993). The number of deaths reported to coroners has increased through the twentieth and twenty first century. In 2014, 223,841 deaths were reported to coroners in (MOJ 2015a): 9). The registrar (of births, deaths and marriages) is placed under a statutory duty to report certain types of deaths of which he/she is informed to the coroner (The Registration of Births and Deaths Regulations 1987 (S.I. 1987 No. 2088) reg. 41(1)). However, while the Registrar may be informed of all deaths, he/she cannot possess all the details of every case, and as such, the coroner's system 'stands or falls on the co-operation of the medical profession' (Buchanan and Mason 1995: 145). Doctors are under no equivalent statutory requirement to report and their obligation is based on a doubtful common law or moral obligation to assist (Leadbetter and Knight 1993). For the deaths of individuals who have been attended in their last illness by a registered medical practitioner, the practitioner is obliged to sign and transmit to the registrar of birth and deaths a certificate on a prescribed form, stating the cause of death (Births and Deaths Registration Act 1953, s.22(1)). Most coroners follow a working rule that all deaths occurring within 24 hours of emergency admission ought to be reported.

A study by Start et al. in 1993 suggested that there are several parts of the coronial system that are poorly understood by doctors. A postal questionnaire was completed by 135 clinicians, asking them which of the fictitious case histories they would report to the coroner. Worryingly, clinicians of all grades only identified half of the reportable cases, with 97 per cent of General Practitioners unable to recognise all cases requiring reporting. In particular, cases of deaths associated with possible adverse drug reactions remain under reported (Start et al. 1993; Luce 2003). This is significant given the high proportion of adverse events that surround the prescription and administering of medication (The Health Foundation 2011). An analysis of reported deaths between 2011 and 2010 found considerable variation between reporting of registered deaths (between a low of 12 per cent and a high of 87 per cent (Mclean et al. 2013). This under-reporting is likely to be explained by a combination of the culture of non-criticism and the misperception of the coroner as a blame-allocating institution.

Despite the limited remit of coroners to investigating facts surrounding death, it is understandable that professionals fear any connection with it. The minimal medico-legal teaching within the medical curriculum and knowledge of different working practices of local coroners is also likely to play a part here. Thus one of the main defects in the system is that the coroner is only empowered to investigate when a death is reported. Sections 18 and 19 of the Coroners and Justice Act 2009 make provision for reporting to be compulsory and for the appointment of Medical Examiners who would scrutinise all deaths, although neither of these provisions are in force. Such a system seems all the more pressing given that the NHS appears to investigate a relatively small number of deaths, even for those classed as unexpected. For example, a freedom of information request by *The Guardian* newspaper revealed that NHS trusts have investigated 209 out of 1,463 deaths of inpatients with learning disabilities since 2011. And of those deaths deemed unexpected, only 36 per cent were investigated (*The Guardian* 21 December 2015).

Inquests and Patient Safety

Coronial investigations, in dealing with a high number of deaths associated with negligent or sub optimal medical treatment, are potentially important from a patient safety perspective. Analysis of inquest files from three coroner's offices over a ten-year period showed a threefold increase in complaints to coroners and the police from bereaved relatives about standards of medical care. Similarly, the number of inquests into medical deaths has increased twofold in the period 2004–8 compared with 1999–2003 (Griffiths and Sanders 2013: 118). Coroners are in a position to provide some sort of accountability to grieving families and make reports in order to help improve patient safety. In fact, providing accountability and justice to families is seen as increasingly important function of the coronial system (Davis et al. 2002, and see *Khan v Sec of State for Health* [2003] EWCA Civ 1129). Deaths associated with police negligence or malpractice, such as the killing of John Charles de Menezes and Ian Tomlinson (*The Guardian* 12 December 2013 and 3 May), and the Hillsborough stadium disaster, are powerful examples of inquests satisfying the search for truth by families. This function of 'public justice for the public' has been emphasised by the Chief Coroner (Thornton 2012).

The coronial system also has a public health and safety function in terms of helping to prevent similar deaths in the future. Whilst the provision of health data for preventing disease has been part of the coroner's role since the Victorian era (Thornton 2012: 4) it has been criticised for not realising its potential in this respect (Smith 2003). In the context of improving the safety of healthcare, coroners clearly have the potential for issuing reports that can inform the safety of care, although it has been argued that the system prioritises legal accountability over public health improvement (McGowan and Viens 2010). Whilst these two aims – legal accountability to families and a broader epidemiological duty   have been seen as competing ones, this need not necessarily be so. Given the evidence that families of bereaved or harmed patients

are motivated by trying to prevent others suffering the same fate
(see Chapter 9), this duty to try and learn lessons and improve safety is
consistent with the aim of accountability. The mechanism by which
coroners can impact on the safety of care is through issuing 'Regulation
28 reports' (what were previously called 'Rule 43 reports'), which will be
examined below.

Whilst inquests answer the need for accountability and offer an
opportunity for patient safety learning, strictly speaking, the main
function of the coroner is to establish the cause of violent or unnatural
deaths. The purpose of coronial investigations, as per Section 5 of the
2009 Act, is to deal with four factual questions: who the deceased was,
and how, when and where the deceased came by his or her death.
The question of 'how' the deceased died is not designed to discuss
searching and far-reaching issues, but limited to 'the means' by which
the deceased came by his death. However, the remit of certain inquests
has been extended by the impact of the jurisprudence surrounding
Article 2 of the ECHR. This demands that for deaths with reasonable
grounds for suggesting that the state bears some responsibility, for
example, deaths in police custody or in NHS hospitals, there should
be an effective and independent means of investigating the circumstances of that death. This is known as the procedural or adjectival
aspect of Article 2. In order to comply with Article 2, the House of
Lords has ruled that certain inquests may adopt a broader approach to
exploring the 'how' question to include 'by what means and in what
circumstances' (R v Middleton [2004] UKHL 10 para. 35). The decision
whether Article 2 is engaged at an inquest is a decision for the coroner
open to challenge by means of Judicial Review. Coroners will often
announce at an early stage of the investigation process that they are
proceeding on the basis that Article 2 is engaged or is not engaged but
go on to say that they will keep the matter under constant review.
However, in practice the difference in scope between an 'Article 2'
inquest and a non-'Article 2' inquest is narrowing. A decade prior to
Middleton it had been held that the scope of an inquest could be wider
than the statute strictly required. In R v Inner West London Coroner ex
parte Dallaglio [1994] 3 All ER 139 Simon Brown LJ (as he then was)
said:

> It is, in short, for the individual Coroner to recognise and resolve the
> tension existing between ss 8(3) and 11(5)(b) of the 1988 Act and r36.
> The inquiry is almost bound to stretch wider than strictly required for the

purposes of a verdict. How much wider is pre-eminently a matter for the Coroner whose rulings on the question will only exceptionally be susceptible to judicial review.

How does this wider remit apply to deaths associated with alleged medical negligence? What types of cases will permit an enhanced 'Middleton' inquest where wider circumstances may be probed? The position is not entirely clear, but the key question, to be decided by coroners, is whether 'the system as a whole, including both any investigation initiated by the State and the possibility of civil and criminal proceedings and/or a disciplinary process, satisfies the requirements of Article 2' (*R (Takoushis) v H M Coroner for Inner North London* [2006] 1 W.L.R. 461, at 493. In a medical context, it appears that whether Article 2 is engaged depends on the *degree* of alleged negligence involved in a case. Thus a case of simple negligence would not engage Article 2, but conduct potentially constituting gross negligence manslaughter might. This raises the issue of distinguishing between simple and gross negligence explored in the previous chapter and to how such determinations are made by coroners, in addition to consistency between different coroners. There is also authority that Middleton-type inquests are warranted in cases involving systemic (rather than individual) neglect, for example where there is a 'failure to provide suitable facilities or adequate staff or appropriate systems of operation' (*Humberstone* [2010] EWCA Civ 1479 at [58]). However, this is rather problematic in that by necessity it calls for a coronial assessment *before* a full investigation is made. It is arguable that Article 2 should apply to all cases involving deaths associated with medical harm (McIntosh 2012). It remains to be seen whether in the future, the enhanced 'and in what circumstances' type of investigation might apply to all deaths investigated by coroners, irrespective of whether they are related to agents of the state. Whilst this would seem appropriate in terms of providing accountability and also in terms of learning from events, this would require considerable extra resources to enable the system to provide this service.

When coroners are notified of deaths, they may either decide that no inquest or post-mortem examination is necessary or ask a pathologist to conduct a post-mortem. If that examination does not reveal a natural cause of death or suggests that the death was violent or unnatural, then the coroner is likely to open an inquest. Coroner's inquests are high profile and attract substantial media coverage. The number of inquests held has increased gradually over the past decade, although this trend appears to have been halted by the implementation of the Coroners and

Justice Act 2009 in 2013. In 2014, there were 25,889 inquests (MOJ 2015a: 9). The decision not to hold an inquest may be challenged by way of judicial review. Coroners and courts have struggled to come to terms with the notion of 'unnatural death' (Roberts et al. 2000), which remains a question of fact for coroners who have generally approached this in terms of a single dominant cause. This is problematic for deaths associated with potential medical error where there are typically multiple causes. In *R v Poplar Coroner ex parte Thomas* [1993] 2 W.L.R. 547 the deceased died from a severe asthma attack and there was evidence suggesting that she would not have died but for the ambulance arriving after a 33 minute delay. The Court of Appeal concluded that the coroner had been entitled to regard the death as caused by the asthma and thus natural and not demanding an inquest. However, Simon Brown LJ suggested that he would have regarded the death as unnatural (at 555):

> if the late arrival of the ambulance had constituted a more extreme failure of the service, [and concluded that] cases may well arise in which human fault can and properly should be found to turn what would otherwise be a natural death into an unnatural one, and one into which therefore an inquest should be held.

The significance of these comments became apparent in *R v HM Coroner's Court of St Pancras, Ex Parte Touche* [2001] Lloyd's Rep Med 67. After giving birth to twins, Laura Touche died from a cerebral haemorrhage following severe hypertension. The evidence suggested that had her blood pressure been monitored earlier she would probably not have died. The question arose as to whether her death was unnatural and thus calling for an inquest under s.8 (1) of the Coroners' Act 1988. The coroner's decision that Mrs Touche died a natural death and thus not meriting an inquest was set aside by the Divisional Court, following an application for judicial review. As Kennedy LJ explained (at 69):

> [where] a patient is in hospital suffering from a condition which if not monitored and treated in a routine way will result in death, and, for whatever reason, the monitoring and treatment is omitted, then ... the Coroner must hold an inquest unless he can say that there are no grounds for suspecting that the omission was an effective cause of death.

This was upheld by the Court of Appeal, which accepted the argument that there was reasonable cause to suspect that Mrs Touche's death was contributed to by 'neglect' and thus merited an inquest. It might have been expected that the effect of this decision would be that hospital deaths caused by failure to provide routine treatment would be classified as unnatural and thus requiring an inquest. However, this does not appear to have been the case.

The conclusions available at inquests reflect the fundamental tension between its fact-finding purpose and its historical association with blame and criminal justice. In an attempt to further distance coronial investigations from the criminal justice system, the term *verdict* has been replaced by the more neutral one of *conclusion*. Clearly, how the conclusion is framed is important to both relatives and any health professionals involved. This is particularly so given the emotive connotations, if not strict legal meaning, that such verdicts possess. Coroners (and rarely juries) must decide between the following short-form conclusions: I. Accident or misadventure, II. Alcohol / drug related III. Industrial disease IV. Lawful/unlawful killing V. Natural causes VI. Open VII. Road traffic collision VIII. Stillbirth IX. Suicide. As an alternative or in addition to one of the short-form conclusions, the coroner (or jury) may make a brief narrative conclusion. Such conclusions offer a short descriptive account explaining the circumstances surrounding the death, but tend to be worded in quite neutral terms and avoid attributing blame to individuals. Narrative conclusions have increased from 7 per cent in 2005 to 18 per cent in 2014 (MOJ 2015a: 20).

The conclusion of natural causes and, more rarely, the conclusion of accident/misadventure can be qualified as being contributed by neglect or in the case of natural causes, self-neglect. This generally refers to the absence of care, and thus usually concerns an omission. In terms of medical cases it has been interpreted as a gross failure to provide or procure basic medical attention. This may never be a conclusion on its own, and cannot form part of a conclusion unless a clear causal connection between the conduct and cause of death is established (*R v H M Coroner for North Humberside and Scunthorpe, ex parte Jamieson* [1994] 3 All E.R. 972, 990–1). Such a verdict would seem to be impliedly criticising individuals, and would certainly be perceived as such by the relatives and professional(s) in question. A conclusion of natural causes is appropriate where the facts show that the acts of individuals, such as medical professionals, played no significant part in the death, in other words, death resulted from an underlying disease. This is the most common conclusion returned, accounting for 29 per cent in 2012 (MOJ 2013a: 14). This is followed by accident or misadventure (26 per cent) which may follow inappropriate treatment, or rough handling. However, it may also be an appropriate conclusion where the treatment, or consequence of treatment, has caused the death, even if it is accepted that it is of a high standard. Lawful killing is appropriate where there is no question of criminal responsibility for the death in question. Unlawful killing arises in all cases of homicide (excluding accidents and cases where the killing was justified, for example, self-defence). This includes murder, manslaughter and infanticide. This is the most emotive conclusion, although it has no real legal effect. Although Section 10(2) (old Rule 42) prohibits a conclusion to appear to determine criminal liability on part of a named person, there will be cases where it will be obvious that a particular individual was responsible for the death and an unlawful killing conclusion must be recorded if appropriate. Unlawful killing and suicide require the criminal standard of proof, whereas the civil standard applies to others.

In order to comply with the enhanced Article 2 style inquests, the House of Lords has approved the use of narrative verdicts. Such verdicts, recorded as 'unclassified' in official coronial statistics, have risen markedly between 2007 and 2011 and accounted for 15 per cent of the total in 2012 (MOJ 2013a: 15), and to 18 per cent in 2014 (MOJ 2015a): 20). They are likely to appeal to coroners in offering an escape from the blamist language of some of the short-form conclusions, and may also offer a more detailed and satisfactory explanation for families. Analysis (by two retired coroners) of a random sample of 2,196 unclassified verdicts in that period found that 25 per cent of unclassified verdicts were cases involving medical or surgical treatment. This has led to the suggestion of introducing a new verdict of 'Medical or surgical intervention unsuccessful' (MOJ 2013a: 25). Such neutral language would be consistent with euphemistic terms such as 'lost opportunities' which tend to feature as part of narrative verdicts, though may be a source of frustration for families in cases where they suspect neglect or suboptimal care.

One of the reasons for such euphemism is the effect of Sections 5 and 10(2) of the Coroners and Justice Act 2009 (which were previously covered by rules 36 and 42 of the Coroners Rules 1984). Section 5(3) prohibits coroners and juries from expressing any opinion 'on any *other* matters' although it has been held that this should not be interpreted so as to defeat the purpose of holding an inquest. The inquiry is not, therefore, restricted to the 'last link in the chain of causation' (*R v Inner West London Coroner, ex p. Dallaglio* [1994] 4 All ER 139). Section 10(2) states that a conclusion 'may not be framed in such a way as to appear to determine any question of (a) criminal liability on the part of a named person, or (b) civil liability'. In this vein, judges have stressed that 'It is not the function of a Coroner's inquest to provide a forum for attempts to gather evidence for pending or future criminal or civil proceedings' (per Dillon LJ in *R v Poplar Coroners Court ex parte Thomas* [1993] 2 WLR 547, 553). To be sure, whilst inquest evidence is not admissible of the facts stated therein, it might properly form the *basis* for further inquiries leading to civil or criminal proceedings. Research conducted by Slapper (1999) suggests that judges have adopted a narrow approach to the facts surrounding death. This has led to an overly hostile stance towards advocates treading close to the prohibitions of Sections 5 and 10(2). However, there remains some confusion surrounding the precise effect of Section 10(2). The coroner or jury are entitled to *explore* facts bearing on such liability, but not *frame* the conclusion in such a way. For example, it had been found that a verdict of 'lack of care' did not contravene the old Rule 42 by appearing to determine civil liability. In *R v Surrey Coroner, ex parte Campbell* [1982] Q.B. 661, 676 the Divisional Court approved a passage from Jervis on coroners asserting that:

> to avoid such conflict the verdict is careful to refrain from stating that the death was aggravated by the lack of care of any particular person or persons and merely states that it was aggravated by lack of care. There is, therefore, no suggestion that any person owed a duty of care towards the deceased, breach of which would render that person liable for civil or criminal negligence.

The Court of Appeal has confirmed this (*R v H M Coroner for North Humberside and Scunthorpe, ex parte Jamieson* [1994] 3 All E.R. 972) yet it is surely asking too much for both relatives and any professionals involved to divorce this verdict/conclusion from a sense of blame. Whilst coroners are careful to comply with the rules in Sections 5 and 10 of the Act, conclusions such as 'unlawful killing' will understandably have strong implications of blame and responsibility. The increasing use of narrative conclusions are important here, allowing coroners to satisfy the need for families to have a fuller explanation into how a loved one died, and allowing coroners to make criticisms, albeit phrased in neutral terms such as noting 'missed opportunities'.

Prevention of Future Deaths Reports

Rule 43 of the 1984 Coroners Rules enabled a coroner to report matters in writing to a person or authority who may have power to prevent the recurrence of fatalities similar to that which the inquest is investigating. This is now covered by paragraph 7 of Schedule 5 of the 2009 Act and Regulations 28–9 of the Investigation Regulations, and these are referred to as prevention of future deaths reports. Recent reforms recognise the potential of these reports for improving public health in terms of enabling learning and prevention around patient safety. It was amended in 2008 so that reports could be made to prevent future (not necessarily similar) deaths (The Coroners (Amendment) Rules 2008). Under the 2009 reforms, coroners now have a duty rather than a power to make a report, with a view to preventing other deaths. This gives greater prominence and importance for these reports to improve public health and safety. In the case of hospital deaths, these reports are sent to NHS Trusts, usually addressed to the Chief Executive, and also to the Chief Coroner and the grieving family. Some reports that raise issues of general relevance about the provision of safe care are addressed to the Department of Health or to healthcare regulators. Whilst recipients of such reports are not obliged to implement the recommendations which may be implicit in the reports, they are expected to reply within 56 days (Regulation 29(3)(a)). The number of such reports is relatively low in proportion to the number of inquests held: there were 186 in the six-month period between April and September 2012 (MOJ 2013b). The fact that the coronial system has suffered from a lack of resources is likely to partly explain this low number. Interestingly, the majority of such reports relate to hospital deaths and thus NHS Trusts received the largest number of Regulation 28 reports (44 per cent). These deaths are classified as Hospital Death (clinical procedures and medical management) related. The other category relevant to patient safety is that of Care Home Health Related Deaths. The Chief Coroner's office intends to make all reports made since 25 July 2013 available online.

These reports offer considerable potential for implementing changes that will improve patient safety. Common issues that have emerged since such data has been kept include problems over note taking, staffing ratios, communication, training and the recording of medication (MOJ 2013b: 7). A study of a sample of 30 Regulation 28 reports published between 9 July and 2 November 2015 reveals the wide array of patient safety issues leading to critical comment by coroners. These included a failure to administer a whooping cough vaccine to a pregnant mother (with consequent death of her baby who contracted the virus), the failure to diagnose deep vein thrombosis, and numerous failures to safely observe particularly vulnerable patients. A basic analysis of these

30 cases, listed in Table 7.1 below, enables the identification of common safety problems (note that some cases contained a number of concerns expressed by coroners, thus the 33 concerns (made in the 30 cases) listed below):

- lack of guidance, discrepancy between local/national guidance, failure to implement guidance (9)
- communication errors (4)
- failure to follow care plans (4)
- failures to observe particularly vulnerable patients (3)
- medication errors (3)
- poor note keeping and maintenance of medical records (3)
- safe levels of staffing and bed space (3)
- lack of a learning environment, including the failure to heed previous prevention of future deaths reports (3)
- diagnostic errors (1)

What is striking is the apparently high number of cases where the deaths appeared avoidable if appropriate action was taken, especially in terms of following good practice guidelines. This confirms an important finding from existing patient safety research noted in Chapter 2 about the problem of implementation. That is, in many areas guidelines exist for the most appropriate and safest way to manage specific situations, but all too often those guidelines are not implemented or inadequately implemented. There are likely to be many occasions when failure to follow such guidelines does not lead to patient harm and so are merely classified as 'near misses'. However, when such failures do lead to harm, coroners are able to note these concerns in Regulation 28 reports and use their status in order to help influence changes. Akin to other mechanisms which have been discussed in the previous two chapters, there is a lack of evidence about how the work of coroners in this context might contribute towards improving patient safety. Coroners retain wide discretion in how they discharge their duties, and the lack of consistency between coroners makes any general observations difficult to make. However, unlike civil and criminal cases, which are primarily concerned with awarding compensation and attributing responsibility, the coronial jurisdiction, via Regulation 28 reports, is able to make a much more targeted contribution in terms of addressing specific failures and raising concerns, and thus is much more likely to make a positive impact.

Table 7.1 *Sample of Coronial Prevention of Future Death Reports between 9 July to 2 November 2015*

Deceased	Date of Report	Coroner's Concerns
Connor Sparrowhawk	2 November 2015	Observation of an epileptic patient in the bath
Vasilis Ktorakis	18 October 2015	Medication (oxytocin) administered to new born baby, and the failure of staff to learn lessons from mismanagement
Adrian Smith	16 October 2015	Request to perform an MRI scan not followed
Alan Tear	16 October 2015	Post-operative instructions not followed by nursing staff
Patrick Carrick	9 October 2015	Departure from management plan and blood test results not actioned
Suzanne Greenwood	9 October 2015	Monitoring of a psychiatric patient
Liam Smith	18 September 2015	Following guidelines
Thelma Jones	12 August 2015	No co-ordinated care or treatment plans
Lorraine Bird	10 August 2015	Failure to diagnose DVT and the lack of a protocol
Amanda Ellams	7 August 2015	Poor note keeping and a lax attitude to measuring blood oxygen saturation levels.
Kathleen Neville	7 August 2015	Prescription error and failure to follow NICE guideline
Robert Hogg	6 August 2015	Failure to implement pathways for identifying very sick children
Thomas Thurling	6 August 2015	Monitoring new medication for psychiatric patient and staff shortages
Michael Quinn	3 August 2015	Safe blood glucose levels prior to surgery and discrepancy between local/ national guidance
Anthony Dwyer	30 July 2015	Adequacy of national guidance for management of tracheostomy patients
Casey Garrett	30 July 2015	Inappropriate midwifery care – poor foetal monitoring, failure escalate level of care – poor learning environment

Table 7.1 (cont.)

Deceased	Date of Report	Coroner's Concerns
Williams Bows	28 July 2015	Lack of guidance for advising Primary Care doctors on monitoring patients on particular drug
Arthur Cook	27 July 2015	Low staffing levels, poor pressure ulcer documentation, continuity between primary and secondary care
Lynn Poyser	23 July 2015	Adverse interaction of two drugs and available guidance
Rachel Hollister	21 July 2015	Obstetric haemorrhage protocol not meet the RCOG guidelines
Masoud Ghaderi	17 July 2015	Inadequate care records and lack of risk assessment
Isabella Drew	16 July 2015	Failure to follow guidance for pertussis vaccination of pregnant women, and poor communication between parts of ante natal care
John Lloyd	16 July 2015	Failure to notify GP of hospital admission and consequences for ongoing treatment (accidental opiate overdose)
Stanley Oliver	16 July 2015	Safe staffing ratios (specialist radiologists)
Joyce Hartford	15 July 2015	Inadequate nursing records
Emma Carpenter	14 July 2015	Funding and bed space for treating anorexic patients
Barbara Harrison	13 July 2015	Theatre equipment, post-operative care (infection), management and communication of care plan
Dorothy McDermott	10 July 2015	Need for guidance on suitable placement of vulnerable patients (residential/nursing care) pressure sore management
Michael George	9 July 2015	Failure to heed earlier Prevention of Future Death reports. Failure to have effective system for blood glucose monitoring on a ward
Tony Piel	9 July 2015	Failure to observe NICE guideline about considering patient's home environment when discharging

Conclusion

The work of coroners can make an important contribution towards improving patient safety. Whilst such investigations are limited to answering the four factual questions of who the deceased was, and when, where and how they died, the last of these allows for a more searching examination of the circumstances surrounding deaths, many of which might have been avoided. Article 2 of the European Convention on Human Rights has been an important mechanism for ensuring that deaths involving State responsibility are permitted this wider remit. Unnatural deaths which take place within the NHS are an important example of this. Whilst coronial work is not, strictly speaking, of a regulatory nature, nevertheless such investigations are an increasingly important part of the regulatory environment. The ability to issue Regulation 28 'prevention of future death' reports to a range of recipients, including hospital Chief Executives, professional regulators and the Department of Health, enables coroners to comment about specific failures and call for urgent change. In many ways, the ethos of coronial investigations is consistent with the preferred approach to patient safety failures explored in Chapter 2, which is to eschew individual blame and concentrate instead on system problems and the capacity for learning and prevention. Whilst coroners are able to comment critically about the conduct of individuals, the reports examined and summarised in Table 7.1 focus on identifying failures to follow protocols or system problems such as safe levels of staffing and effective systems of monitoring vulnerable patients. Whilst coronial work will continue to provide explanations and some form of accountability to the family of the deceased, it is also able to perform an important public health role in terms of identifying the causes of safety failings and calling for preventative action to learn lessons from past tragedies.

8

Professional Responsibility

Speaking Up and Saying Sorry

The final two chapters of this book consider the role that professionals and patients can play in improving safety. The previous chapters have evaluated the work of formal regulators such as the General Medical Council (GMC) and the Care Quality Commission (CQC), as well as exploring the potential of civil, criminal and coronial mechanisms for preventing unsafe practices. Whilst well-designed regulation and law are important in terms of establishing rules, encouraging compliance and ensuring accountability, we have seen that there are limits to what they can achieve. This is partly explained by the reality that regulators and regulations may be rather distant concerns to everyday medical work. As Chapter 4 noted, there is no strong evidence about whether, and in what ways, formal regulation impacts on professional behaviour, or indeed the extent to which professionals engage with codes of conduct and ethics. There is therefore a need to understand the contribution (and potential contribution) of those delivering and receiving healthcare services, as a type of informal regulation. The role of patients and carers will be examined in the next chapter. The current chapter will consider the important day-to-day role of professionals in monitoring safety, whether through raising concerns about clinical competence or unsafe working environments caused by staff shortages or inadequate equipment. It describes the accounts of high-profile healthcare whistle-blowers who have raised safety concerns. The culture of the medical profession, and indeed the health service, is central to this, particularly as it applies to the sensitive subject of safety.

Creating a culture of safety depends on a number of elements, but openness and honesty are critical. This chapter focuses on two aspects of openness most significant for this book. First is the need for professionals to raise safety concerns, whether about individual incompetence or organisational failings that cause or risk avoidable harm to patients. This has traditionally been labelled as whistle-blowing, but has also been described in more neutral terms as the freedom to 'speak up' about safety. Secondly, and closely connected to this, is the need for professionals to openly disclose medical harm to their patients. After a long campaign, a duty on healthcare organisations to openly disclose incidents that have harmed patients is now enshrined in law and enforced by the Care Quality Commission. The creation of this duty of candour encountered medical resistance, but this chapter argues that the strong signal sent by a statutory duty can help encourage greater openness and learning about safety and be a trigger for cultural change. Whilst understanding and changing culture is extremely challenging, until candour and transparency become the norm, efforts to improve patient safety are unlikely to succeed, or only realise limited progress.

Medical Culture and Safety

In dealing with risk on a daily basis, doctors have developed a language and culture that normalises medical mistakes. While all professions construct 'vocabularies of realism' (Stelling and Bucher 1973), this is particularly well-rooted in medicine, where high risk and harm are inherent features of work. This normalisation of mistakes has been extensively observed through ethnographic studies by medical sociologists. Classic works from the United States include Eliot Freidson's *Doctoring Together* (1975), which observed the distinction drawn between 'normal' and 'deviant' mistakes and a general reluctance to confront poor performance. Similarly, Charles Bosk's *Forgive and Remember* (1979) found that surgeons forgave technical errors such as surgical slips but not normative errors such as failing to be honest or accept responsibility. Millman (1977: 91) studied the 'various processes by which medical mistakes are systematically ignored, justified or made to appear unimportant or inconsequential by the doctors who have made them or those who have noticed they have been made'. The denial or neutralisation of medical errors was further observed in studies by Terry Mizrahi (1984) and Marianne Paget (1988). In the United Kingdom, Marilynn Rosenthal (1987) found similar themes around professional loyalty and the norm of non-criticism, often captured by the expression 'there but for the grace of God go I'.

These aspects of medical culture, particularly the fear of blame and a closed culture that resists external non-medical evaluation have also been observed by more recent studies (Waring 2005; Dixon-Woods 2010). These show how doctors identify the uncertainty of medicine, professional loyalty, and the perceived pointlessness of reporting errors as reasons for not engaging with patient safety initiatives. These are strong features of the professional dominance model of professionalism and are illustrated by the treatment of healthcare whistle-blowers described below. Culture is clearly extremely complicated and multi-layered, and in the context of an increasingly specialised medical profession, generalisations are inappropriate. However, the lack of an established culture of safety in medicine has been powerfully illustrated by events such as those at Bristol and Mid Staffordshire, which were outlined in Chapter 1. The public inquiry report into paediatric cardiac surgery at the Bristol Royal Infirmary observed a 'club culture' that was resistant to criticism (Kennedy 2001: 2). Similarly, the Mid Staffordshire NHS Foundation Trust report criticised a culture that failed to listen and respond appropriately to the concerns of staff and carers, with consequent harm to hundreds of patients (Francis 2013).

This norm of non-criticism has also been reflected in guidance issued by the General Medical Council about appropriate professional duties. Historically, its code of conduct has long cautioned doctors against disparaging other colleagues, on the basis of it being disloyal and unprofessional. It was only in 1987 that its guidance explicitly placed a duty on doctors to act on suspicion that colleagues were a threat to patient safety (GMC 1987). A case in 1994 is believed to be the first time the Council condemned a doctor for failing to act in relation to the incompetence of a colleague, although it imposed no punishment (Dyer 1994). Whilst revised versions of this guidance reflect a shift away from discouraging disparagement towards encouraging the reporting of concerns about patient safety (GMC 2013c: paras. 24 and 25), nevertheless, there are few, if any cases where the council have punished practitioners for turning a blind eye (Harris and Slater 2015). This absence of safety culture extends beyond the normalisation of individual mistakes to the toleration of unsafe environments, for example shortages of staff, beds or equipment. This 'mend and make do' mentality, which reveals resilience in the face of difficult circumstances, is clearly admirable. However, it ultimately prioritises a 'culture of pragmatism' over a culture of safety at a cost to patient welfare (Kennedy 2001: Chapters 22–37). Whilst fostering a culture that prioritises safety faces a number of challenges, including the effect of legal and regulatory interventions, this chapter will argue that honesty and openness are the essential starting points and that healthcare professionals must take the lead at championing this.

Speaking Up

The norm of non-criticism observed by medical sociologists has been powerfully illustrated by the treatment of professionals who have gone public with their patient safety concerns – the so-called whistle-blowers. Whistle-blowing has been defined as the 'public disclosure, by a person working within an organization, of acts, omissions, practices, or policies perceived as morally wrong by that person and is a disclosure regarded as wrongful by that organization's authorities' (Hunt 1998). It represents something of a last resort for colleagues between staying silent and other more subtle voice strategies for communicating their concerns (Jones and Kelly 2014). Whilst raising safety concerns is an important matter of professional conscience and ethics, it has not been a strong feature of medical culture. In fact, those raising concerns have invariably encountered resistance and hostility, as well as suffering huge costs in terms of their careers and personal lives. The first part of this chapter will recount the stories of high-profile healthcare whistle-blowers in order to illustrate the negative aspects of medical culture towards those raising concerns. Although staff who speak up are making an important contribution to the safety of care, such behaviour has been viewed negatively in the context of a medical culture sensitive to criticism and accountability. This is reflected in the experiences of the following healthcare whistle-blowers:

- Dr Stephen Bolsin was the consultant anaesthetist who first raised concerns about the quality of paediatric heart operations carried out by two surgeons at the Bristol Royal Infirmary. Dr Bolsin began working at the hospital in 1988 and promptly raised concerns about the length of time it took surgeons to perform 'hole in the heart' and arterial switch procedures. He kept his own audit of these procedures and expressed his concerns to senior management at the hospital. Dr Bolsin felt that his concerns were not being taken sufficiently seriously, and that this was partly because one of the surgeons occupied a powerful position as medical director of the hospital. He maintained that patient safety was being sacrificed for surgical pride and a learning curve (Bolsin 1998b). He continued to collect data which he argued established the poor mortality rate for these two surgeons. Eventually, he went public with his concerns, passing over his evidence to the Department of Health and giving testimony at the GMC hearings against the two surgeons and the public inquiry. After unsuccessfully attempting to obtain work at other NHS hospitals, he continued his medical career in Australia.

- Dr David Drew was dismissed from his post as a consultant paediatrician at Walsall Manor Hospital in 2010. He raised concerns about the competence of a colleague who he felt should have referred an at-risk baby to social services. The baby died after being shaken violently by his stepfather, who was sentenced to jail for manslaughter. Dr Drew blew the whistle on the clinical incompetence of his colleague in not responding to suspicious bruising on the child during an earlier hospital admission, and also about the way that the hospital covered up these failings. He was dismissed from his post for his use of religious materials in his communications with colleagues, but maintains that the die was cast after he blew the whistle about his safety concerns (Drew 2014).

- Another consultant paediatrician, Dr Kim Holt, was suspended for four years after raising concerns about systems problems with the paediatric service at St Ann's Hospital in Haringey. In 2006 she wrote to managers warning that understaffing and poor record-keeping was compromising the safety of children treated in the clinic. A locum doctor working at the clinic failed to spot signs that a 17-month-old baby boy who was on the child protection register had been physically abused, including suffering a broken back. Sadly, the baby (Baby P) was found dead two days later in his cot with severe injuries. Dr Holt maintains that had the concerns expressed by her and by three colleagues been listened to, this death might have been avoided. She was offered £120,000 by the hospital trust to leave her job and remain silent by signing a gagging clause. She refused and instead went public with her concerns, which led to her suspension from work for four years. In 2011, the hospital trust formally apologised to her and she returned to work at a different hospital (*The Guardian* 14 June 2011).

- Dr Raj Mattu, a cardiologist at Walsgrave hospital in Coventry, raised concerns about the practice of squeezing an additional bed into a heart ward designed to be used by four patients. He raised concerns that this stretched essential resources in the ward and compromised safety. After the concerns were not responded to, despite the involvement of the Care Quality Commission, Dr Mattu went public and claimed that this '5 in 4' policy had accounted for the deaths of at least two patients. Numerous allegations were then made against Dr Mattu, ranging from bullying to financial irregularities, none of which were substantiated, and he was suspended and then sacked in 2010. He was successful in his claim for unfair dismissal and awarded £1.22 million in damages (*The Guardian* 4 February 2016).

- Helene Donnelly worked as an accident and emergency (A&E) nurse at Mid Staffordshire NHS Foundation Trust. She raised over a hundred complaints about the treatment of patients at the hospital. Specifically, she repeatedly warned hospital managers about faulty equipment, untrained staff and staff shortages, but her concerns were not acted upon. She was a key witness to the Francis Inquiry and gave evidence about nurses being pressured to break rules in order to meet targets, even falsifying records to make it appear that patients had been seen within the four-hour waiting time target. The following quote from nurse Donnelly illustrates the negative aspects of a culture which was resistant to junior staff raising concerns with senior colleagues (Francis, 2013 Volume 1: 108):

> The culture in the department gradually declined to the point where all of the staff were scared of the Sisters and afraid to speak out against the poor standard of care the patients were receiving in case they incurred the wrath of the Sisters. Nurses were expected to break the rules as a matter of course in order to meet targets, a prime example of this being the maximum four-hour wait time target for patients in A&E. Rather than 'breach' the target, the length of waiting time would regularly be falsified on notes and computer records. I was guilty of going along with this if the wait time was only being breached by 5 ... or 10 minutes and the patient had been treated ... [but] when wait times were being breached by 20–30 minutes or more and the patient had still not been seen, I was not prepared to go along with what was expected. I was concerned about the terrible effect that our actions were having on patient care. I did raise this with Sisters [X] and [Y], however their response was extremely aggressive, basically telling me that they were in charge and accusing me and anyone else who agreed with me of not being team players.

- Jennie Fecitt, a nurse with 23 years of clinical experience, worked as a clinical coordinator for three NHS walk-in centres in Manchester. She raised concerns about a colleague who wrongly claimed to have certain qualifications, and the implications of this for the safety of patients. The following quote provides another example of a culture resistant to the concerns voiced by nurse Fecitt and two colleagues (*The Independent* 31 October 2011):

> We were worried about our patients, who we have a duty to protect. It was a question of integrity: if he could lie about his qualifications, what else would he lie about? What we didn't know until the tribunal was that senior managers knew he didn't have the correct qualifications two years earlier and that a competence assessment was never carried out. But other nurses thought we were on a witch hunt and started shutting doors in our faces and ignoring us. My daughter received a threatening phone call. We kept reporting that we were being victimised, but nothing happened; we took out formal grievances but they were parked.

Nurse Fecitt was redeployed to another position by NHS Manchester and unsuccessfully claimed that her employer had failed to protect her against harassment by colleagues. Regrettably, these are not the only examples of individuals motivated by patient safety being prevented from working, experiencing bullying and in some cases being subject to false accusations after speaking out. The decision to raise concerns has come at a personal cost to these clinicians, both financial and emotional. The treatment of whistle-blowers been described as a 'stain on the NHS' (HCSC 2015) but it is also a financial drain. For example, the legal fees in relation to the dismissal of Dr Raj Mattu have been estimated at six million pounds (*The Guardian* 17 April 2014). Whilst such cases are inevitably complex and some will involve issues beyond safety, nevertheless they reveal negative aspects of workplace culture in the NHS that are detrimental to patient safety and also to the well-being of those staff who raise concerns.

Whistle-Blowing and the Law

Whilst legislation has existed to protect whistle-blowers since 1998, in the form of the Public Interest Disclosure Act (PIDA), it has had a limited effect in preventing the negative aspects of medical workplace culture revealed by these stories. The PIDA amends the Employment Rights Act 1996 in order to provide statutory protection for 'good faith' whistle-blowing, what it calls 'protected disclosures'. The preamble to the Act declares that it aims 'to protect individuals who make certain disclosures of information in the public interest; to allow individuals to bring such action in respect of victimisation'. There is no doubt that raising concerns about matters which have compromised patient safety amount to a 'qualifying disclosure' under Section 43B of the 1996 Act. Whilst six situations justifying disclosure are specified, paragraph (d) is the most pertinent to patient safety in noting that 'the health or safety of any individual has been, is being or is likely to be endangered'.

The act envisages three types of disclosures: internal (to the employer), external (to regulators) and public (most commonly to the media). There is an institutional 'ladder' from internal disclosures to public disclosures with the requirements becoming harder to satisfy upon climbing this ladder (Gobert and Punch 2000). This is designed to encourage internal disclosures and a degree of self-regulation around such concerns, perhaps reflecting an underlying disquiet about 'going public'. Under Section 43C(1), internal disclosures to employers originally needed to be made in 'good faith', which meant that they were made with an honest belief in the truth of the allegation. The need for 'good faith' was removed by the Enterprise and Regulatory Reform Act 2013 and is thus not applicable for disclosures made from 25 June 2013. Instead, tribunals are now able to reduce any compensation payable where workers acted without good faith. For external disclosures to prescribed persons such as regulators, the worker must additionally believe that the allegation is 'substantially true' (Section 43F). Under Section 43G, public disclosures must satisfy an additional hurdle that the worker must not be acting for gain, and also that the worker reasonably believes that disclosure to the employer would lead to detriment, concealment of the evidence or that previous disclosures about the same information were made. The latter requirements are not necessary in the event of disclosures about 'exceptionally serious failures' (Section 43H). The General Medical Council was not originally included as a 'prescribed person' for the purposes of external disclosures, and was only added in 2013 by The Public Interest Disclosure (Prescribed Persons) (Amendment) Order 2013. Until this change, any disclosures to the regulator would therefore need to have satisfied the heavier burden of external disclosure in Section 43G. The fact that the GMC was not a prescribed person for the first 15 years of the PIDA is arguably further evidence of a culture and regulatory system that has been wary of whistle-blowers.

Section 47B of the 1996 Act (as amended by the PIDA) gives workers the 'right not to be subjected to any detriment' by employers. A loophole in the law meant that the Act's protection did not extend to suffering detriment by colleagues, as opposed to employers. This became apparent in the case brought by nurse Jennie Fecitt, where it was held that the Act imposed no duty on employers to prevent colleagues from causing detriment to each other, for example through bullying or harassment (*Fecitt & Others v NHS Manchester* [2011] EWCA Civ 1190.) In response to this decision, Section 19 of the Enterprise and Regulatory Reform Act 2013 has amended the 1996 Act so that whistle-blowers are now protected from detriment from colleagues, as well as from employers. Whilst employment tribunals have the authority to reinstate a dismissed employee, given the breakdown of trust on both sides, this may not be attractive to either party and is rarely used. Reflecting the reality that reinstatement is unlikely, the Public Interest Disclosure (Compensation) Regulations 1999 does not specify an upper limit on the amount of compensation payable to those suffering detriment.

From 2013 to 2014 there were 2,212 applications made to an Employment Tribunal under the Public Interest Disclosure Act. The success rate of cases that proceed to hearings is low – approximately from 3 to 5 per cent – with the majority being settled by ACAS (Advisory, Conciliation and Arbitration Service), settled privately or withdrawn (Ashton 2015: 38). Whether the reforms introduced by PIDA have been successful in helping change workplace culture remains an open question (Lewis 2010; Ashton 2015). In the context of patient safety, NHS bodies have been obliged by the Department of Health to establish whistle-blowing policies within the framework of the PIDA. Connected to this, guidance issued after the introduction of the Act also prohibited NHS employers from using so-called gagging clauses to attempt to silence employees from speaking up (Health Service Circular 1999). However, the whistle-blowing stories summarised above suggest that such policies have at times been circumvented and that the act has had limited impact in encouraging greater transparency and protection for those raising concerns. Survey research tends to corroborate this: in 2012 a survey by the Medical Protection Society reported that only 11 per cent of respondents said they would be confident of the process if they blew the whistle (MPS 2012).

Further evidence about a workplace culture that is resistant to colleagues raising concerns was revealed in a report by Robert Francis QC into creating an open and honest reporting culture in the NHS (Francis 2015). The review received submissions from 600 individuals and 43 organisations. More than 19,500 responded to staff surveys. This high number in itself reflects the level of concern amongst healthcare professionals about the safety of raising concerns. The report confirms that the two main reasons staff give for not speaking up are the fear of personal repercussions and the futility of so doing. More broadly, it notes 'a culture within many parts of the NHS that deters staff from raising serious and sensitive concerns and which not infrequently has negative consequences for those brave enough to raise them' (Francis executive summary 2015: 8). The report calls for a culture that embraces safety, speaking up about concerns, and one which is free from bullying. The Department of Health accepted the recommendations in the Francis report, including the appointment of a 'freedom to speak up guardian' in every NHS organisation, overseen by a national guardian, as part of the CQC. It also recommends that every NHS organisation provides training to its staff in raising concerns and responding appropriately (DOH 2015d).

Whilst such initiatives are encouraging, it remains to be seen whether they are able to alter entrenched aspects of medical culture observed by the empirical studies noted above and further illustrated by the documented experiences of whistle-blowers. This culture has been resistant to criticism and external accountability and has been marked by a lack of openness around safety failings. What strategies are likely to transform medical workplace culture so that staff are encouraged to raise concerns and feel supported and protected when they do? This is clearly far from easy and depends on a number of factors. It involves the input of law and regulation in setting out rules that protect whistle-blowers. The treatment of whistle-blowers described in this chapter suggest that such laws have had limited effect in enabling staff to safely raise concerns. Stronger laws may be part of the solution. For example, Norway appears to have a much higher rate of healthcare workers raising concerns and seeing those concerns being acted upon, which may be explained by laws that offer greater protection for those raising concerns in Norway (Skivenes and Trygstad 2010). It may also be that such laws are more likely to be effective within the context of a no-fault system of medical liability, a version of which has existed in Norway under its Patient Injury Compensation Act 2001 (Johnsen 2006). However, creating an environment conducive to safely raising concerns will also depend on having managers and organisations that constantly and consistently value and respond promptly to such concerns. Above all, it depends on a system of medical education, training and socialisation that values vigilance and the raising of concerns and shuns secrecy and silence. It is here that the modern form of professionalism outlined in Chapter 1 is so important. Patient safety scholars have noted that successful change tends to happen at a local level and must be led by those working and receiving care (Vincent et al. 2013). There is ample evidence that the success of safety initiatives, guidelines or policies depend to a large extent on their legitimacy with professionals (Currie et al. 2009; Martin et al. 2015). The peer pressure form of control, evident in the ethnographic studies summarised at the start of this chapter, remains highly significant even in a reformed medical professionalism. Rules and policies that encourage staff to raise concerns therefore need to be accepted and supported by professionals. It is only when raising concerns is considered to be a desirable professional norm that legal and regulatory mechanisms will be most effective. This connection between regulation and professionalism is also true in relation to being open with patients who have suffered medical harm, which will now be discussed.

Saying Sorry

Raising concerns or speaking up is an important aspect of a culture that prioritises safety. Being honest with patients in the aftermath of medical harm is also an integral feature of this culture. The ethical case for doctors to disclose errors to patients is clear and based on the importance of truth-telling and respect for persons (Berlinger 2005; Smith and Forster 2000). However, this apparent ethical consensus has not prevented an 'ethically embarrassing debate' within healthcare about whether or not to disclose such harmful events (Leape and Berwick 2005: 2388). Whilst the evidence suggests that the principle of disclosure is widely supported by professionals, nevertheless, there is a large gap between principle and practice. A National Audit Office report (2005: 4) revealed that only 24 per cent of English hospital trusts routinely informed patients who had been victims of adverse incidents. Research from the United States has suggested a disclosure rate of between 30 and 40 per cent (Blendon et al. 2002; Lopez et al. 2009). This evidence also suggests that doctors are less likely to disclose when errors are not obvious to patients or when they have more serious consequences. Regrettably, disclosure is often half-hearted and based on half-truths (O'Connor et al. 2010).

Although informing patients that medical treatment has caused them harm is clearly 'the right thing to do', a complex range of factors conspire to explain this disclosure gap. Proponents of disclosure cannot ignore the medico-legal fears that *might* serve to discourage disclosure. Survey research in the United States and Australia confirms the suspicion that the fear of law is the main barrier to the practice of open disclosure (Gallagher et al. 2003; Studdert et al. 2010). Whilst the same sort of survey research evidence is currently lacking in the UK, the statutory assurance under Section 2 of the Compensation Act 2006, that an apology or offer of redress is not an admission of liability or breach of statutory duty, is unlikely to reassure professionals who are considering disclosing. The reluctance to disclose such events to patients is not only explained by the fear of litigation, or indeed of other forms of accountability. It might also reflect a sense of misplaced paternalism that such disclosures might harm patients psychologically and damage their trust. Another factor is the reality that disclosing and apologising is time-consuming for busy

professionals who may have moved onto the next patient. More fundamentally, it is explained by the shortcomings of medical education, which
has not prioritised the necessary communication skills necessary for effective disclosure (Leape et al. 2010).

Efforts to encourage candour by regulators (GMC 2008) and patient
safety agencies (NPSA 2009) are of recent origin. Interestingly, tort law
has long considered the *possibility* that that professionals ought to be
under a legal duty of candour in relation to their work. For example, in
Lee v South West Thames Regional Health Authority [1985] 1 W.L.R. 845
Sir John Donaldson MR stated that 'some thought should be given to
what is the duty of disclosure owed by a doctor and a hospital to a patient
after treatment', albeit that this issue wasn't central to the appeal in that
case. In *Naylor v Preston* [1987] 1 W.L.R. 958, the same judge went
further in stating that 'in professional negligence cases, and in particular
in medical negligence cases, there is a duty of candour resting on the
professional man' (at p. 967). Such a duty should hardly be considered
radical – after all, the duty of care in negligence, as discussed in Chapter 5,
now endorses the prudent patient test for determining the standard of
care in relation to information disclosure *before* medical intervention, so
it could be argued that this should also include communication *after*
treatment.

However, the law of tort has not evolved to create such a legal duty for
post-treatment disclosure. The most egregious example of the failure of
the courts to endorse such a duty arose in the sad story of Robbie Powell,
who died in 1990 after doctors failed to diagnose his Addison's disease.
Whilst the Health Authority admitted liability and made a payment of
£80,000 in respect of the death, in *Powell v Boladz* (1998) 39 BMLR 35,
which was an action for psychiatric harm suffered by his parents, the
Court of Appeal held that no duty of care existed between the doctor and
Robbie's parents. Regrettably, the court held that the doctors were not
legally obliged to explain the circumstances surrounding the death of
Robbie to his parents, thus further illustrating tort law's ambivalent
relationship with patient safety. Whilst the General Medical Council
responded to the case by revising its guidelines to oblige candour in
such circumstances (GMC 2008), the Powells were refused leave to
appeal to the House of Lords. Their case was unsuccessful at the
European Court of Human Rights, which endorsed the shameful situation that 'doctors have no duty to give parents of a child who died as
a result of their negligence a truthful account of the circumstances of
the death, nor even to refrain from deliberately falsifying records'

(*Powell v UK* Application no. 45305/99 admissibility decision of 4 May 2000). Whilst the decision of the Court of Appeal in *Powell v Boladz* has since been overruled by the House of Lords in a different context (*Customs and Excise Commissioners v Total Network SL* [2008] UKHL 19), the common law has yet to establish a duty of candour, despite the long campaign led by Mr William Powell (Powell 2014).

Tort law is a limited and reactive mechanism for encouraging candour, and less preferable to a duty enshrined in statute. Such a duty is now contained in Regulation 20 of the Health and Social Care Act 2008 (Regulated Activities) Regulations 2014. This is an obligation on health service bodies (as opposed to individuals) to act in an open and transparent way in relation to care and treatment, and specifically to inform patients of a 'notifiable safety incident'. The potential benefits of such a duty will be considered further below. But before doing so, it is worth reflecting on the medical resistance to creating a legal duty of candour, which further illustrates the lack of a developed culture of safety. For example, a statement by the Medical Defence Union (2009) in response the House of Commons Health Committee recommendation for introducing a statutory duty of candour in 2009 is revealing and worth quoting in full:

> We do not support the Committee's recommendation that the CMO's proposal for a statutory duty of candour be considered. The inference of the recommendation is that no effective duty of candour currently exists, but this is not the case for doctors who already have an ethical duty and our experience is that doctors do raise concerns. We do not know what the sanction would be if such a legal duty were introduced, but doctors can already be erased from the medical register if their fitness to practise is impaired because they have not complied with GMC guidance. Surely that is sanction enough?

This statement was problematic in a number of respects. The claim that an ethical duty of candour is effective is inconsistent with the research evidence, which reveals a relatively low rate of disclosure to patients (O'Connor 2010). Relying on the General Medical Council to enforce the ethical duty also appears to be somewhat misplaced. A parliamentary debate in 2010 revealed that the GMC had not dealt with a single case for breach of the duty contained in its guidance (HC Debate 1 December 2010, cols 276WH.) Despite these less than convincing objections, the government initially ruled out legislation and instead attempted to encourage greater openness through a contractual obligation on providers. This requires providers to publish a 'declaration of a commitment to openness' on their websites, failure of which could lead to financial deductions (DOH 2011). This contractual duty is limited in that it does not apply to primary care contractors – thus excluding GPs, dentists, and opticians from the requirements, but more fundamentally, undervalues the significance of openness by confining it within a term of a contract.

As with many of the reforms to the regulation of patient safety, it was ultimately the power of events that led to the decision to draft a statutory duty – in particular, recommendation number 181 of the Francis inquiry report into Mid Staffordshire (2013). Whilst not the first official report to call for a legal duty (see Kennedy 2001; DOH 2003; HCHS 2009), the combination of the media coverage of the Mid Staffordshire report and the campaigning efforts of William Powell and the patient safety charity Action Against Medical Accidents (AvMA) persuaded the Government to legislate (DOH 2014c: 11). The Department of Health had initially intended (in line with the Francis recommendation) that such a duty would be limited to cases where death or serious harm was caused. However, intervention by AvMA persuaded the Secretary of State for Health to commission a review on whether the threshold for the duty should be lowered to include moderate harm. Debating the degree of harm necessary to trigger a legal duty to tell the truth is somewhat unedifying, as is the prospect of hospitals waiting to discover the outcome of substandard care before disclosing. The case for being candid should not depend on whether the harm caused is classified as serious or moderate, which is objectionable in principle and also counterproductive to the aim of encouraging greater openness to patients and opportunities for learning (Quick 2014). Thankfully, a subsequent review concluded strongly in favour of setting the threshold for triggering the duty at moderate harm (Dalton and Williams 2014).

The details of the duty are contained in Regulation 20 of the Health and Social Care Act 2008 (Regulated Activities) Regulations 2014. It applies to NHS hospital trusts in England from 1 October 2014 and to all other care providers registered with the CQC from 1 April 2015. It imposes a general duty to act in an open and transparent way in relation to care and treatment provided to patients. More specifically, patients or their carers must be informed that a 'notifiable safety incident' has occurred, which entails being given an account of what happened, advice on what further inquiries are deemed appropriate and also include a verbal and written apology. A notifiable safety incident is defined as an unintended or unexpected incident which could or has resulted in death, severe harm, moderate harm or prolonged psychological harm. The threshold of moderate harm is defined as 'any patient safety incident that resulted in a moderate increase in treatment (return to surgery, unplanned readmission, prolonged episode of care, extra time in hospital) and which caused significant but not permanent harm' (NPSA 2009). The duty is placed on organisations rather than individuals, though it is hoped that patients are informed by doctors involved in their care. Receiving an explanation and apology from someone unconnected to the delivery of care, such as an administrative officer, is less likely to satisfy patients or help encourage the required cultural change in patient-professional relationships. Ultimately, research will be needed to evaluate the implementation of the duty of candour and whether its enforcement is effective in terms of encouraging greater openness around patient safety incidents.

However, there are reasons to be positive about the potential transformative power of this legal duty created by Parliament. It sends a strong signal to organisations and individuals about acceptable behaviour and is more likely to attract attention and affect behaviour than the preexisting unenforceable aspirations contained in documents such as the NHS constitution, or guidelines developed by the National Patient Safety Agency (2009). This is not to suggest that a legal duty of candour is in any way a solution to problems such as those that caused the failures at Mid Staffordshire. It is part of the broader question of what is the optimum amount and type of law and regulation for helping to secure safer healthcare. However, whilst candour is only one part of this, it is arguably a very significant one. For example, although cultural change is likely to evolve from locally led initiatives and teams of professionals engaging with the science of safety, nevertheless, law has an important role in setting standards and accelerating progress. And in the spirit of smart regulation, legal duties should be consistent with ethical responsibilities. As noted in Chapter 4, behavioural change is much more likely when various sources of influence such as law, medical education, regulation, guidelines and peer group norms are consistent in requiring openness around safety.

Being candid about safety issues has significance beyond ethical and legal implications. Arguably, honesty also has the potential to alter the dynamics of power and trust within patient-professional relationships. Requiring professionals to offer face-to-face explanations to patients and their families for medical harm can help transform the culture within healthcare, which has been characterised by weak forms of accountability and a lack of openness. One of the main criticisms of the prevailing culture in medicine has been the reluctance to be open and speak up about safety issues. By requiring disclosure as a matter of law, it is to be hoped that this will help create the open and learning culture which, as we have seen, is necessary for improving safety. However, some have expressed concern that a legal duty might be counterproductive to openness by actually discouraging the admission of mistakes. This argument is based more on fear and supposition as opposed to any credible evidence. In fact, it could be argued that any prevailing culture of openness is currently so weak that there is little that a legal duty could actually damage. This may or may not be true, but debates about the duty of candour have given undue weight to the unproven claim that creating a legal duty would be detrimental to safety culture. This ignores the possibility that sending out a strong signal in favour of honesty, coupled with appropriate safeguards for individual professionals who raise concerns, may accelerate cultural change. This begs the question about what safeguards are appropriate in order to strike a balance between protecting staff who speak up and ensuring transparency and accountability to patients. Some have argued for a Chinese wall between systems for learning and those of accountability and discipline, with only limited exceptions for gross or criminal behaviour (Legemaate 2011). With this in mind, Australia and Canada have introduced qualified privilege laws that protect disclosures from discovery in legal proceedings. In Australia, whilst protections differ between different states, the laws do not protect professionals in relation to all aspects of disclosure, and are a limited shield from liability (Studdert and Richardson 2010). The Canadian compromise of disclosing facts to patients but keeping opinions private for professional review is a difficult and unjustifiable distinction to draw (Gilmour 2011). At the time of writing, the Department of Health in England has announced its intention to create a Health Investigation Safety Branch to investigate patient safety incidents. The Secretary of State for Health has stated that disclosures will 'not normally be able to be used in disciplinary or legal proceedings' unless disclosure is ordered by a court (DOH 2016). It remains to be seen how the details of this will be worked out and whether it supports or contradicts the duty of candour.

It could be argued that the lack of empirical evidence about the deterrent effect of tort law on unsafe practice might suggest that a duty of candour will also be ineffective. But this is to confuse the different concepts of competency and honesty. Putting it simply, being honest is easier than being error-free. Arguably, one of the reasons for legitimately doubting the safer medicine thesis in relation to negligence actions is that errors are an inevitable feature of medical work. This is likely to be the main reason why the incidence of adverse events has no clear connection to systems of fault or no fault liability. The apparent failure of the tort system to discourage unsafe practices does not mean that a duty of candour will be similarly unsuccessful. But a duty of candour is more likely to be effective as part of a system that abandons the fault and blame aspects of negligence. In particular, it would ideally be introduced alongside a no-fault compensation scheme, akin to those operating in New Zealand and the Nordic countries as discussed in Chapter 5. Professionals might be thought more likely to disclose harmful events with the reassurance that they will not face legal or regulatory repercussions, unless the conduct in question suggests criminal behaviour or a continued risk to the safety of others.

Interestingly, the fear that disclosure may decrease trust or trigger complaints appears to be exaggerated. Indeed, there is some evidence that disclosure may actually increase patients' perception of the quality of care received. For example, Lopez et al. (2009) found that disclosure of adverse events doubled the odds of patients giving high ratings to the quality of care – even amongst patients suffering harm as a result. This raises the possibility that disclosure may not only be ethically appropriate but also effective in decreasing the risk of litigation and improving patient feedback. However, the empirical evidence for this remains thin: for example, Studdert et al. (2007), in a study drawing on the opinions of 78 experts, suggest that disclosure is an implausible risk management strategy in that greater disclosure is likely to mean increased litigation and costs. This is supported by Wu et al. (2009) in a study suggesting that whilst disclosure increases patient trust and their ratings of physicians, it does not decrease the propensity to sue. Overall, there is limited evidence, and what exists is only based on hypothetical as opposed to real experience of adverse events (O'Connor et al. 2010).

A notable exception to this, and a model for others to follow, is the University of Michigan Health System (UMHS). Since 2001 it has operated an 'open disclosure with offer' system for responding to medical harm causing injury. This aims to compensate patients quickly and fairly when 'unreasonable medical care' causes injury, to support patients in the aftermath of harm and to reduce injuries by learning from patients' experiences (Boothman et al. 2012). This early settlement model has no compensation cap, but an accepted offer waives the legal right to sue (Mello and Gallagher 2010). In a retrospective before-after analysis from 1995 to 2007, Kachalia et al. (2010) present empirical evidence that the number of claims, rate of lawsuits, time for resolution and the costs have all decreased significantly. Comparisons of before and after the introduction of this system found that the UMHS reduced its average monthly rate of new claims from 7.03 to 4.52 and the number of legal actions from 2.13 to 0.75 per 100,000 patient encounters. Whilst the authors do not to claim a clear causal link here, given that claims declined in general in Michigan in the latter half of the study period, they are nevertheless able to conclude that such a system does not increase costs, and indeed quite possibly reduces them. Perhaps most importantly, such initiatives appear to help professionals and managers move away from a 'deny and defend' culture and embrace a culture of honesty and shared learning around patient safety.

Conclusion: Towards a Culture of Safety

Most studies and inquiries into patient safety have concluded by calling for cultural change. However, trying to change entrenched attitudes and practices is extremely challenging. Any attempt to transform culture has to begin by properly understanding the prevailing 'shop floor culture of medicine' (Bosk 2005: 10). In his public inquiry report into paediatric heart surgery at Bristol, Ian Kennedy also acknowledges the need to honestly appraise culture, including its problematic aspects, in order to accept the need for change (2001: Chapter 22.15).

> To change a culture takes time; it takes a sense of direction and it takes determination. There are no short cuts. Patience is required. And, during this process of change, understanding by all of all is essential. If a way forward is to be charted, the first stage must be an open and honest appraisal of the culture in which healthcare is practised and an acceptance that it must develop. This process is not free from pain, particularly when those who work in the NHS already feel bruised and hurt. But it is a process which must be negotiated, for change depends on a recognition of the need to change.

This chapter has explored aspects of medical culture that clearly require change. The negative experiences of individuals who have blown the whistle about clinical incompetence and unsafe systems offer powerful examples of this culture. Whilst speaking up about safety concerns is ethically appropriate, it nevertheless disturbs well-established norms of professional loyalty, hierarchy and etiquette. Similarly, whilst professionals have tended to support the principle of open disclosure to patients, this has not translated into routinely admitting such mistakes.

A culture of safety depends on a variety of factors including honesty, openness, accountability, teamwork and a commitment to learning. Such a culture would welcome those who raise concerns rather than ignoring or penalising them. It would also encourage staff to fully comply with the legal duty of candour. In short, a safety culture must be intolerant of unsafe practices and environments and be honest with patients about medical harm. However, creating a culture and system of regulation that prioritises safety has been described as a 'humanitarian, sociological, and anthropological long game' (McCartney 2016). Whilst this is clearly reliant on the input of those who manage and monitor healthcare, it also requires those who deliver care and treatment to take the lead in behaving in ways that are compatible with safety. Being vigilant about safety and being open with patients is essential to the model of professionalism outlined in Chapter 1. It also requires professionals to encourage patients and their carers to be more active in terms of helping secure the safety of care, which is the focus of the final chapter.

9

Patients, Carers and Safety

This final chapter argues that patients and their families should be encouraged and empowered to play a greater role in ensuring the safety of care. Involving patients with decisions about their treatment is now accepted as the norm in modern healthcare systems, reflecting the principle of patient autonomy. Indeed, this is arguably the greatest achievement of the disciplines of medical law and ethics (Kennedy 1991; Jackson 2001; Maclean 2013). However, the idea that patients and their carers might also help secure the *safety* of care is much more radical. It runs counter to the perception of patients (and their carers) as passive recipients of healthcare who lack the required knowledge and expertise to make a meaningful contribution to safety. This is related to the concern that greater patient and carer involvement risks encroaching on professional autonomy over the technical aspects of medical work, and also that it risks or reflects an erosion of patients' trust in healthcare professionals. The professional dominance thesis outlined in Chapter 1 left little space for active patients, especially with regard to monitoring and evaluating the quality and safety of care. In this dominant theory of medical professionalism, doctors control the technical autonomy of work, including the way that mistakes and safety incidents are defined and dealt with. This model of professionalism leaves little room for the valuable role that patients and their carers can play in enhancing safety.

Efforts to improve safety have tended to focus exclusively on the education, training and regulation of professionals, and more recently on the regulation of healthcare organisations. However, this chapter will argue that it is legitimate and necessary to involve patients and their carers in attempts to ensure the safety of care. Patients are uniquely placed to comment about and question the safety of care, given their involvement in all aspects of care, unlike the wide range and number of healthcare professionals treating them at different times. The individual patient 'is the one common denominator across all their care experiences, making them a natural source for information across healthcare boundaries, health professionals, services and care settings' (O'Hara and Isden 2013: 4). In England, patient involvement in healthcare decisions is now a legal requirement, both in terms of the common law of informed consent (discussed in Chapter 5) and the Health and Social Care Act 2012, which amended Section 14 of the NHS Act 2006 and placed a duty on commissioners to promote the involvement of patients and their carers in decisions about prevention, diagnosis, care and treatment. However, whilst this is now a matter of legal obligation, the question of *how* to engage patients and their families remains problematic in practice. Successfully engaging patients with the safety of their care challenges the prevailing culture of medicine where doctors have dominated and left insufficient space for the input of patients and their carers. This chapter will examine how patients and carers can make valuable contributions to the study and delivery of safer healthcare, with reference to some powerful examples of failures to involve patients and carers sufficiently.

The Role of Patients and Carers

The role of patients and carers may be seen as a type of informal regulation of safety and quality. Patients may be involved before, during and after treatment, whether through discussing treatment options, asking safety relevant questions, providing feedback, and even helping design service delivery and regulation. On a more formal level, patients and carers have mobilised themselves into pressure groups to campaign about problems at particular hospitals or in relation to specific issues, such as the call for a duty of candour in healthcare. A review of the available evidence reveals that the main approaches to involving patients in safety improvement include: collecting feedback retrospectively (whether through surveys or complaints), involving patients in planning service change, and encouraging patients to help identify risks during their care (Health Foundation 2013). A more detailed explanation of the ways in which patients can engage with the safety of their care is provided by Coulter (2011: 110):

- choosing a safe healthcare provider
- helping with an accurate diagnosis
- participating in treatment decisions
- contributing to safe medication use

- participating in infection control initiatives (especially by monitoring hand hygiene)
- checking the accuracy of medical records
- observing and checking care processes
- identifying and reporting complications and adverse events
- effective self-care and monitoring treatments, feedback and advocacy on safety issues.

Most grievances from patients and their families about safety problems revolve around poor communication. The literature about why people complain and turn to law strongly supports this (Genn 1999; Mulcahy 2003). In the healthcare context, the most common examples of this include insufficient discussion about treatment options, including where treatment takes place and who carries it out, and inadequate attention to concerns expressed by patients and their families, especially in relation to the standard of care and to explanations about failures of care. A range of factors might explain why professionals tend to underplay the concerns of patients and their families, but this is closely tied up with notions of expertise and legitimacy. Under a system of professional dominance, lay concerns can be dismissed as unfounded or purely based on emotion rather than the more detached and valued clinical assessment. As Coulter puts it, patient expertise is often seen as a 'fluffy notion that lacks the solid underpinning of scientific rigour on which medical care is supposedly built' (2011: Preface). The tendency to undervalue concerns expressed by patients and their carers can be regarded as a distinctive type of epistemic injustice called 'testimonial injustice'. This concept is used to describe situations where 'a speaker receives an unfair deficit of credibility from a hearer owing to prejudice on the hearer's part' (Fricker 2007: 9). The patient-professional relationship is a classic example where such testimonial injustice is allowed to exist, that is, where too much credibility is given to the words of doctors and too little credibility to the words spoken by patients because of prejudices about their appropriate roles as professionals or patients. Unfortunately, this can have negative implications for the safety of care.

Whilst the research evidence on the impact of involving patients is currently thin (Health Foundation 2013), nevertheless, there remain good reasons why patients and their families should be involved much more with the safety of care. In terms of the ethics of care, it is clear that patients should be centrally involved in treatment decisions and therapies that concern their well-being. This is based on the principle of patient autonomy and has been nicely reflected in the expression 'no decision about me without me' (DOH 2012). Some have questioned the automatic prioritisation of autonomy over other ethical concepts (Brazier 2006), and others doubted whether the meaning of autonomy in healthcare contexts has been appropriately interpreted (Entwistle et al. 2010a). However, it is arguable that healthcare professionals who show respect for ethical principles such as patient autonomy and beneficence are more likely to be behaving in a way which respects patient safety (Hoppe 2011: 61). There are also practical benefits given that patients are often the first to notice that something is wrong with them and best understand their experience of ill health. Importantly, families who have observed harms caused by safety shortfalls appear willing to report their concerns to medical staff, which is in contrast to the relatively low level of reporting of safety concerns by doctors (Vincent and Davis 2012; Daniels et al. 2012). Patients and families who do speak up are able to express anger or amazement at issues such as insufficient bed space or unsafe staffing levels, which are often seen as 'normal' by those familiar with the system (Morris 2014).

Active patients may also be safer patients. There is some evidence that patients who participate more actively in their own care may be around 50 per cent less likely to suffer an adverse event during their hospital stay. Interestingly, such patients also judged the quality of care more favourably. This study by Weingart et al. (2011: 273) suggests that 'participatory patients observed, identified and communicated potential problems before they resulted in medical injuries' and that safety is thus a product of the interaction between patients, their families and the professionals and hospitals treating them. However, the authors acknowledge that the impact of patient participation on patient safety is complex and methodologically challenging (2011: 275). Overall, the amount and quality of evidence about this point is quite thin, which in itself reflects the fact that insufficient attention has been given to the perspective of patients. Nevertheless, it is clear that understanding the patient and carer experience is ethically important in terms of the commitment to creating a culture of openness and learning around patient safety.

A further attraction of greater patient involvement with safety is the capacity it has for enabling a healthier form of professional accountability. When things go wrong with healthcare treatment, patients and their families are the most important audience in terms of accountability. As argued in the previous chapter, being honest with patients about medical harm has the capacity for allowing a healthy face-to-face form of accountability to develop in professional-patient relationships. Regulators are (by definition) distant organisations who are removed from the day-to-day provision of care. The idea of greater face-to-face accounting to patients is likely to be far more effective than the impersonal approach of complains procedures and litigation. This is not to deny that many patients and carers prefer not to speak up about their concerns due to the fear of being seen as challenging or awkward. Unfortunately, patients worry that by speaking up they will be perceived negatively as 'complainants' (as opposed to 'engaged patients'), and that this may adversely affect the quality of care received. For example, Entwistle et al. (2010b) found that such reluctance by patients was explained by the fear that they would be deemed difficult and that this might affect the therapeutic relationship. Whilst the hurt and emotions involved in particularly serious incidents might mean that face-to-face discussions are difficult and might not result in a satisfactory resolution for all concerned, it should at least form the starting point. Based on the conceptualisation of trust advanced in Chapter 3, openly involving patients arguably has the potential for leading to healthier trusting relationships between professionals and patients. This requires that medical education and training places greater emphasis on the skills that are necessary for informing patients about adverse events and caring for them in the aftermath of this.

In order to understand the experience of patients and their carers, a number of case studies are now considered. These are all instances where the legitimate safety concerns of carers were not appropriately acted upon. They are sometimes emotionally charged examples of strong individuals who have suffered significantly yet nevertheless campaigned vigorously for accountability and improvements to safety. They serve as a reminder of the profound effect that safety failures have on patients and their families, illustrating the harms caused not just by safety lapses, but by a culture that struggles with fallibility and honesty. They also suggest the steps that are needed to make long-term improvements to the safety of patients. The secondary harm caused by concealing the truth has long been acknowledged. For example, Jean Robinson, former chair of the Patients Association and a lay member of the General Medical Council, reflecting on her experience of disciplinary cases, commented that: 'What impressed me was not just the extent of the medical disasters, but also the profound additional damage inflicted when patients and the bereaved failed to get answers and were met with a stone wall of silence or outright lies' (Robinson 1999: 246) This is not only painful for families but is also wasteful of an invaluable resource about the patient's experience of illness and the quality and safety of care delivered. These accounts illustrate ineffective systems for handling concerns and tragedies suffered by families and also reveal the limited progress that has been made towards normalising the patient or carer centred view of healthcare. But whilst these are ultimately sad stories of failure and harm, they have also led to positive changes to the regulatory and legal landscape of patient safety. It is the determination of these courageous individuals that has driven such change.

Bristol Heart Children's Action Group (BHCAG)

This action group with over 300 members was set up in response to concerns about the mortality rate for paediatric heart surgery at Bristol Royal Infirmary between 1988 and 1995. The background to what became known as the 'Bristol babies' story was described in Chapter 1. Stephen Bolsin, a consultant anaesthetist at the hospital, began recording surgical results to test his unease over the length and outcomes of operations performed by two consultant surgeons, James Wisheart and Janardan Dhasmana. He raised his concerns with the hospital chief executive, and after failing to get a satisfactory response, passed on his concerns to the Department of Health. The story was first reported by Dr Phil Hammond writing in *Private Eye* on 8 May 1992, but it was not until early 1995 that the surgeons were prevented from operating at the hospital. There followed the largest and most expensive disciplinary case in the history of the General Medical Council. The surgeons were charged with serious professional misconduct for continuing to perform surgery despite high mortality rates; Mr Wisheart also stood accused of misleading parents by underestimating the risks that children would be exposed to. After a 65-day hearing in which 67 witnesses responded to more than 2,500 questions, the allegations were found to have been proven. James Wisheart was erased from the medical register whilst Janardan Dhasmana was prevented from operating on children for three years (Quick 1999).

The BHCAG group successfully campaigned for a public inquiry, which was led by the distinguished medical lawyer Professor Ian Kennedy (2001). The main grievances of the families were that surgeons continued to perform operations despite knowing about their higher than average mortality rates. In terms of the role of carers in helping to ensure patient safety, the most relevant issue here is that of choosing a safe healthcare provider. Many parents argued that had they been aware about the high complication rates for paediatric heart surgery at Bristol, and given the option of referral elsewhere at units with better outcomes, they would have chosen that option. In a paper submitted to the Kennedy inquiry, the BHCAG stated clearly that: 'We, as parents, without exception, would have taken our children anywhere in the world to secure the highest standards of medical care, circumstances may dictate otherwise, but that is for the parent to decide!' (BHCAG 2000). Parents were also frustrated that their expertise as parents of their children, in terms of sensing a worsening of their condition, was often ignored. As the BCHAG pointed out in a position paper submitted to the second phase of the inquiry 'it is here that the parents have the expertise and not the medical profession' (BHCAG 2000). This underplaying of parental concerns, partly because they were expressed by emotional parents rather than detached professionals, is a good example of what Fricker (2007) has called testimonial injustice.

William Powell and the Campaign for Robbie's Law

William Powell led one of the longest campaigns for patient safety reform following the death of his son Robbie in 1990, after the failure to diagnose his Addison's disease. The paediatrician who examined Robbie at hospital had suspected Addison's disease as a possible diagnosis and wrote to his GP advising that a test be conducted should Robbie continue to have symptoms. The test was never carried out and the information about this suspected diagnosis was never given to his parents. Had they known of this (which arguably they should have), they would have been able to request that the test (which may have saved Robbie's life) be performed sooner. Robbie was examined by a number of GPs both at the practice and at the family home, but the concerns of the family were not treated sufficiently seriously. Regrettably, the last GP to examine Robbie at home refused to call an ambulance to take him to hospital, leaving his parents to drive him there. He died shortly after being admitted. Whilst the Health Authority admitted liability and made a payment of £80,000 in respect of the death, in an action for psychiatric harm suffered by his parents the Court of Appeal held that no duty of care existed between the doctor and the parents (*Powell v Boladz (1998) 39 B.M.L.R. 35*). In denying that doctors were legally obliged to explain the circumstances surrounding the death of Robbie to his parents, this was a further illustration of tort law's weak relationship with patient safety, as explored in Chapter 5. This was duly recognised in the revised GMC guidelines to practitioners in the aftermath of this case (GMC 1998), yet the Powells were refused leave to appeal to the House of Lords and were unsuccessful at the European Court of Human Rights, which endorsed the shameful situation that 'doctors have no duty to give parents of a child who died as a result of their negligence a truthful account of the circumstances of the death, nor even to refrain from deliberately falsifying records' (*Powell v UK* Application no. 45305/99 admissibility decision of 4 May 2000). In fact, there followed a review by the Crown Prosecution Service about whether any offences of forgery or perverting the course of justice were committed in terms of the contents of Robbie's medical records, in addition to the offence of manslaughter by gross negligence. Although no prosecutions were brought, the fact that this was considered indicates the seriousness of this case. Mr Powell has been an active campaigner for a statutory duty of candour, which he has called 'Robbie's Law' in honour of his son (Powell 2014). His considerable efforts in publicising the story of his son's sad death and campaigning for reform were instrumental in exerting pressure to create the legal duty of candour discussed in Chapter 8.

Julie Bailey and Cure the NHS

Cure the NHS was founded by a small group of relatives and patients who successfully campaigned for a public inquiry into the failings of care at Mid Staffordshire NHS Foundation Trust between January 2005 and March 2009. The Health Care Commission investigated the hospital in 2009 and estimated that it had higher than average mortality rates and allowed 'appalling care' to continue (Francis 2013). Julie Bailey, who lost her mother Bella Bailey due to the allegedly poor care at the hospital, was an active leader of this campaign group. The public inquiry, led Robert Francis QC, lasted 31 months and was highly critical of numerous failings at the trust. These included basic failures of care to keep patients clean, nourished and hydrated and also to provide timely pain relief. A shortage of staff, particularly nurses, was identified as one of the major causes of this substandard care. The trust was also criticised for a lack of leadership and for not listening and responding to the feedback from patients and their families. Indeed, a frustrating feature of the Mid Staffordshire story, which is common to the other stories described here, is that carers had noticed and pointed out the examples of unsafe care at the hospital, but these concerns had fallen on deaf ears. As the Francis report noted:

> Trust management had no culture of listening to patients. There were inadequate processes for dealing with complaints and serious untoward incidents (SUIs). Staff and patient surveys continually gave signs of dissatisfaction with the way the Trust was run, and yet no effective action was taken and the Board lacked an awareness of the reality of the care being provided to patients. The failure to respond to these warning signs indicating poor care could be due to inattention, but is more likely due to the lack of importance accorded to these sources of information' (Francis 2013, executive summary 1.9).

Again, this appears to be a classic example of testimonial injustice whereby the concerns of patients and family carers were undervalued. Carers such as Julie Bailey spoke up at the time to voice their concerns about the standards of care received, but the hospital trust failed to respond appropriately. Whilst this failure to act on these concerns may be explained by a number of reasons, chief among them is the absence of a culture whereby concerns voiced by patients and carers are taken sufficiently seriously. The high-profile campaign group led by Julie Bailey was influential in persuading the government to establish a public inquiry and the powerful evidence given was instrumental to the 290 recommendations made in the report. The Government accepted the vast majority of these recommendations (DOH 2014), including implementing the recommended criminal offence of ill treatment or wilful neglect, as discussed in Chapter 6.

James Titcombe and the Morecambe Bay NHS Foundation Trust Inquiry

James Titcombe campaigned about failures in care at the maternity unit of Furness General Hospital, part of the Morecambe Bay NHS Foundation Trust. This followed the death of his baby son Joshua from untreated pneumococcal septicaemia. Joshua's mother, Hoa, and James had been unwell with sore throats and headaches in the days leading up to Joshua's birth, and whilst Hoa had been given antibiotics, none were administered to baby Joshua. Joshua developed sepsis and, despite being transferred to a specialist unit in Newcastle, died aged nine days old. The trust acknowledged that there was a 90 per cent chance that Joshua would have survived had he been treated appropriately and promptly with antibiotics. It also admitted that midwives were not trained to spot the signs of sepsis, which included the low temperature which Joshua had. The aftermath of this tragedy, including the extraordinary lack of transparency and accountability over the substandard care at the maternity unit has been documented in a book called *Joshua's Story*, written by James Titcombe (2015). A frustrating feature of this tragedy is that the concerns raised by James Titcombe were not acted upon by staff. Specifically, his question about why Joshua was not being treated with antibiotics given that his wife was receiving them was wrongly dismissed as being unnecessary. His request that Joshua be reviewed by a paediatrician was also not acted upon. At the inquest into Joshua's death, where a narrative verdict noted the missed opportunities to diagnose and treat his infection, the coroner, Mr Ian Smith, found that there 'was a failure to listen to and understand what the family said, what their concerns were about their own illness and whether that might pass on to Joshua' (Titcombe 2015: 124). Whilst there are sure to be many reasons which may explain why staff failed to take these reasonable questions sufficiently seriously, it is again hard to deny the relevance of the concept of testimonial injustice here: the lay concerns of a loving father were too readily dismissed by the midwifery staff.

James Titcombe's pursuit of the truth about the death of his son led to communications with the hospital, the Health and Safety Executive, the Nursing and Midwifery Council, the National Health Service Litigation Authority, the Care Quality Commission, the local coroner, the police and the ombudsman. However, despite the involvement of so many agencies the search for answers and accountability for the avoidable death of his baby son proved extremely challenging and all-consuming. Although the initial complaint to the ombudsman about the hospital's investigation (including the disappearance of crucial medical records) was dismissed, a second complaint was upheld and found that the response to complaints by the authorities demonstrated a lack of openness and that this caused further pain for the family (PHSO 2014b).

Sadly, Joshua Titcombe was not the only avoidable death at the Furness General Hospital maternity unit. Concerns about the standards of care at the unit voiced by a campaign group led by James Titcombe led to an independent investigation into the management, delivery and outcomes of care provided by the maternity and neonatal services at the Trust from January 2004 to June 2013. The inquiry report was highly critical of clinical staff, the hospital and also the system of regulation (Kirkup 2015). In particular, the report was critical of a culture that tolerated poor quality care and failed to be open and honest with those suffering harm:

> What is inexcusable, however, is the repeated failure to examine adverse events properly, to be open and honest with those who suffered, and to learn so as to prevent recurrence. Yet this is what happened consistently over the whole period 2004–12, and each instance represents a significant lapse from the professional duty of NHS staff (Kirkup 2015: 183).

Whilst this is a sad story of failure it has had some positive outcomes. Somewhat unusually, James Titcombe has been employed by the Care Quality Commission as a National Advisor on Patient Safety, Culture & Quality, and has been active in sharing his experiences and campaigning for patient safety (Titcombe 2015). The decision to recruit a bereaved father and campaigner for patient safety to work for the sector regulator is clearly of great symbolic importance in underlining the value of the carer experience. But it is also important from a practical perspective in terms of ensuring that such a powerful story is not forgotten and that not only are lessons learned at one hospital unit, but that more widespread cultural changes are encouraged. The capacity of those affected by patient safety failures to channel their grief in order to advocate reform has the potential to help prevent others suffering similar tragedies.

Professional Dominance and Patient Activism

Taken as a whole, these very different examples demonstrate both how unwilling professionals have sometimes been to take patient and carer testimony into account in their treatment and how damaging this can be in practice. They also, however, suggest how powerful individual cases can be in effecting real change in this context. They are all examples whereby the experiential knowledge of patients and their carers has the potential for contributing towards learning and change. However, the ability of patients and their carers to contribute to the safety of care depends on a culture that embraces such involvement. No matter how confident and sophisticated patients and carers may be, they will struggle to make an impact if professionals are not receptive to their involvement. The ability of health professionals to listen effectively depends on many factors such as training and personal communication skills. It requires openness, humility and a willingness to recognise patients as true partners in the delivery of care and treatment. But it also rests on factors beyond their control, such as general workload and the constraints of time within the dedicated appointments system. In short, less time and resources is likely to mean less room for patient engagement. Thus, poor staffing ratios and a general lack of resources are not the ideal conditions for enabling open communication and shared decision making.

The research evidence suggests that the following factors influence the degree of patient engagement with their own safety: illness severity, individual cognitive characteristics, patient-professional relationships and organisational factors (Health Foundation 2013). Clearly, some of these factors are beyond the control of individual professionals. However, they do have significant control over the quality of the patient-professional relationship, specifically, the ability to create an environment where patients and their families are encouraged to play an active role in terms of safety. Patients are generally uncomfortable asking professionals awkward questions about their individual performance or whether they have washed their hands. However, professional encouragement appears to increase the willingness of patients to ask sensitive questions (Davis et al. 2011). In order for patients and carers to be fully engaged and vigilant about safety, the professionals responsible for their care need to be open to such involvement.

Chapter 1 noted how the professional dominance model left insufficient space for the concerns of patients and their families to be taken seriously. This is largely explained by the high degree of autonomy and trust enjoyed by the profession relative to patients. Patient activism around safety clearly challenges professional dominance. Whilst this book has argued that professional dominance is becoming outdated, this does not mean that the alternative is patient dominance. Williamson is correct to note that 'Patient activists, patients trying to improve healthcare for other patients, do not want healthcare professionals to lose their skills, their expertise and their sense of self-worth. Patient activists respect professionals' wish to do good. They wish patients to share professionals' power, making healthcare better for both patients and professionals' (2010: 2).

The tension between professional autonomy and patient participation is a complex one. Recognising patients as experts is counter to the training of health professionals, which reinforces their role as knowledgeable experts and patients as relatively ignorant and inexpert. But this is a somewhat simplistic distinction. Patient centredness is not the same as patient dominance. Patients may only wish to be involved in certain aspects of their care, for example, negotiating visiting hours rather than discussing technical aspects of care. Some patients will choose not to have an active involvement in their treatment (Sieff 2014). But some will (and arguably all should) want to know about the safety of their care and feel able to ask safety relevant questions, including sensitive questions about how many procedures a doctor has performed and how their outcomes compare to others. In order for patients to feel comfortable asking such pertinent questions, the onus is on professionals to communicate effectively with patients and understand what is important for them.

However, the idea of patients and families routinely evaluating the safety of care is a radical departure from the professional dominance thesis. This requires a new style of professionalism that prioritises the safety of patients. At the heart of efforts to engage patients with healthcare, and also to encourage a culture of safety, is the idea of recognising that patients are persons (Entwistle and Watt 2013). This may seem like an odd thing to say – of course patients are people – but the constraints of delivering healthcare services, coupled with the advance of high technology, often means that the patient as a person gets forgotten. Part of this may be attributed to the successes of medicine, especially in treating diseases such as cancer and cardiovascular disease. However, this can sometimes lead to a sense that professionals are dealing with diseases rather than treating people with diseases (Leape, personal communication 8 June 2010). A familiar feature of the case studies set out above revolves around the failure to take sufficient account of patients and carers as people with feelings, emotions and choices to make. As explored in Chapter 2, this has led some to dislike the term 'patient safety' for encouraging a managerial approach concerned with completing paper work and meeting targets rather than caring for people (Kennedy 2006: 29). Kennedy explains that this is about more than just semantics: 'if you see someone as an appointment at 3-o'clock, or a case to treat, or a kidney problem, it requires an effort of mental re-orientation to see a person in front of you. Good professionals, of course, make that effort. But the default person is the atomised un-person . . . the generalist, the professional who still sees people as people, can be regarded by some as anachronistic, someone who cannot keep up with the pace' (Kennedy 2006: 31).

The experiences and successes of patient activists, such as those discussed above, has led some to conceptualise such patient activism as an emancipation movement (Williamson 2010). This radical position suggests the potential for patient activists and groups to challenge medical dominance and ensure a rebalancing of power better to serve the interests of patients. According to Williamson, radical patient activists and patient groups actually create new knowledge to challenge the dominance of medical profession. This is knowledge based on the experiences of patients and their carers, not only with their own ill health, but with the quality and safety of the healthcare received. Williamson analyses events such as those which occurred at the Bristol Royal Infirmary described above as an example of the dominant power of the medical profession in repressing the rights of parents to know the truth. Whilst acknowledging that repression is a strong term in the caring context, she argues that patients' interests can be repressed in three main ways. First, through withholding information denying them the ability to articulate their own interests; secondly, through lack of social and political arrangements for promoting patients' interests; and thirdly through unwillingness to listen to or act on what patients say (2010: 23). Williamson regards such behaviour as coercive as it fails to respect the autonomy of patients. For example, a surgeon who doesn't inform a patient that he has never performed a particular procedure before fails to respect his patient's safety and autonomy (2010: 59.) Similarly, a doctor who underestimates the risks associated with a particular procedure can be said to be repressing his patient's interests. In line with the argument in Chapter 3, withholding information is also arguably a sign of a lack of trustworthiness in health professionals, and potentially renders patients' trust in them 'misplaced' or even 'rotten' (Baier 1986; O'Neill 2002).

However, it is worth noting that patients and their carers may ask safety relevant questions which require little, if any, knowledge about medicine or healthcare. For example, questions about whether the correct drug or dosage has been prescribed or whether staff have complied with hand hygiene protocols do not require any expertise other than the understandable desire to help ensure safe outcomes. The question asked by James Titcombe about whether his son Joshua might need antibiotics, given that his mother had been prescribed them, is another good example. Such questions may not always be warmly welcomed by healthcare professionals who may not appreciate what might be regarded as excessive vigilance or an intrusion on their professional judgement. But such questions are entirely legitimate and do not require any special knowledge. Neither should they be regarded as challenging expert authority. Arguably, such questions should be encouraged as part of a culture and professionalism that prioritises safety.

Conclusion

The idea that patients, in their role as consumers of healthcare, can have something important to say about the quality of care is not new (Donabedian 1992). Nor is the idea that people as moral agents should exercise some control over important issues that affect them. 'Patient centred healthcare' or 'patient engagement' has long been part of the rhetoric of government and regulatory policy statements. Regrettably, the active involvement of patients and carers has tended to be looked down upon as an unwelcome intrusion into professional terrain. Echoing Ivan Illich's blast against the ills of medicalisation and the consequent inability of patients to care for themselves, Williamson has said that 'Falling back on patients for some important task is like falling back on women to replace men in factories during the Second World War. Such moves can be liberating. But they are a mark of how far freedom to contribute responsibly to society has been denied' (2010: 122). This has led Leape et al. to criticise the dysfunctional culture of disrespect that has prioritised individual professional autonomy above teamwork, collaboration and inclusiveness, noting that: 'Doctors, nurses, and other health professionals have been trained to provide care that is patient-centred, but most do not regard patients as true partners in all of the activities and decisions related to their care' (NPSF 2014: 19). This is a shame given the possible benefits of a patient centred approach to delivering healthcare. Focusing on the role of patients and carers reminds us of the ethics of care and compassion that should be central to medical encounters (Held 2006). Importantly, this involves recognising that patients are human beings with a crucial perspective on their own care needing to be recognised and embraced rather than ignored. Patients need to feel that it is not only legitimate but helpful for them to be closely involved in securing the safety of care, which should be the dominant concern.

~

Conclusion

As we have seen throughout this book, patient safety is not easy. It involves complex issues of care, competency, culture, communication and cost. It is also a site of conflict between professionals, patients, managers, organisations, regulators and politicians. Improving safety in healthcare is difficult in ideal conditions, but is particularly challenging in the real world of under-resourced health systems struggling to cope with ageing populations and the increase of chronic conditions (WHO 2011). This book does not claim to have the formula for safer care. There is no one-size-fits-all guide for individuals and institutions to improve the quality and safety of what they do. Patient safety is an emerging field of inquiry and even documented success stories have not fully unlocked the reasons behind their risk reduction and improved outcomes (Pronovost et al. 2011). The question about how care can be made safer remains somewhat elusive. This is not to say that increased efforts to research and reduce medical harm have been futile. Leading safety researchers have concluded that care is getting safer, albeit that presenting clear evidence for this is not straightforward (Vincent and Amalberti 2016). However, the increased desire to understand patient safety and prevent medical harm is in itself something to celebrate; it was not that long ago that regulators and medical commentators resisted and even resented the need to investigate medical harm. Whilst there is much progress to be made, in particular with safety in primary care and social care, patient safety does now attract significant research, is a priority for regulators and is on the political agenda.

However, the problem of patient safety is too complex to be managed by one organisation or a single regulator. This may partly explain why so many actors are involved in monitoring the quality and safety of care. At the coalface, this starts with a multi-disciplinary team of healthcare professionals and healthcare administrators who attempt to provide and organise safe care. Above them are multiple regulators who make up a somewhat crowded and confusing environment. This begins with professional regulators such as the General Medical Council, whose functions include investigating the fitness to practise of its registrants. For most of its existence, the GMC has not concerned itself with questions about the quality and safety of care of medical practitioners. However, as explored in Chapter 4, structural and procedural reforms have led to a GMC with a much stronger focus on protecting patients from unsafe practitioners. These reforms, driven by a crisis of trust in self-regulation, also led to the creation of the Professional Standards Authority for Health and Social Care in order to monitor the effectiveness of professional regulators. Both the GMC and PSA are primarily concerned with the competency and safety of individual practitioners. The more complex and ambitious task of ensuring that healthcare organisations provide safe and effective care is discharged by the Care Quality Commission. On the periphery of regulation, there are medical royal colleges and defence unions who seek to educate and advise their members about appropriate standards of care. A range of activity is sponsored by charitable organisations such as the Health Foundation and the King's Fund, who ensure that the research agenda evolves. Finally, pressure for reform is exerted by patient advocacy groups such as Action Against Medical Accidents (AvMA), which has been relentless (and successful) in campaigning for patient safety reforms.

There is thus no shortage of actors with some responsibility for patient safety or for seeking to influence change. Some have described this as an example of the 'problem of many hands'. This arises when multiple actors, both individuals and organisations, contribute to something, in this case patient safety, but it is difficult to hold any one actor responsible for the effects of their combined actions. Unsurprisingly, this has the effect of frustrating system-level actions that are required in order to manage risk more effectively (Dixon-Woods and Pronovost 2016). Furthermore, there is no coherent system or shared values for trying to ensure patient safety in the first place and plenty of scope for confusion, conflict and inconsistency. This is no surprise given the different aims of various regulatory and legal mechanisms, some prioritising learning and prevention whilst others designed to attribute responsibility and ensure justice between aggrieved parties. However, this should not prevent examination of how existing mechanisms might be better utilised in order to help improve patient safety.

This book has tried to do three things. First, it has explained why the vision of professionalism that characterises the professional dominance model is ill-suited to the needs of patient safety. This is because dominance defends a system where there is too much trust in medical authority, too little involvement of patients and insufficient engagement with the subject of error and harm. As explored in Chapters 1 and 8, this is explained by various aspects of medical culture, including the norm of non-criticism, professional loyalty, the fear of blame and the perceived pointlessness of reporting errors. This is not to say that all aspects of this 'old' professionalism are bad or not well intentioned. For example, the decision not to burden patients with full disclosure of all safety relevant information can also be explained by a paternalistic desire not to create anxiety and distrust amongst patients. However, it is undeniable and regrettable that the dominant profession has not engaged with the study of error and safety, whether through lack of time, knowledge of the key concepts and methods for undertaking such work or for fear of the negative consequences of unearthing problems (Davies 2007). Engaging professionals with the science of improvement and implementation faces considerable challenges, not least because doctors are trained and socialised in a biomedical model and may struggle to relate to knowledge and language from the social sciences, which is necessary for doing improvement science (Marshall and Mountford 2013).

The rise of consumerism, managerialism and regulation has long challenged the dominance thesis and it is now accepted that the state-profession dynamic has significantly altered. This has led some to exaggerate the extent to which the profession has been pushed out of the picture (Furedi 2006). Whether or not professional dominance has in fact diminished is perhaps not critical; it is certainly something which is difficult to evidence. Of more relevance is exploring how professionalism can evolve to embrace patient safety as its dominant concern. This book has argued for a new vision of professionalism that prioritises the safety of patients. Fundamentally, this involves revising the conventional perception of what constitutes a good doctor.

For too long, patients have tolerated clinicians who they regard as technically competent, even if those staff have poor communication skills. This is often reflected in terms of someone being a 'good doctor' but with awful 'bedside manner'. This character, familiar to us all, does not belong in a model of professionalism which is sensitive to the needs of individual patients and requires soft communication skills for explaining risks and medical harm. The model professional should be emotionally intelligent, patient-centred and fully engaged with technological innovations and initiatives in patient safety research.

Modern professionalism must also embrace features of modern health-care systems, such as the emphasis on evidence-based practice and a commitment to accountability and regulation (Martin et al. 2015). It must welcome teamwork and respond positively to the suggestions and scrutiny of others, including those traditionally lower down the power hierarchy. Whilst there are encouraging signs that this shift is already underway, there is much more progress to be made on this front and indeed a risk that talk of a new professionalism remains rhetoric rather than reality. It is crucial that patient safety is not overly medica-lised but rather embraces the active involvement of patients as well as the input and insights of researchers from a range of disciplines.

Secondly, this book has argued that law can do more for patient safety than has generally been accepted. The prevailing position within patient safety research has been to dismiss the role of law as unhelpful and even counterproductive to the aim of improving care. This is partly because law has been viewed negatively and narrowly in terms of legal actions in civil and criminal negligence. Many have claimed that the threat of such actions prevent a culture of safety by making staff less likely to talk openly about error and safety. Both of these legal mechanisms may well hinder efforts to encourage professionals to be more candid, although there is no clear evidence about the connection between such mechanisms and the safety of care. The debate about whether tort law and the threat of litigation deters unsafe care is one that is likely to continue, though as discussed in Chapter 5, the best evidence suggests that it has no or little effect on producing safer care.

However, there is more to law than cases of civil or criminal negli-gence. Chapter 6 explored less visible legal mechanisms, described as regulatory offences, and considered their potential for supporting patient safety improvements. Unlike tort and criminal law, these mechanisms are designed with the overriding aim of improving safety. Health and Safety law, whilst designed in terms of protecting employees as opposed to patients, is nevertheless well suited to managing and minimising the risks within healthcare organisations. This branch of the law, and its enforcement officers, possess the necessary expertise in risk management and ensuring compliance. In focusing squarely on safety, and particularly the contribution of flawed systems, such prosecutions offer a more appropriate response as opposed to mechanisms that focus on individual fault. As the advance of improvement science leads to the greater use of safety protocols and checklists, inspectors would be equipped with more detailed best practice guidelines to supplement the broadly drafted sections of the 1974 Act. However, this would require the H&SE to take on a greater role in terms of investigating patient safety incidents, which seems unlikely given the role of the Care Quality Commission for enforcing breaches of safe standards of care. The criminalisation of these safety breaches is symbolically important in expressing the seriousness of patient safety. Whether or not such measures are effective in helping to improve safety remains to be seen and will largely depend on the enforcement approach of the CQC. Crucially, both these types of offences are aimed at organisations, and thus more likely to have a deterrent effect, in that organisations are better able to implement policies and reward practices that prioritise safety.

The work of coroners is another example where law has the potential for improving patient safety. Whilst coronial investigations are generally limited to ascertaining basic facts about unnatural deaths, the question about 'how' someone died has the potential for broadening out such investigations to consider various circumstances surrounding these deaths. In the context of deaths associated with medical care, the ability of coroners to make 'prevention of future deaths reports' and to communicate these widely is an important function carried out in the name of public health. Chapter 7 explored the wide range of issues identified in such reports, including communication problems, failures to implement guidance or follow care plans, staffing ratios, inadequate training and poor medical record keeping. The ethos of coronial investigations is also consistent with the preferred approach to patient safety failures explored in Chapter 2, which is to eschew individual blame and concentrate instead on system problems and the capacity for learning and prevention. The increase in complaints to coroners and the police from bereaved relatives about standards of medical care, and an increase of inquests into deaths associated with such care suggest that coroners are likely to have plenty to say about the safety of patients.

This is not to overstate the capacity of law for improving patient safety. Reformed medical education, training, greater resources and the creation of a shared culture of safety are much more integral. However, it would be wrong to dismiss law as irrelevant to this. Indeed, such a position overlooks the possibility that some legal duties may help encourage the shift towards a culture of safety. There are countless examples, from other contexts, where law reform has made an obvious contribution to safety culture. Laws mandating the wearing of seatbelts in cars and laws prohibiting smoking in public places have undoubtedly been successful in affecting behavioural change (DFT 2015; LGAR 2007). Of course, healthcare is much more complex than wearing seat belts or not smoking; as Vincent and Amalberti have remarked, it is akin to 20 industries under one banner (2016: 7). However, as argued in Chapter 3, when ethical statements and policy goals are also reflected in legal obligations, then those goals arguably stand a better chance of being realised.

The creation of a legal duty of candour is a good example of this. As discussed in Chapter 8, placing candour on a legal footing encountered much medical resistance. This was partly based on the view that existing duties in professional codes of conduct were sufficient. However, evidence about the low rate of disclosure in practice (O'Connor 2010) and the fact that the GMC has not investigated practitioners for the breach of this duty suggests otherwise. A legal duty created by Parliament has a higher profile and sends a strong signal to organisations and individuals about the need for openness and honesty. This is more likely to be taken seriously than unenforceable aspirations contained in policy statements or ethical guidelines, although this will require evaluation of the implementation of this duty. Candour is also significant in terms of developing the patient-centred model of professionalism discussed throughout this book. Arguably, it also has the potential to alter the dynamics of power and trust within patient-professional relationships. Encouraging professionals to offer face-to-face explanations to patients and their families about medical harm can help transform a culture which has been characterised by weak forms of accountability and a lack of openness. One of the main criticisms of the prevailing culture in medicine has been the reluctance to be open and speak up about safety issues. By requiring disclosure as a matter of law, it is to be hoped that this will help speed up the shift to an open and learning culture. This requires appropriate safeguards for staff who 'risk' being honest with patients about medical harm. Finding an appropriate balance here between providing patients with the whole truth and protecting candid professionals from legal sanctions will be a key task for the newly created Healthcare Safety Investigation Branch.

Finally, this book has argued that patient safety requires the active engagement of patients and their carers. Patients are uniquely placed to comment about and question the safety of care, given their involvement in all aspects of care, unlike the wide range and number of healthcare professionals treating them at different times. The professional dominance model left little space for patients to actively participate in ensuring the safety of their care. As Chapter 9 argued, the alternative is not patient dominance but rather patient centredness. This requires closer and more equal relationships between patients and professionals. This has variously been described as the 'therapeutic alliance' (Teff 1985), 'collaborative consent' (Donabedian, 1992: 249) and 'shared decision making' (Elwyn et al. 2010). For such concepts to be more than just attractive sounding aspirations, there needs to be a genuine recognition of the value of the patient (and carer) experience of healthcare, including the safety of care. Shared decision-making can be rewarding for patients, carers and professionals alike. Berwick (2013: 18) has nicely summarised the main objectives of greater patient involvement in their own care:

> The goal is not for patients and carers to be the passive recipients of increased engagement, but rather to achieve a pervasive culture that welcomes authentic patient partnership – in their own care and in the processes of designing and delivering care. This should include participation in decision-making, goal-setting, care design, quality improvement, and the measuring and monitoring of patient safety. Patients and their carers should be involved in specific actions to improve the safety of the healthcare system and help the NHS to move from asking, "What's the matter?" to, "What matters to you?" This will require the system to learn and practice partnering with patients, and to help patients acquire the skills to do so.

However, whilst the idea of shared decision-making is promising, it may not always be suitable in terms of ensuring the safety of patients. Patients will sometimes need to ask tough questions of those treating them, for example, about the outcomes of their individual care or whether they have complied with hand hygiene protocols. This may not feel like a shared process for professionals who may find such questioning uncomfortable. Patients who ask sensitive questions about the issue of safety can create a sense of uncertainty and awkwardness within therapeutic relationships, and professionals may interpret such vigilance as distrust. However, patients deserve to know the truth about safety and trust in professionals to be honest with them. It may be thought that policy initiatives that seek to encourage such patient engagement may inappropriately shift responsibility for safety from the health service and professionals to patients (Entwistle et al. 2005). Ultimate responsibility for safety should rest with healthcare professionals and healthcare organisations. However, there is a pressing need for patients and their carers to be allowed – indeed encouraged – to help ensure their own safety. Although we cannot mandate patient involvement in healthcare safety, and some patients will prefer not to be so involved, we can legitimately expect professionals to create the conditions where patients feel comfortable taking an active role (Watt 2009: 5). Many patients will need educating and guiding on how they can 'look out' for themselves in terms of helping ensure the safety of their care. The recent publication of an excellent guidebook on how to 'stay safe' in hospitals is a reflection of this need (Warren, Franklin and Vincent 2015).

It is understandable that professionals worry that patients who know too much about safety risks and problems may lose trust. However, this ignores the possibility that involving patients in the safety of their care has the potential for enhancing trusting relationships. As discussed in Chapter 3, patients and their carers might reasonably be expected to have a greater degree of trust in treatment in which they feel fully involved, and where their safety concerns are not ignored. The stories summarised in Chapter 9 reveal the natural feelings of distrust caused by a lack of honesty and a failure to listen to the concerns of patients and their carers. Ensuring that patient engagement helps preserve healthy trust and improve safety is challenging. It requires patients to accept the reality that medicine is a high-risk setting that will never be harm free. It also requires that professionals openly acknowledge safety issues and accept that patients are entitled to ask difficult or sensitive questions. Healthcare professionals who listen carefully to patients and carers, recognising their valuable role in the care process, are likely to be delivering safer care. Patient safety should, after all, be primarily about patients.

BIBLIOGRAPHY

Abbott, A. (1988). *The System of Professions: An Essay on the Division of Expert Labor*, Chicago: University of Chicago Press.

Alghrani, A. et al. (2011). 'Healthcare scandals in the NHS: crime and punishment'. *Journal of Medical Ethics*, 37, 230–2.

Allen, N. (2013). 'Psychiatric care and criminal prosecution'. In D. Griffiths and A. Sanders, eds., *Bioethics, Medicine and the Criminal Law*. Vol. II of *Medicine, Crime and Society*, Cambridge: Cambridge University Press, pp. 159–73.

Annas, G. (2006). 'The patient's right to safety – improving the quality of care through litigation against hospitals'. *New England Journal of Medicine*, 354, 2063.

Archer, J., De Bere, S. R., Brennan, N. and Lynn, N. (2013). *Evaluating the strategic impact of medical revalidation: Building an evaluation framework* (Final Report).

Arlidge, A. (1998). 'Criminal negligence in medical practice'. *Medico-Legal Journal*, 1, 3–14.

Ashton, J. (2015). '15 Years of whistleblowing protection under the public interest disclosure act 1998: are we still shooting the messenger?' *Industrial Law Journal*, 44 (1), 29–52.

Ashworth, A. and Horder, J. (2013). *Principles of Criminal Law*, 7th edn, Oxford: Oxford University Press.

Ashworth, A. and Zedner, L. (2008). 'Defending the criminal law: reflections on the changing character of crime, procedure and sanctions'. *Criminal Law and Philosophy*, 2(1), 21–51.

Aveling, E. L., Parker M. and Dixon-Woods, M. (2016). 'What is the role of individual accountability in patient safety? A multi-site ethonographic study'. *Sociology of Health and Illness*, 38(2), 216–32.

Ayres, I. and Braithwaite, J. (1992). *Responsive Regulation: Transcending the Deregulation Debate*, Oxford: Oxford University Press.

Baier, A. (1986). 'Trust and antitrust'. *Ethics*, 96 (2), 231–60.

Baier, A. (1994). *Moral Prejudices: Essays on Ethics*, London: Harvard University Press.

Baker, T. (2005). *The Medical Malpractice Myth*, Chicago: University of Chicago Press.

Ballatt, J. and Campling, P. (2011). *Intelligent Kindness: Reforming the Culture of Healthcare*, London: Royal College of Psychiatrists.

Barber, B. (1983). *The Logic and Limits of Trust*, New Jersey: Rutgers University Press.

Barello, S. et al. (2014). 'The challenges of conceptualizing patient engagement in health care: lexicographic literature review'. *Journal of Participatory Medicine*, 6 (June 11).

BHCAG (2000). 'Service – empowering the public in the healthcare process'. Position Paper prepared for Phase 2 of the BRI Inquiry.

Beck, U. (1992). *Risk Society: Towards a New Modernity* (translated by M. Ritter), London: Sage Publications.

Berlant, J. L. (1975). *Profession and Monopoly: A Study of Medicine in the United States and Great Britain*, Berkeley: University of California Press.

Berlinger N. (2005). *After Harm: Medical Error and the Ethics of Forgiveness*, Baltimore: Johns Hopkins University Press.

Berwick, D. (2013). *A Promise to Learn – A Commitment to Act: Improving the Safety of Patients in England*, National Advisory Group on the Safety of Patients in England (London).

Berwick, D. M. (1989). 'Continuous improvement as an ideal in health care'. *New England Journal of Medicine*, 320 (1), 53–6.

Bilton, D. and Cayton, H. (2013). *Asymmetry of Influence: The Role of Regulators in Patient Safety*, London: Health Foundation.

Black, J. (2002). 'Critical reflections on regulation'. *Australian Journal of Legal Philosophy*, 27, 1–37.

Black, N. (2010). 'Assessing the quality of hospitals hospital standardised mortality ratios should be abandoned'. *British Medical Journal*, 340, c2066.

Blendon R. J. et al. (2002). 'Views of practicing physicians and the public on medical errors'. *New England Journal of Med*, 347(24), 1933–40.

Bliss, M. (2005). *Harvey Cushing: A Life in Surgery*, New York: Oxford University Press.

Bogner, M. S. (1994). *Human Error in Medicine*, Hillsdale, New Jersey: Lawrence Erlbaum Associates.

Bolsin, S. (1998a). 'The Bristol cardiac disaster'. *British Medical Journal*, 317, 1579–82.

Bolsin, S. (1998b). 'Professional misconduct: the Bristol case'. *Medical Journal of Australia*, 169, 369–72.

Boothman, R. C. et al. (2012). 'Nurturing a culture of patient safety and achieving lower malpractice risk through disclosure: lessons learned and future directions'. *Frontiers of Health Services Management*, 28(3), 13–28.

Bosk, C. L. (1979). *Forgive and Remember: Managing Medical Failure*, Chicago: University of Chicago Press.

Bosk, C. L. (2005). 'Continuity and change in the study of medical error: the culture of safety on the shop floor', www.sss.ias.edu/files/papers/paper20.pdf.

Boyce, T. et al. (2010). *Choosing a High Quality Hospital: The Role of Nudges, Scorecard Design and Information*, London: King's Fund.

Brazier, M. (2006). 'Do no harm – do patients have responsibilities too?' *Cambridge Law Journal*, 65(2), 397–422.

Brazier, M. and Miola, J. (2000). 'Bye-bye Bolam: A medical litigation revolution?' *Medical Law Review*, 8(1), 85–114.

Brazier, M. and Alghrani, A. (2009). 'Fatal medical malpractice and criminal liability'. *Professional Negligence*, 25(2), 51–67.

Brennan, T. A. et al. (1991). 'Incidence of adverse events and negligence in hospitalised patients: results of the Harvard Medical Practice Study I'. *New England Journal of Medicine*, 324, 370–6.

British Medical Journal (1977). 'Royal Commission on the NHS: Report of Council to the Special Representative Meeting', 6056, 299–334.

British Medical Journal (1981). 'Medical audit: voluntary, confidential, unconditional and non-directive', 283, 253.

Brownlie, J., Greene, A. and Howson, A. (2008). *Researching Trust and Health*, New York: Routledge.

Brownsword, R. (2008). *Rights, Regulation and the Technological Revolution*, Oxford: Oxford University Press.

Buchanan, D. R. and Mason, J. K. (1995). 'The Coroner's office revisited'. *Medical Law Review*, 3(2), 142–60.

Calnan, M. and Rowe, R. (2008). 'Trust relations in a changing health service'. *Journal of Health Services Research & Policy*, 13 Suppl. 3: 97–103.

Care Quality Commission (2014). Annual report and accounts 2013/14 HC 295.

Care Quality Commission (2015a). Enforcement Policy.

Care Quality Commission (2015b). Memorandum of Understanding between CQC, the H&SE and Local Authorities in England.

Carthey, J., Walker, S., Deelchand, V., Vincent, C. and Harrop Griffiths, W. (2011). 'Breaking the rules: understanding non-compliance with policies and guidelines'. *British Medical Journal*, 343, 621–3.

Case, P. (2011). 'Putting public confidence first: doctors, precautionary suspension and the General Medical Council'. *Medical Law Review*, 19(3), 339–71.

Cayton, H. (2014). 'Asymmetry of influence: the role of regulators on patient safety'. King's Fund conference – 'One year on from Francis' London.

Chalmers, J. and Leverick, F. (2013). 'Tracking the creation of criminal offences'. *Criminal Law Review*, 7, 543–60.

CHPI (2014). *Patient Safety in Private Hospitals – the Known and the Unknown Risks*, London: Centre for Health and the Public Interest.

CHRE (2010). Right Tough Regulation (London: Council for Healthcare Regulatory Excellence).

CHRE (2012). Handling concerns about the regulators: proposals for commencing sections 27(2)and 28 of the National Health Service Reform and Health Care Professions Act 2002.

Christmas, S. and Millward, L. (2011). *New Medical Professionalism: A Scoping Report for the Health Foundation*, London, Health Foundation.

Clarkson, C. M. V. (2000). 'Context and culpability in involuntary manslaughter: principle or instinct?' In A. Ashworth and B. Mitchell, eds., *Rethinking English Homicide Law*, Oxford: Oxford University Press, pp. 133–65.

Clwyd, A. and Hart, T. (2013). *A Review of the NHS Hospitals Complaints System Putting Patients Back in the Picture.*

Codman, E. A. (1984). *The Shoulder.* F. L. Malabar, R. E. Kreiger, quoted in V. A. Sharpe and A.I. Faden (1998). *Medical Harm: Historical, Conceptual and Ethical Dimensions of Iatrogenic Illness,* Cambridge: Cambridge University Press.

Collins, M. E. et al. (2009). 'On the prospects for a blame-free medical culture'. *Social Science & Medicine,* 69, 1287–90.

Corfield, P. J. (1995). *Power and the Professions in Britain 1700–1850,* London: Routledge.

Coulter, A. (2011). *Engaging Patients in Healthcare.* Maidenhead: Open University Press.

Council for Healthcare Regulatory Excellence. (2009). CHRE Policy Framework.

Currie, G., Humphreys, M., Waring, J. and Rowley, E. (2009). 'Narratives of professional regulation and patient safety: the case of medical devices in anaesthetics'. *Health, Risk & Society*, 11(2), 117–35.

Dalton, D. and Williams, N. (2014). *Building a Culture of Candour: A Review of the Threshold for the Duty of Candour and of the Incentives for Care Organisations to be Candid,* London: Royal College of Surgeons.

Daniels, J. P. et al. (2012). 'Identification by families of pediatric adverse events and near misses overlooked by health care providers'. *Canadian Medical Association Journal,* 184(1), 29–34.

Davies, A. C. L. (2000). 'Don't trust me, I'm a doctor: medical regulation and the 1999 NHS reforms'. *Oxford Journal of Legal Studies,* 20(3), 437–56.

Davies, H. T. O. and Shields, A. V. (1999). 'Public trust and accountability for clinical performance: lessons from the national press reportage of the Bristol hearing'. *Journal of Evaluation in Clinical Practice,* 5(3), 335–42.

Davies, H., Powell A. and Rushmer, R. (2007). 'Healthcare professionals' views on clinician engagement in quality improvement: a literature review'. London: The Health Foundation.

Davies, H. T. O. (2007). 'Why don't clinicians engage with quality improvement?' *Journal of Health Services Research & Policy,* 12(3) July, 129.

Davies, M. (2010). 'The demise of professional self-regulation? Evidence from the "ideal type" professions of medicine and law'. *Professional Negligence,* 26(1), 3–38.

Davis, G. et al. (2002). *Experiencing Inquests.* Home Office Research Study 241, London: Home Office.

Davis, P. et al. (2002). 'Adverse events in New Zealand public hospitals I: occurrence and impact'. *New Zealand Medical Journal*, 115(1167), U271.

Davis, P. et al. (2003). 'Acknowledgement of "no fault" medical injury: review of patients' hospital records in New Zealand'. *British Medical Journal*, 326(7380), 79.

Davis, R. E. et al. (2011). 'Patient involvement in patient safety: How willing are patients to participate?' *BMJ Quality & Safety*, 20(1), 108–14.

Dawda, P., Jenkins, R. and Varnam, R. (2010). Quality improvement in general practice: Discussion Paper, London: King's Fund.

Department of Health (1999). NHS Performance Assessment Framework. Department of Health.

Department of Health (2000). An organisation with a memory: report of an expert group on learning from adverse events in the NHS chaired by the Chief Medical Officer. London: The Stationery Office.

Department of Health (2003). Making amends: a consultation paper setting out proposals for reforming the approach to clinical negligence in the NHS, Department of Health.

Department of Health (2011). 'Implementing a "Duty of Candour"; a new contractual requirement on providers' proposals for consultation.

Department of Health (2012). Liberating the NHS: no decision about me without me: government response to the consultation on proposals for greater patient involvement and more choice.

Department of Health (2014a). New offence of ill-treatment or wilful neglect: consultation document.

Department of Health (2014b). Criminal offence of ill-treatment or wilful neglect: impact assessment.

Department of Health (2014c). Hard truths: the journey to putting patients first: volume one of the government response to the Mid Staffordshire NHS Foundation Trust Public Inquiry Cm 8777-I.

Department of Health (2015a). 2015/16 Choice framework.

Department of Health (2015b). Regulation of health care professionals regulation of social care professionals in England. The Government's response to Law Commission report 345, Scottish Law Commission report 237 and Northern Ireland Law Commission report 18 (2014) Cm 8839 SG/2014/26. Cm 8995.

Department of Health (2015c). Triennial review of the NHS Litigation Authority review report.

Department of Health (2015(d)). Learning not blaming: The government response to the Freedom to Speak Up consultation, the Public Administration Select Committee report 'Investigating clinical incidents in the NHS', and the Morecambe Bay Investigation (Cm 9113).

Department of Health (2016). 'From a blame culture to a learning culture'. Speech by Secretary of State for Health to a Global Patient Safety Summit on 10 March 2016.

Department for Transport (2015). Statistical release: seat belt and mobile phone use surveys: England and Scotland, 2014.

Dingwall, R. (1994). 'Litigation and the threat to medicine'. In J. Gabe et al., eds., *Challenging Medicine*. London: Routledge, pp. 46–64.

Dingwall, R. (1999). 'Professions and social order in a global society'. *International Review of Sociology*, 9(1), 131–40.

Dingwall, R. (2006). 'The enduring relevance of professional dominance'. *Knowledge, Work and Society*, 4(2), 77–98.

Dixon-Woods, M. (2010). 'Why is patient safety so hard? A selective review of ethnographic studies'. *Journal of Health Services Research & Policy*, 15 (Suppl. 1), 11–16.

Dixon-Woods, M. and Pronovost, P. J. (2016). 'Patient safety and the problem of many hands'. *BMJ Quality & Safety*, Published online first: [24 February 2016] doi:10.1136/bmjqs-2016-005232.

Dixon-Woods, M., Yeung, K. and Bosk, C. L. (2011). 'Why is UK medicine no longer a self-regulating profession? The role of scandals involving "bad apple" doctors'. *Social Science & Medicine*, 73, 1452–9.

Donabedian, A. (1992). 'Quality assurance in health care: consumers' role'. *Quality in Health Care*, 1, 247–51.

Dopson, S. (2009). 'Changing forms of managerialism in the NHS: hierarchies, markets and networks'. In J. Gabe and M. Calnan, eds., *The New Sociology of the Health Service*. Abingdon: Routledge.

Draycott, T. et al. (2015). 'The role of insurers in maternity safety. Best practice & research'. *Clinical Obstetrics and Gynaecology*, 29(8), 1126–31.

Drew, D. (2014) *Little Stories of Life and Death*, Leicester: Matador.

Dunn, P. (1998). 'The Wiseheart affair: paediatric cardiological services in Bristol 1990–5'. *British Medical Journal*, 317, 1144–5.

Durkheim, E. (1964). *The Division of Labour in Society*, New York: Free Press.

Dyer, C. (1994). 'Consultant found guilty of failing to act on colleague'. *British Medical Journal*, 308, 809.

Dyer, C. (1997). 'Two surgeons are accused of ignoring high death rates'. *British Medical Journal*, 315, 1691.

Dyer, C. (2015). 'Evidence of hospital failures was not disclosed at surgeon's manslaughter trial'. *British Medical Journal*, 351, h4229.

Dyer, C. (2016). 'Breast surgeon faces 21 charges of unlawfully wounding 11 patients'. *British Medical Journal*, 532: i343.

Earle, T. C. and Cvetkovich, G. T. (1995). *Social Trust: Toward a Cosmopolitan Society*, Westport, Connecticut: Praeger.

Elston M. A. (2009). 'Remaking a trustworthy medical profession in twenty-first century Britain?'. In J. Gabe and M. Calnan, eds., *The New Sociology of the Health Service*, Abingdon: Routledge, pp. 17–36.

Elston, M. A. (1991). 'The politics of professional power: medicine in a changing health service'. In J. Gabe, M. Calnan and M. Bury, eds., *The Sociology of the Health Service*, London: Routledge, pp. 55–88.

Elwyn, G. et al. (2010). 'Implementing shared decision making in the NHS'. *British Medical Journal*, 341, c5146.

Emslie, S. (2005). *International Perspectives on Patient Safety*, London: National Audit Office.

Entwistle, V. et al. (2010a). 'Supporting patient autonomy: the importance of clinician-patient relationships'. *Journal of General Internal Medicine*, 25(7), 741–5.

Entwistle, V. et al. (2010b). 'Speaking up about safety concerns: multi-setting qualitative study of patients' views and experiences'. *Quality and Safety in Health Care*, 19, e33.

Entwistle, V., Mello, M. M. and Brennan, T. A. (2005). 'Advising patients about patient safety: current initiatives risk shifting responsibility'. *Joint Commission Journal on Quality and Safety*, 31(9) September, 483–94.

Entwistle, V. and Watt, I. (2013). 'Treating patients as persons: a capabilities approach to support delivery of person-centred care'. *The American Journal of Bioethics*, 13(8), 29–39.

Evetts, J. (2006). 'Short note: the sociology of professional groups'. *Current Sociology*, 54(1), 133–43.

Evetts, J. (2009). 'The management of professionalism: a contemporary paradox'. In Gewirtz, S. et al., eds., *Changing Teacher Professionalism: International Trends, Challenges and Ways Forward*. Routledge: Abingdon, pp. 19–31.

Farnham, D. and Horton, S. (1993). *Managing the Public Services*. London: Macmillan.

Farrell, A. M. and Devaney, S. (2007). 'Making amends or making things worse?' *Legal Studies*, 27(4), 630–48.

Feinberg, J. (1970). 'The expressive function of punishment'. In J. Feinberg, *Doing and Deserving*. Princeton, NJ: Princeton University Press, pp. 95–118.

Feng, X. Q., Acord, L., Cheng, Y. J., Zeng, J. H. and Song, J. P. (2011). 'The relationship between management safety commitment and patient safety culture'. *International Nursing Review*, 58, 249–54.

Fenn, P. et al. (2000). 'Current cost of medical negligence in NHS hospitals: analysis of claims database'. *British Medical Journal*, 320, 1567–71.

Fenn, P. et al. (2002). 'Deterrence and liability for medical negligence: theory and evidence'. Paper presented at the 19th Annual Conference of the European Association of Law and Economics, Athens, 19–21 September 2002.

Ferguson, A. L. and Braithwaite, E. (2012). 'Putting Things Right in Wales'. *Clinical Risk*, 18, 6–8.

Ferner, R. and McDowell, S. (2006). 'Doctors charged with manslaughter in the course of medical practice, 1795–2005: a literature review'. *Journal of the Royal Society of Medicine*, 99, 309–14.

Ferner, R. and McDowell, S. (2013). 'Medical manslaughter'. *British Medical Journal* 347, f5609.

Field, R. I. (2007). *Health Care Regulation in America: Complexity, Confrontation and Compromise*, New York: Oxford University Press.

Fitzpatrick, M. (2000). *The Tyranny of Health: Doctors and the Regulation of Lifestyle*, London: Routledge.

Fox, D. M. (1994). 'Medical institutions and the state'. In W. F. Bynum and R. Porter, eds., Volume II of *Companion Encyclopedia of the History of Medicine*, London: Routledge, pp. 1204–30.

Francis, R. (2013). The report of the Mid Staffordshire NHS Foundation Trust Public Inquiry. London: The Stationery Office, HC 898 I-III.

Francis, R. (2015). Freedom to speak up: An independent review into creating an open and honest reporting culture in the NHS. London: The Stationery Office.

Freidson, E. (1970a). *Profession of Medicine: A Study of the Sociology of Applied Knowledge*, New York: Harper and Row.

Freidson, E. (1970b). *Professional Dominance: The Social Structure of Medical Care*, Chicago: Aldine.

Freidson, E. (1975). *Doctoring Together: A Study of Professional Social Control*, New York: Elsevier.

Freidson, E. (1986). 'The medical profession in transition'. In L. H. Aitken and D. Mechanic, eds., *Applications of Social Science to Clinical Medicine and Health Policy*, New Brunswick, New Jersey: Rutgers University Press, pp. 63–79.

Freidson, E. (1994). *Professionalism Reborn: Theory, Prophecy and Policy*, Cambridge: Polity Press.

Freidson, E. (2001). *Professionalism: The Third Logic*, Oxford: Polity Press.

Fricker, M. (2007). *Epistemic Injustice: Power and the Ethics of Knowing*, Oxford: Oxford University Press.

Frontier Economics. (2014). Exploring the costs of unsafe care in the NHS. A report prepared for the Department of Health.

Fukuyama, F. (1995). *Trust: The Social Virtues and the Creation of Prosperity*, New York: The Free Press.

Furedi, F. (1999). *Courting Mistrust*, London: Centre for Policy Studies.

Furedi, F. (2006). 'The end of professional dominance'. *Social Science and Modern Society*, 43(6), 14–18.

Gallagher, T. H. et al. (2003). 'Patients' and physicians' attitudes regarding the disclosure of medical errors'. *Journal of the American Medical Association*, 289, 1001–7.

Gambetta, D. (1988). 'Can we trust trust?', In D. Gambetta, ed., *Trust: Making and Breaking Cooperative Relations*, Oxford: Blackwell, pp. 213–37.

Gawande, A. (2003). *Complications: A Surgeon's Notes on an Imperfect Science*, London: Profile.

Gawande, A. (2007). *Better: A Surgeon's Notes on Performance*, London: Profile.

Gawande, A. (2009). *The Checklist Manifesto: How to Get Things Right*, London: Profile.

Genn, H. (1999). *Paths to Justice: What People Do and Think About Going to Law*, Oxford: Hart.

Giddens, A. (1990). *The Consequences of Modernity*, Cambridge: Polity Press.

Gilmour, J. (2011). 'Patient safety and clinical risk in Canada', Chapter 12. In J. Tingle and P. Bark, eds., *Patient Safety, Law Policy and Practice*, Abingdon: Routledge.

Glaeser, E. and Sunstein, C. R. (2014). 'Regulatory review for the states', *National Affairs*, 20, 37–54.

Glover Thomas, N. and Fanning, J. (2010). 'Medicalisation: the role of e-pharmacies in iatrogenic harm', *Medical Law Review* 18(1), 28–55.

GMC (1979). *Professional Conduct and Discipline: Fitness to Practise*, London: General Medical Council.

GMC (1985). *Professional Conduct and Discipline: Fitness to Practise*, London: General Medical Council.

GMC (1987). *Professional Conduct and Discipline: Fitness to Practise*, London: General Medical Council.

GMC (1998). *Good Medical Practice*, London: General Medical Council.

GMC (2000). *Revalidating Doctors: Ensuring Standards, Securing the Future: Consultation Document*, London: General Medical Council.

GMC (2001). *Acting Fairly to Protect Patients: Reform of the GMC's Fitness To Practise Procedures*, London: General Medical Council.

GMC (2008). *Good Medical Practice*, London: General Medical Council.

GMC (2012). *Raising and Acting on Concerns About Patient Safety*, London: General Medical Council

GMC (2013a). *The State of Medical Education and Practice in the UK in 2012*, London: General Medical Council.

GMC (2013b). *The Good Medical Practice Framework for Appraisal and Revalidation*, London: General Medical Council.

GMC (2013c). *Good Medical Practice*, London: General Medical Council.

GMC (2014a). *The State of Medical Education and Practice in the UK in 2014.* London: General Medical Council.

GMC (2014b). *2013 Annual Statistics for Our Investigations into Doctors' Fitness to Practice*, London: General Medical Council.

GMC (2015). *Reforming Our Fitness to Practise Investigation and Adjudication Processes: A Public Consultation on Changes to Our Rules*, London: General Medical Council.

Gobert, J and Punch, M (2000). 'Whistleblowers, the Public Interest, and the Public Interest Disclosure Act 1998', 63(1), *Modern Law Review*, 25–54.

Goldberg, R. (2013). *Medicinal Product Liability and Regulation*, Oxford: Hart.

Gooderham, P. (2011). '"No-one fully responsible": a "collusion of anonymity" protecting health-care bodies from manslaughter charges?' *Clinical Ethic*, 6, 68–77.

Gorovitz, S. and MacIntyre, A. (1976). 'Toward a theory of medical fallibility', *The Journal of Medicine and Philosophy*, 1(1), 51–71.

Grabosky, N. (1995). 'Counterproductive regulation'. *International Journal of the Sociology of Law*, 23, 347–69.

Griffiths, D. and Sanders, A. (2013). 'The road to the dock: prosecution decision-making in medical manslaughter cases'. In *Medicine, Crime and Society*. Cambridge: Cambridge University Press.

Griffiths, R. (1983). NHS Management Inquiry, London: Department of Health and Social Security.

Groopman, J. (2007). *How Doctors Think*, London: Houghton Mifflin.

Grubb, A. (1993). *Medical Law Review*, 1, 241.

Gunningham, N. and Grabosky, P. (1998). *Smart Regulation: Designing Environmental Policy*, Oxford, Clarendon Press.

Hall, J. (1972). 'Negligence and the general problem of criminal responsibility', *Yale Law Journal*, Vol. 81, 912.

Hammond, P. (1992). *Private Eye*, May 8.

Harpwood, V. (2007). *Medicine, Malpractice and Misapprehensions*, Abingdon: Routledge-Cavendish.

Harris, R. and Slater, K. (2015). Analysis of cases resulting in doctors being erased or suspended from the medical register. Report prepared for: General Medical Council, DJS research.

Hart, H. L. A. (1968). 'Negligence, mens rea and criminal responsibility'. In *Punishment and Responsibility: Essays in the Philosophy of Law*, Oxford: Oxford University Press, pp. 136–57.

Haug, M. R. (1973). 'Deprofessionalisation: an alternate hypothesis for the future'. In P. Halmos, ed. *The Sociological Review Monograph* 20: Professionalisation and Social Change. Keele: University of Keele, pp. 195–211.

Haug, M. R. (1988). 'A re-examination of the hypothesis of physician deprofessionalization'. *The Milbank Quarterly*, 66(2), 48–56.

Hawkins, K. (2002). *Law as Last Resort: Prosecution Decision Making in a Regulatory Agency*, Oxford: Oxford University Press.

HC Debate. 1 December 2010, cols 276WH.

Health and Care Professions Council. (2016). Standards of conduct, performance and ethics.

Health Foundation. (2011). Evidence scan: levels of harm in primary care.

Health Foundation. (2013). Involving patients in improving safety.

Health Service Circular 1999/198. The Public Interest Disclosure Act 1998. Whistleblowing in the NHS (London: Department of Health).

Healthcare Commission. (2009). The Healthcare Commission 2004–2009: Regulating healthcare – experience and lessons.

Healy, J. (2011). *Improving Health Care Safety and Quality: Reluctant Regulators*, Farnham: Ashgate.

Heimer, C. A. (2008). 'Thinking about how to avoid thought: deep norms, shallow rules, and the structure of attention'. *Regulation & Governance*, 2, 30–47.

Held, V. (2006). *The Ethics of Care*, New York: Oxford University Press.

Heywood, R. (2010). 'Non-delegable duties and hospitals'. *Professional Negligence*, 26 (1), 49–55.

Hilfiker, D. (1984). 'Facing our mistakes'. *New England Journal of Medicine*, 310, 118–22.

Hogan, H. et al. (2012). 'Preventable deaths due to problems in care in English acute hospitals: a retrospective case record review study'. *BMJ Quality & Safety*, 21, 737–45. doi:10.1136/bmjqs-2012–001159.

Hogan, H. et al. (2015). 'Avoidability of hospital deaths and association with hospital-wide mortality ratios: retrospective case record review and regression analysis'. *British Medical Journal*, 351, h3239.

Hood, C. (1991). 'A public management for all seasons?', *Public Administration*, 69 Spring, 3–19.

Hoppe, N. (2011). 'Medical ethics and patient safety'. In J. Tingle and P. Bark, eds., *Patient Safety, Law Policy and Practice*, Routledge: Abingdon, pp. 53–63.

Horder, J. (1997). 'Gross negligence and criminal culpability' *U. Toronto L. J*, 47, 495.

Horder, J. et al. (1986). 'Ways of influencing the behaviour of general practitioners'. *Journal of the Royal College of General Practitioners*, 36, 517–21.

Horton, R. (1998). 'How should doctors respond to the GMC's judgements on Bristol?' *The Lancet*, 351, 1900.

Horton, R. (2005). 'Trust me, I'm a doctor', *Times Literary Supplement*, June 17.

House of Commons Health Committee (2009). Patient safety: sixth report of session 2008–9. HC 151–1, London, TSO.

House of Commons Health Committee (2011). Complaints and litigation sixth report of session 2010–12, Volume I. HC 786-I, London: The Stationery Office.

House of Commons Health Committee (2015). Complaints and raising concerns, HC, 350, 2014–15.

Hughes, E. C. (1958). *Men and Their Work*, Westport, Connecticut: Greenwood Press.

Huising, R. and Silbey, S. S. (2011). 'Governing the gap: forging safe science through relational regulation'. *Regulation and Governance*, 5, 14–42.

Hunt, G. (1998). 'Whistle-blowing'. In *Encyclopaedia of Applied Ethics*. Volume IV San Diego: Academic Press, 525–35.

Husak, D. (2008). *Overcriminalization: The Limits of the Criminal Law*, New York: Oxford University Press.

Hutter, Bridget M. (2001). *Regulation and Risk: Occupational Health and Safety on the Railways*, Oxford: Oxford University Press.

Illich, I. (1977a). *Limits to Medicine: Medical Nemesis: The Expropriation of Health*, London: Pelican Books.

Illich, I. (1977b). *Disabling Professions*, London: Boyars.

Institute of Customer Service (2010). National Complaints Culture Survey.

IOM. (1999). *To Err Is Human: Building a Safer Health System*, Washington DC: National Academy Press.

IOM. (2001). *Crossing the Quality Chasm: A New Health System for the 21st Century*, Washington DC: National Academy Press.

Ipsos MORI (2013). www.ipsos-mori.com/researchpublications/researcharchive/15/Trust-in-Professions.aspx?view=wide.

Irvine, D. (2003). *The Doctors' Tale: Professionalism and Public Trust*, London: Radcliffe Publishing.

Jackson, E. (2001). *Regulating Reproduction: Law, Technology and Autonomy*, Oxford: Hart Publishing.

Jackson, E. (2006). '"Informed consent" to medical treatment and the impotence of tort'. In S. McLean, ed. *First Do No Harm: Law, Ethics and Healthcare*, Aldershot: Ashgate, pp. 273–86.

Jackson, E. (2010). 'Top-up payments for expensive cancer drugs: rationing, fairness and the NHS'. *Modern Law Review*, 73(3), 399–427.

Jackson, E. (2012). *Law and the Regulation of Medicines*, Oxford: Hart.

Jacobs, R., Mannion, R., Davies, H.T.O. et al. (2013). 'The relationship between organizational culture and performance in acute hospitals'. *Social Science & Medicine*, 76, 115–25.

Jewson, N. D. (1974). 'Medical knowledge and the patronage system in 18th Century England'. *Sociology*, 8, 369–85.

Johnsen, J. R. (2006). Health systems in transition: Norway. Vol. 8, No. 1. (edited by E. Bankauskaite). *European Observatory on Health Systems and Policies.*, Denmark: WHO Regional Office for Europe.

Johnson, T. (1972). *Professions and Power*, London: Macmillan.

Jones, A. and Kelly, D. (2014). 'Deafening silence? Time to reconsider whether organisations are silent or deaf when things go wrong'. *BMJ Quality & Safety*, 23, 709–13.

Jones, K. (1998). 'Trust'. In E. Craig, ed., *Routledge Encyclopaedia of Philosophy*, London: Routledge.

Jutel, A. and Lupton, D. (2015). Digitizing diagnosis: a review of mobile applications in the diagnostic process. *Diagnosis*, 2(2), 89–96.

Kachalia, A. et al. (2010). 'Liability claims and costs before and after implementation of a medical error disclosure program'. *Annals of Internal Medicine*, 153, 213–21.

Kaye, R. (2006). 'Stuck in the middle: the rise of meso-regulators'. *Risk and Regulation*, 6, 23–35.

Kennedy, I. (1991). *Treat Me Right: Essays in Medical Law and Ethics*, Oxford: Clarendon.

Kennedy, I. (2001). The report of the public inquiry into children's heart surgery at the Bristol Royal Infirmary 1984–1995: Learning from Bristol (Cmnd. 5207 (I)).

Kennedy, I. (2006). *Learning from Bristol: Are We?* London: self-published.

Kennedy, I. and Grubb, A. (2000). *Medical Law*, 3rd edn, London: Butterworths.

Kirkup, B. (2015). The Report of the Morecambe Bay Investigation.

Klein, R. (1974). 'Accountability in the National Health Service'. *Political Quarterly*, 42, 363–75.

Klein, R. (1995). *The New Politics of the NHS*, 3rd edn, London: Longman.

Kuhlmann, E. (2006a)). *Modernising Healthcare: Reinventing Professions, the State and the Public*, Bristol: Policy Press.

Kuhlmann, E. (2006b). 'Traces of doubt and sources of trust: health professions in an uncertain society'. *Current Sociology*, 54, 607.

Kuhlmann, E. et al. (2013). '"A manager in the minds of doctors:" a comparison of new modes of control in European hospitals'. *BMC Health Services Research*, 13, 246.

LÖF (2015) Annual Report (Stockholm, LÖF).

Lacey, N. (2004). 'Criminalisation as regulation: the role of criminal law', In C. Parker et al., eds., *Regulating Law*. Oxford University Press, pp. 144–67.

Lacey, N., Wells, C. and Quick, O. (2010). *Reconstructing Criminal Law*, Cambridge: Cambridge University Press.

Larson, M. S. (1977). *The Rise of Professionalism: A Sociological Analysis*, Berkeley: University of California Press.

Law Commission. (1996). Involuntary Homicide Bill Clause 2(1): Law Commission Legislating the Criminal Code: Involuntary Manslaughter Law Commission No 237

Law Commission. (2005). Consultation Paper 177. A New Homicide Act for England and Wales?

Law Commission. (2012). Regulation of Health Care professionals. Regulation of Social Care Professionals in England. Joint Consultation Paper LCCP 202/ SLCDP 153/NILC 12 (2012).

Leadbetter, S. and Knight, B. (1993). 'Reporting deaths to coroners', 306 *British Medical Journal* 1018.

Leape, L. (1994). 'Error in medicine'. *Journal of the American Medical Association*, 272(23), 1851–7.

Leape, L. (1997). 'A systems analysis approach to medical error'. *Journal of Evaluation in Clinical Practice*, 3(3), 213–22.

Leape, L. and Berwick, D. (2005). 'Five years after To Err Is Human: what have we learned?' *Journal of the American Medical Association*, 18 May, 293(19), 2384–90.

Leape, L. et al. (2009). 'Transforming healthcare: a safety imperative', *Quality and Safety Health Care*, 18, 424–8.

Leape, L. et al. (2010). Unmet Needs: Teaching Physicians to Provide Safe Patient Care. Report of the Lucian Leape Institute Roundtable on Reforming Medical Education.

Legemaate, J. (2011). 'Blame free reporting: international developments'. Chapter 6 in J. Tingle and P. Bark, eds., *Patient Safety, Law Policy and Practice*, Abingdon: Routledge.

Lewis, D. (2010). 'Ten years of Public Disclosure Act 1998 claims: what can we learn from the statistics and recent research?' *Industrial Law Journal*, 39(3), 325–8.

Lewis, R., Morris A. and Oliphant, K. (2006). 'Tort personal injury claims statistics: is there a compensation culture in the United Kingdom?' *Torts Law Journal*, 14(2), 158–75.

Light, D. (1995). 'Countervailing powers: a framework for professions in transition'. In T. Johnson, G. Larkin and M. Saks, eds., *Health Professions and the State in Europe*, London: Routledge, pp. 25–41.

Light, D. (2011). *The Risks of Prescription Drugs*, New York: Columbia University Press.

Lilford, R. and Pronovost, P. (2010). 'Using hospital mortality rates to judge hospital performance: a bad idea that just won't go away'. *British Medical Journal*, 340, 2016.

Lloyd Bostock, S. and Mulcahy, L. (1994). 'The social psychology of making and responding to hospital complaints: an account model of complaint processes', *Law & Policy*, 16(2), 123.

Lloyd-Bostock, S. (2010). 'The creation of risk related information: The UK General Medical Council's electronic database'. *Journal of Health Organization and Management*, 24(6), 584–96.

Lloyd-Bostock, S. and Hutter, B. (2008). 'Reforming regulation of the medical profession: the risks of risk based approaches'. *Health, Risk & Society*, 10(1), 69–83.

Local Government Analysis and Research. (2007). Smokefree legislation compliance data. Report covering 1st–13th July 2007 (Period 1).

Lopez, L. et al. (2009). 'Disclosure of hospital adverse events and its association with patients' ratings of the quality of care'. *Quality of Care Arch Intern Med*, 169(20), 1888–94.

Lord Pearson. (1978). Royal Commission on Civil Liability and Compensation for Personal Injury Cmnd 7054.

Lord Young of Graffham. (2010). Common Sense Common Safety: A report by Lord Young of Graffham to the Prime Minister following a Whitehall-wide review of the operation of health and safety laws and the growth of the compensation culture. London, Cabinet Office.

Loudon, I. (1992). 'Medical practitioners 1750–1850 and the period of medical reform in Britain'. In A. Wear, ed., *Medicine in Society: Historical Essays*, Cambridge: Cambridge University Press, pp. 219–47.

Luce, T. (2003). Death certification and investigation in England, Wales and Northern Ireland: The report of a fundamental review. CM 5831. London: The Stationery Office, 2003.

Luhmman, N. (1988). 'Familiarity, confidence, trust: problems and alternatives'. In D. Gambetta, ed., *Trust: Making and Breaking Cooperative Relations*, Oxford: Blackwell, pp. 94–107.

Luthander, C. M. et al. (2016). 'Results from the National Perinatal Patient Safety Program in Sweden: the challenge of evaluation'. *Acta Obstetricia et Gynecologica Scandinavica*, 95(5), 596–603.

Maclean, A. (2013). *Autonomy, Informed Consent and Medical Law: A Relational Challenge*, Cambridge: Cambridge University Press.

Macrae, C. (2014). *Close Calls: Managing Risk and Resilience in Airline Flight Safety*, Basingstoke: Palgrave Macmillan.

Makary, M. A. and Daniel, M. (2016). 'Medical error—the third leading cause of death in the US'. *British Medical Journal*, 353, i2139.

Mallon, W. J. (2000). *Ernest Amory Codman: the End Result of a Life in Medicine*, Philadelphia: W. B. Saunders.

Mannion R, et al. (2005). *Cultures for Performance in Health Care*, Maidenhead: Open University Press.

Manthorpe, J. and Samsi, K. (2014). 'Care professionals' understanding of the new criminal offences created by the Mental Capacity Act 2005'. *International Journal of Geriatric Psychiatry*, published online 30 May.

MARSH. (2011). Department of Health NHS Litigation Authority Industry Report.

Marshall, M. and Mountford, J. (2013). 'Developing a science of improvement'. *Journal of the Royal Society of Medicine*, 106(2) February, 45–50.

Marshall, M., Pronovost, P. and Dixon-Woods, M. (2013). 'Promotion of improvement as a science'. *The Lancet*, 381(9864), 419–21.

Martimianakis, M. et al. (2009). 'Sociological interpretations of professionalism'. *Medical Education*, 43, 829–37.

Martin, G. P. et al. (2015). 'Professionalism redundant, reshaped, or reinvigorated? realizing the "third logic" in contemporary health care'. *Journal of Health and Social Behavior*, 56(3), 378–97.

McCall Smith, A. (1993). 'Criminal negligence and the incompetent doctor'. *Medical Law Review*, 1 Autumn, 336–49.

McCartney, M. (2016). 'Regulation doesn't guarantee safety'. *British Medical Journal*, 352, i96.

McGowan, C. R. and Viens, A. M. (2010). 'Reform of the coroner system: a potential public health failure'. *Journal of Public Health*, 32(3), 427–30.

McIntosh, S. (2012). 'Fulfilling their purpose: inquests, article 2 and next of kin'. *Public Law*, July, 3, 407–15.

McIntyre, N. and Popper, K. (1983). 'The critical attitude in medicine: the need for a new ethics'. *British Medical Journal*, 287, 1919–23.

McKinlay, J. B. and Stoeckle, J. D. (1988). 'Corporatization and the social transformation of doctoring'. *International Journal of Health Services*, 18(2), 191–205.

Mclean, M. (2015). 'Coroner consistency – The 10-jurisdiction, 10-year, postcode lottery?' *Medicine, Science and the Law*, 55(2), 102–12.

Mclean, M. Roach, J. and Armitage, R. (2013). 'Local variations in reporting deaths to the coroner in England and Wales: a postcode lottery?' *Jounal of Clinical Pathology*, 66, 933–6.

Mechanic, D. (1996). 'Changing medical organization and the erosion of trust'. *The Milbank Quarterly*, 74(2), 171–89.

Mechanic, D. and McAlpine, D. (2010). 'Sociology of health care reform'. *Journal of Health and Social Behavior*, 51(S1), S147–59.

Medical Defence Union. (2009). Press release 3 July 2009.

Medical Protection Society (MPS). (2012). Whistleblowing Doctors Afraid to Speak Out. London: MPS.

Mello, M. and Studdert, D. (2008). 'Deconstructing negligence: the role of individual and system factors in causing medical injuries'. *Georgetown Law Journal*, 96(2), 599–623.

Mello, M. et al. (2006). 'Health courts' and accountability for patient safety, *The Milbank Quarterly*, 84(3), 459–92.

Mello, M., Kachalia, A. and Studdert, D. (2011). *Administrative Compensation for Medical Injuries: Lessons from Three Foreign Systems*, New York: Commonwealth Fund.

Mello, M. M. and Brennan, T. A. (2002). 'Deterrence of medical errors: theory and evidence for malpractice reform'. *Texas Law Review*, 80, 1595.

Merrison, A. (chair). (1975). Report of the Committee of Inquiry into the Regulation of the Medical Profession Cmnd 6018. London: HMSO.

Merry, A. and McCall Smith, A, (2001). *Errors, Medicine and the Law*, Cambridge University Press.

Millenson, M. L. (2002). 'Pushing the profession: how the news media turned patent safety into a priority'. *Quality and Safety in Health Care*, 11(1), 57–63.

Millman M. (1977). *The Unkindest Cut: Life in the Backrooms of Medicine*, New York: Morrow Quill.

Mills, D. H. (1978). 'Medical insurance feasibility study'. *Western Journal of Medicine*, 128, 360–5.

Ministry of Justice. (2013a). Coroners Statistics 2012 England and Wales. Ministry of Justice Statistics Bulletin.

Ministry of Justice. (2013b). Summary of Reports and Responses under Rule 43 of the Coroners Rules.

Ministry of Justice. (2015a). Coroners Statistics 2014 England and Wales. Ministry of Justice Statistics Bulletin.

Ministry of Justice. (2015b). Frequently Asked Questions about the Chief Coroner and the Coroner Service (2015).

Miola, J. (2011). 'The tort of negligence and patient safety'. In J. Tingle and P. Bark, *Patient Safety, Law Policy and Practice*, Abingdon: Routledge, pp. 41–52.

Mizrahi T. (1984). 'Managing medical mistakes: ideology, insularity and accountability among internists-in-training'. *Soc Sci Med*, 19(2), 135–46.

Mold, A. (2010). 'Patient groups and the construction of the patient-consumer in Britain: an historical overview'. *Journal of Social Policy*, 39(4), 505–21.

Mollberg, M., Lagerkvist, A. L., Johansson, U. et al. (2008). 'Comparison in obstetric management on infants with transient and persistent obstetric brachial plexus palsy'. *Journal of Child Neurology*, 23, 1424–32.

Möllering, G. (2001). 'The nature of trust: from Georg Simmel to a theory of expectation, interpretation and suspension'. *Sociology*, 35(2), 403–20.

Möllering, G. (2006). *Trust: Reason, Routine and Reflexivity*, Oxford: Elsevier.

Möllering, G. (2008). 'Foreword'. In J. Brownlie, A. Greene and A. Howson, eds., *Researching Trust and Health*, New York: Routledge, vii–x.

Montgomery, J. (1989). 'Medicine, accountability, and professionalism'. *Journal of Law and Society*, 16(2), 319–39.

Morris, A. (2011). '"Common sense common safety": the compensation culture perspective'. *Professional Negligence*, 27(2), 82–96.

Morris, S. (2014). 'Coroner: opportunities were lost in care of boy who died at Bristol hospital'. *The Guardian*, 23 January 2014.

Mulcahy, L. and Allsop, J. (1996). *Regulating Medical Work: Formal and Informal Controls*, Buckingham: Open University Press.

Mulcahy, L. (2000). 'From fear to fraternity: a socio-legal analysis of doctors' responses to being called to account'. Unpublished PhD thesis, University of North London.

Mulcahy, L. (2003). *Disputing Doctors: The Socio-Legal Dynamics of Complaints about Medical Care*, Buckingham: Open University Press.

Mulcahy, L. (2014). 'The market for precedent: shifting visions of the role of clinical negligence claims and trials'. *Medical Law Review*, 22(2), 274–90.

National Audit Office. (2005). *A Safer Place for Patients: Learning to Improve Patient Safety*, London: The Stationery Office.

National Audit Office. (2011). Care Quality Commission: regulating the quality and safety of health and adult social care. Report by the Comptroller and Auditor General (HC 1665 Session 2010–2012, 2 December 2011).

National Audit Office. (2015). Care Quality Commission: Capacity and capability to regulate the quality and safety of health and adult social care. Report by the Comptroller and Auditor General (HC 271 Session 2015–16, 22 July 2015).

National Patient Safety Agency. (2004). *Seven Steps to Patient Safety*, London: National Patient Safety Agency.

National Patient Safety Agency. (2009). National Clinical Assessment Service: The First Eight Years. London: NPSA.

National Patient Safety Foundation. (2014). Safety is personal: partnering with patients and families for the safest care. Report of the Roundtable on Consumer Engagement in Patient Safety.

National Patient Safety Foundation (Lucian Leape Institute Roundtable). (2010). Unmet needs: teaching physicians to provide safe patient care. report on reforming medical education. Boston: NPSF.

NHS England. (2013). NHS England Medical Appraisal Policy. Policy for the appraisal of licensed medical practitioners who have a prescribed connection to NHS England Version 1, October 2013.

NHSLA. (2012). Report and Accounts 2008–12.

NHSLA. (2013a). Framework agreement between the Department of Health and the NHSLA.

NHSLA. (2013b). NHSLA Risk Management Standards 2013–14.

NHSLA. (2015). Report and Accounts 2014/15 HC 293.

NICE. (2015). Safe midwifery staffing for maternity settings. NICE guideline 4.

Nightingale, F. (1863). *Notes on Hospitals*, 3rd edn, London: Longman.

Norman, D. A. (1988). *The Psychology of Everyday Things*, New York: Basic Books.

NPSA. (2009). Being open: communicating patient safety incidents with patients, their families and carers. National Patient Safety Agency.

Nuffield Trust. (2013). *Rating Providers for Quality: A Policy Worth Pursuing?* Nuffield Trust: London.

O'Connor, E. et al. (2010). 'Disclosure of patient safety Incidents: a comprehensive review'. *International Journal for Quality in Health Care*, 22(5), 371–9.

O'Hara, J. and Isden, R. (2013). *Identifying Risks and Monitoring Safety: The Role of Patients and Citizens*. London: Health Foundation.

O'Neill, O. (2002). *A Question of Trust: THE BBC Reith Lectures 2002*, Cambridge: Cambridge University Press.

Ogus, A. I. (1994). *Regulation: Legal Form and Economic Theory*, Oxford: Clarendon.

Oliphant, K. (2007). 'Beyond misadventure: compensation for medical injuries in New Zealand'. *Medical Law Review*, 15(3), 377–91.

Oliphant, K. (2009). 'Compensation, ideology and patient safety in New Zealand's no-fault system', *Opinio Juris in Comparatione*, 3, 1–19.

Paget, M. A. (1988). *The Unity of Mistakes: A Phenomenological Interpretation of Medical Work*, Philadelphia: Temple University Press.

Parand, A. (2013). *The Role of Acute Care Managers in Quality of Care and Patient Safety*, PhD thesis, Imperial College London.

Parliamentary and Health Service Ombudsman. (2014a). The Ombudsman's Annual Report and Accounts 2013–14. 'A voice for change'. HC536.

Parliamentary and Health Service Ombudsman. (2014b). Four investigation reports concerning the University Hospitals of Morecambe Bay NHS Foundation Trust.

Parsons, T. (1947). 'Introduction'. In M. Weber, ed. *The Theory of Economic and Social Organisation*. Translated by A. R. Henderson and T. Parsons, London: William Hodge.

Patients Association. (2016). Press release. Patients Association calls for 'never' incidents to cease. 18 February 2016. Harrow, UK.

Pellegrino, E. (2004). 'Prevention of medical error: where professional and orga-nisational ethics meet'. In V. A. Sharpe, ed., *Accountability: Patient Safety and Policy Reform*, Washington: Georgetown University Press, pp. 83–98.

Percival, T. (1849). *Medical Ethics*, 3rd edn, Oxford: John Henry Parker.

Perkin, H. (1990). *The Rise of Professional Society: England Since 1880*, London: Routledge.

Phillips, D. F. (1999). 'New look reflects changing style of patient safety enhancement'. *Journal of the American Medical Association*, 281(3), 217–19.

Pinkus, R. L. (2001). 'Mistakes as a social construct: an historical approach'. *Kennedy Institute of Ethics Journal*, 11(2), 117–33.

Pittet, D. and Donaldson, L. (2006). 'Challenging the world: patient safety and health care-associated infection'. *International Journal for Quality in Health Care*, 18, 4–8.

Pollock, A. (2005). *NHS Plc: The Privatisation of Our Health Care*, London: Verso.

Porter, M. et al. (2016). 'Standardizing patient outcomes measurement'. *New England Journal of Medicine*, 374, 504–6.

Powell, W. (2014). 'Robbie's Law: Lack of candour – the impact on patients and their families. *Clinical Risk*, 3 February 2014.

Power, M. (1997). *The Audit Society: Rituals of Verification*, Oxford: Oxford University Press.

Pronovost, P. and Vohr, E. (2010). *Safe Patients, Smart Hospitals*, New York: Penguin.

Pronovost, P. Berenholtz, S. and Morlock, L. (2011). 'Is quality of care improving in the UK?' *British Medical Journal*, 342, 341–2.

Prosser, T. (2010). *The Regulatory Enterprise: Government, Regulation and Legitimacy*, Oxford: Oxford University Press.

PSA. (2010a). *Right Touch Regulation*. PSA: London.

PSA. (2010b). The Performance Review Standards: Standards of Good Regulation. Professional Standards Authority.

PSA. (2013. Annual report and accounts and performance review report 2012–13. Volume II, Performance Review Report 2012–13. London: TSO, Professional Standards Authority for Health and Social Care.

PSA. (2015). *Rethinking Regulation*. London: Professional Standards Authority.

Quick, O. (1999). 'Disaster at Bristol: explanations and implications of a tragedy'. *Journal of Social Welfare and Family Law*, 21(4), 307–26,

Quick, O. (2006). 'Outing medical errors: questions of trust and responsibility'. *Medical Law Review*, 14, 22–43.

Quick, O. (2006). 'Prosecuting "gross" medical negligence: manslaughter, discretion and the Crown Prosecution Service'. *Journal of Law and Society*, 33(3), 421–50.

Quick, O. (2008). 'Medical killing: need for a specific offence?' In C. M. V. Clarkson and S. Cunningham, eds., *Criminal Liability for Non-Aggressive Death*, Aldershot: Ashgate, pp. 155–75.

Quick, O. (2010). 'Medicine, mistakes and manslaughter: a criminal combination?' *Cambridge Law Journal*, 69, 186–203.

Quick, O. (2011a). 'A scoping study on the effects of health professional regulation on those regulated'. London: Council for Healthcare Regulatory Excellence.

Quick, O. (2011b). 'Expert evidence and medical manslaughter: vagueness in action'. *Journal of Law and Society*, 38(4), 496–518.

Quick, O. (2014). 'Regulating and legislating safety: the case for candour'. *BMJ Quality & Safety*, 28(8), 614–18.

Quirk, H. (2013). 'Sentencing white coat crime: the need for guidance in medical manslaughter cases'. *Criminal Law Review*, 11, 871–88.

Rasmussen, J. (1990). 'The role of error in organising behaviour'. *Ergonomics*, 33. 1185–99.

Reason, J. T. (1990). *Human Errors*, Cambridge: Cambridge University Press.

Reisman, D. (2010). *Health Tourism: Social Welfare through International Trade*, Cheltenham: Edward Elgar.

Roberts, I. S. D., Gorodkin, L. and Benbow, E. (2000). 'What is a natural cause of death? A survey of how coroners in England and Wales approach borderline case'. *Journal of Clinical Pathology*, 53, 367–73.

Robinson, J. (1999). 'The price of deceit: the reflections of an advocate'. In M. M. Rosenthal, L. Mulcahy and S. Lloyd-Bostock, eds., *Medical Mishaps: Pieces of the Puzzle*, Buckingham: Open University Press, pp. 246–56.

Rosenthal, M. M. (1987). *Dealing with Medical Malpractice: The British and Swedish Experience*, London: Tavistock.

Rosenthal, M. M., Mulcahy, L. and Lloyd-Bostock S., eds., (1999). *Medical Mishaps: Pieces of the Puzzle*, Buckingham: Open University Press.

Rowley, E. and Waring, J. (2011). *A Socio-Cultural Perspective on Patient Safety*, Farnham: Ashgate.

Royal College of Nursing. (2010). A new vision of nursing and midwifery: Royal College of Nursing submission to the Prime Minister's Commission on Nursing and Midwifery.

Royal College of Physicians. (2005). *Doctors in Society: Medical Professionalism in a Changing World*, London: RCP.

Royal College of Physicians. (2010). *Future Physician: Changing Doctors in Changing Times*, London: RCP.

Runciman, B., Merry, A. and Walton, M. (2007). *Safety and Ethics in Healthcare: A Guide to Getting It Right*, Aldershot: Ashgate.

Runciman, W., Hibbert, P., Thomson, R., Van Der Schaaf, T., Sherman, H. and Lewalle, P. (2009). 'Towards an international classification for patient safety: key concepts and terms'. *International Journal for Quality in Health Care*, 21, 18–26.

Salter, B. (1998). *The Politics of Change in the Health Service*, London: Macmillan.

Salter, B. (1999). 'Change in the governance of medicine: the politics of self-regulation'. *Policy & Politics*, 27(2), 143–58.

Schimmel, E. M. (1964). 'The hazards of hospitalisation'. *Annals of Internal Medicine*, 60, 100–10.

Scottish Government. (2014). Consultation on Recommendations for no-fault compensation in Scotland for injuries resulting from clinical treatment. Scottish Government Social Research.

Seldon, A. (2010). *Trust: How We Lost It and How to Get It Back*, London: Biteback.

Seligman, A. B. (1997). *The Problem of Trust*, Princeton, NJ: Princeton University Press.

Sharpe, V. A., ed. (2004). *Accountability: Patient Safety and Policy Reform*, Washington: Georgetown University Press.

Sharpe, V. A. and Faden, A. I. (1998). *Medical Harm: Historical, Conceptual and Ethical Dimensions of Iatrogenic Illness*, Cambridge: Cambridge University Press.

Shaw, G. B. (1931). *Doctors' Delusions, Crude Criminology and Sham Education*, London: Constable.

Sheldon, S. (1997). *Beyond Control: Medical Power and Abortion Law*, London: Pluto.

Shennan, A. and Bewley, S. (2012). 'What has happened to the UK Confidential Enquiry into Maternal Deaths?' *British Medical Journal*, 344, e4147.

Shoushtarian, M. et al. (2014). 'Impact of introducing Practical Obstetric Multi-Professional Training (PROMPT) into maternity units in Victoria, Australia'. *British Journal of Obstetrics and Gynaecology*, 121, 1710–19.

Sieff, A. (2014). Health Foundation Blog. 'Please stop trying to involve me in my healthcare', available at www.health.org.uk/blog/please-stop-trying-to-involve-me-in-my-healthcare/

Simmons, R., Powell, M. and Greener, I. (2009). *The Consumer in Public Services: Choice, Values and Difference*, Bristol: Policy Press.

Skivenes, M. and Trygstad, S. C. (2010). 'When whistle-blowing works: the Norwegian case'. *Human Relations*, 63(7) July, 1071–97.

Skrabanek, P. (1994). *The Death of Humane Medicine*, Social Affairs Unit.

Slapper, G. (1999). *Blood in the Bank: Social and Legal Aspects of Death at Work*, Aldershot: Ashgate.

Smith, C. (2005). 'Understanding trust and confidence: two paradigms and their significance for health and social care', *Journal of Applied Philosophy*. 22(3299), 316.

Smith, J. (2003). The Shipman Inquiry: third report – death certification and the investigation of deaths by coroners. Command paper 5854.

Smith, J. (2004). The Shipman Inquiry: fifth report: safeguarding patients – lessons from the past proposals for the future. Command paper 6394.

Smith, J. C. (1971). 'The Element of Chance in Criminal Liability'. *Criminal Law Review*, February, 63–75.

Smith, M. L. and Forster, H. P. (2000). 'Morally managing medical mistakes'. *Cambridge Quarterly of Healthcare Ethics*, 9, 38–53.

Smith, R. (1990). 'The epidemiology of malpractice'. *British Medical Journal*, 301, 621.

Smith, R. (1998). 'All changed, changed utterly'. *British Medical Journal*, 316, 1917–18.

Smith, R. (2009). 'NHS targets "may have led to 1,200 deaths" in Mid-Staffordshire'. *Daily Telegraph*, 18 March 2009.

Smith, R. G. (1994). *Medical Discipline: The Professional Conduct Jurisdiction of the General Medical Council, 1858–1990*, Oxford: Clarendon.

Snow, R., Humphrey, C. and Sandall, J. (2013). 'What happens when patients know more than their doctors? Experiences of health interactions after diabetes patient education: a qualitative patient-led study'. *British Medical Journal Open*, 3, e003583.

Society for Cardiothoracic Surgery in GB and Ireland. (2011). Maintaining Patients' Trust: Modern Medical Professionalism.

Stacey, M. (1992). *Regulating British Medicine: The General Medical Council*, Chichester: John Wiley & Sons.

Start, R. D. et al. (1993). 'Clinicians and the coronial system: ability of clinicians to recognise reportable deaths'. *British Medical Journal*, 306, 1038–41.

Steel, K. et al. (1981). 'Iatrogenic illness on a general medical service at a university hospital'. *New England Journal of Medicine*, 304, 638–42.

Stelling, J. and Bucher, R. (1973). 'Vocabularies of realism in professional socialization'. *Social Science & Medicine*, 7, 661–75.

Stephen, F., Melville, A. and Krause, T. (2012). A study of medical negligence claiming in Scotland, Scottish Government Social Research.

Studdert, D. and Richardson, M. (2010). 'Legal aspects of open disclosure: a review of Australian law'. *Medical Journal of Australia*, 193(5), 272–76.

Studdert, D. et al. (2006). 'Claims, errors and compensation payments in medical malpractice litigation'. *New England Journal of Medicine*, 354, 2024–33.

Studdert, D. et al. (2007). 'Disclosure of medical injury to patients: an improbable risk management strategy'. *Health Affairs (Milwood)*, 26(1), 215–26.

Studdert, D. et al. (2010). 'Legal aspects of open disclosure II: attitudes of health professionals – findings from a national survey'. *Medical Journal of Australia*, 193(6), 351–5.

Syrett, K. (2007). *Law, Legitimacy and the Rationing of Health Care: A Contextual and Comparative Perspective*, Cambridge: Cambridge University Press.

Tallis, R. (2004). *Hippocratic Oaths: Medicine and Its Discontents*, London: Atlantic.

Tallis, R. and Davis J. (2013). *NHS SOS: How the NHS Was Betrayed – and How We Can Save It*, London: Oneworld.

Taylor, S. (2011). 'Providing redress for medical accidents in France: conflicting aims, effective solutions?' *Journal of European Tort Law*, 2, 57–76.

Teff, H. (1985). 'Consent to medical procedures: paternalism, self-determination or therapeutic alliance'. *Law Quarterly Review*, 101, 432–53.

The Daily Telegraph, 15 October 2015.

The Daily Telegraph, 12 February 2016.

The Guardian, 29 July 2009.

The Guardian, 15 February 2010.

The Guardian, 14 June 2011.

The Independent, 31 October 2011.

The Guardian, 3 May 2013.

The Guardian, 12 December 2013.

The Guardian, 17 April 2014.

The Guardian, 28 April 2014.

The Guardian, 16 December 2015.

The Guardian, 28 January 2016.

The Guardian, 4 February 2016.

Thornton, P. (Chief Coroner). (2012). 'The Coroner System in the 21st Century'. The Howard League for Penal Reform Parmoor Lecture 2012. Available at: www.judiciary.gov.uk/Resources/JCO/Documents/Speeches/Coroner-system -21st-century-chief-Coroner-speech-howard-league.pdf.

Tingle, J. and Bark, P., eds., (2011). *Patient Safety: Law Policy and Practice*, Abingdon: Routledge.

Titcombe, J. (2015). *Joshua's Story: Uncovering the Morecambe Bay NHS Scandal*, Leeds: Anderson Wallace Publishing

Todd, S. (2011). 'Treatment Injury in New Zealand'. *Chicago-Kent Law Review*, 86, 1169.

Trubek, L. G. et al. (2008). 'Health care and new governance: the quest for effective regulation'. *Regulation and Governance*, 2, 1–8.

Ulfbeck, V., Hartlev, M. and Schultz, M. (2012). 'Malpractice in Scandinavia'. *Chicago-Kent Law Review*, 87(1), 111–29.

Van Dijck, G. (2015). 'Should physicians be afraid of tort claims? Reviewing the empirical evidence'. *Journal of European Tort Law*, 6(3), 282–303.

Vaughan, D. (1999). 'The dark side of organizations: mistake, misconduct, and disaster'. In K. Cook and J. Hagan, eds., *Annual Review of Sociology*, 25, 271–305.

Vincent, C. (1989, 'Research into medical accidents: a case of negligence?' *British Medical Journal*, 299, 1150–3.

Vincent, C. (2009). 'Social scientists and patient safety: critics or contributors?' *Social Science & Medicine*, 69, 1777–9.

Vincent, C. (2010). *Patient Safety*, 2nd edn, Edinburgh: Elsevier.

Vincent, C. and Amalberti, R. (2015). 'Safety in healthcare is a moving target'. *BMJ Quality and Safety*, 24, 539–40.

Vincent, C. and Amalberti, R. (2016). *Safer Healthcare: Strategies for the Real World*, New York: Springer International.

Vincent, C. and Davis, R. (2012. 'Patients and families as safety experts'. *Canadian Medical Association Journal*, 184(1), 15–16.

Vincent, C., Neale, G., Woloshynowych, M., (2001). 'Adverse events in British hospitals: preliminary retrospective record review'. *British Medical Journal*, 322, 517–19.

Vincent, C. et al. (1993). *Medical Accidents*, Oxford: Oxford University Press.

Vincent, C. et al. (2008). 'Is health care getting safer?' *British Medical Journal*, 337, 1205–7.

Vincent, C. et al. (2013). The measurement and monitoring of safety, London: Health Foundation.

Vincent, D. (1998). *The Culture of Secrecy Britain, 1832–1998*, Oxford: Oxford University Press.

Waddington, I. (1984). *The Medical Profession in the Industrial Revolution*, Dublin: Gill & Macmillan.

Wallace, H. and Mulcahy, L. (1999). *Cause for Complaint? An Evaluation of the Effectiveness of the NHS Complaints Procedure*, London: Public Law Project.

Walshe K. and Buttery, Y. (1995). 'Measuring the impact of audit and quality improvement activities'. *Journal of the Association for Quality in Healthcare*, 2(4), 138–47.

Walshe, K. (1999). 'Medical accidents in the UK: a wasted opportunity for improvement?' In M. M. Rosenthal, L. Mulcahy and S. Lloyd-Bostock, eds., *Medical Mishaps: Pieces of the Puzzle*. Buckingham: Open University Press, pp. 59–73 at p. 69.

Walshe, K. (2003). *Regulating Healthcare: A Prescription for Improvement*, Maidenhead: Open University Press.

Walton, M., Woodward, H., Van Staalduinen, S. et al. (2010). 'The WHO patient safety curriculum guide for medical schools'. *Quality and Safety in Health Care*, 19, 542–6.

Waring, J. (2005). 'Beyond blame: the cultural barriers to medical incident reporting'. *Social Science and Medicine*, 60, 1927–35.

Waring, J., Dixon-Woods, M. and Yeung, K. (2010). 'Modernising medical regulation: where are we now?' *Journal of Health Organisation and Management*, 24 (6), 540–55.

Warren, O., Franklin, B. D. and Vincent, C. (2015). *Going into Hospital?: A Guide for Patients, Carers and Families*, Saintfield, UK: Eastdown Publishing.

Watt, I. (2009). A review of strategies to promote patient involvement, a study to explore patient's views and attitudes and a pilot study to evaluate the

acceptability of selected patient involvement strategies. Patient Safety Research
Programme PS/034. Patient Involvement in Patient Safety Research Group.

Weber, M. (1968). *Economy and Society: An Outline of Interpretive Sociology*.
G. Roth and C. Wittich, eds. New York: Bedminster Press.

Weingart, S. N. et al. (2011). 'Hospitalised patients' participation and its impact on
quality of care and patient safety'. *International Journal for Quality in Health
Care*, 23(3), 269–77.

Wells, C. (1991). 'Inquests, inquiries and indictments: the official reception of
death by disaster'. *Legal Studies*, 11, 71–84.

Wells, C. (2001). *Corporations and Criminal Responsibility*, 2nd edn, Oxford:
Oxford University Press.

Wells, C. (2013). 'Medical manslaughter: organisational liability'. In D. Griffiths
and A. Sanders, eds., *Bioethics, Medicine and the Criminal Law*, Cambridge
University Press, pp. 192–209.

White, P. (2015). 'More doctors charged with manslaughter are being convicted, shows analysis'. *British Medical Journal*, 351, h4402.

Wilenski, H. L. (1964). 'The professionalization of everyone'. *American Journal of
Sociology*, 70(2), 137–58.

Williams, K. (2005). 'State of fear: Britain's "compensation culture" reviewed'.
Legal Studies, 25(3), 499–515.

Williamson, C. (2010). *Towards the Emancipation of Patients: Patients' Experiences
and the Patient Movement*, Policy Press: Bristol.

Wise, J. (2016). 'The weekend effect—how strong is the evidence?' *British Medical
Journal*, 353, i2781.

Wootton, D. (2006). *Bad Medicine: Doctors Doing Harm since Hippocrates*,
New York: Oxford University Press.

World Health Organisation. (2009). WHO guidelines on hand hygiene in health
care.

World Health Organization. (2011). *Global Health and Aging*.

Wu, A. W. et al. (2009). 'Disclosing medical errors to patients: it's not what you say,
it's what they hear'. *Journal of General Internal Medicine*, 24(9), 1012–7.

Yang, Y. T. et al. (2012). 'Does tort law improve the health of newborns, or
miscarry? a longitudinal analysis of the effect of liability pressure on birth
outcomes'. *Journal of Empirical Legal Studies*, 9(2), 217–45.

Yeung, K. and Dixon Woods, M. (2010). 'Design-based regulation and patient
safety: a regulatory studies perspective'. *Social Science & Medicine*, 71, 502–5.

Yeung, K. and Horder J. (2014). 'How can the criminal law support the provision
of quality in healthcare?' *BMJ Quality & Safety*. Published online first: 5 March
2014, doi:10.1136/bmjqs-2013–002688.

INDEX

Anne-Maree Farrell
The Politics of Blood: Ethics, Innovation and the Regulation of Risk

Stephen Smith
End-of-Life Decisions in Medical Care: Principles and Policies for Regulating the Dying Process

Michael Parker
Ethical Problems and Genetics Practice

William W. Lowrance
Privacy, Confidentiality, and Health Research

Kerry Lynn Macintosh
Human Cloning: Four Fallacies and Their Legal Consequence

Heather Widdows
The Connected Self: The Ethics and Governance of the Genetic Individual

Amel Alghrani, Rebecca Bennett and Suzanne Ost
Bioethics, Medicine and the Criminal Law Volume I: The Criminal Law and Bioethical Conflict: Walking the Tightrope

Danielle Griffiths and Andrew Sanders
Bioethics, Medicine and the Criminal Law Volume II: Medicine, Crime and Society

Margaret Brazier and Suzanne Ost
Bioethics, Medicine and the Criminal Law Volume III: Medicine and Bioethics in the Theatre of the Criminal Process

Sigrid Sterckx, Kasper Raus and Freddy Mortier
Continuous Sedation at the End of Life: Ethical, Clinical and Legal Perspectives

A. M. Viens, John Coggon and Anthony S. Kessel
Criminal Law, Philosophy and Public Health Practice

Ruth Chadwick, Mairi Levitt and Darren Shickle
The Right to Know and the Right Not to Know: Genetic Privacy and Responsibility

Eleanor D. Kinney
The Affordable Care Act and Medicare in Comparative Context

Katri Lõhmus
Caring Autonomy: European Human Rights Law and the Challenge of Individualism

Catherine Stanton and Hannah Quirk
Criminalising Contagion: Legal and Ethical Challenges of Disease Transmission and the Criminal Law